T4-AKK-279

operational **PPBS** for education

SERIES IN ADMINISTRATION   Harry J. Hartley, Consulting Editor

ROBERT F. ALIOTO

Superintendent of Schools
Yonkers, New York

Formerly Superintendent
Pearl River, New York

J. A. JUNGHERR

Director of Finance
City of Newark, New Jersey

Formerly Assistant Superintendent—Business
Pearl River, New York

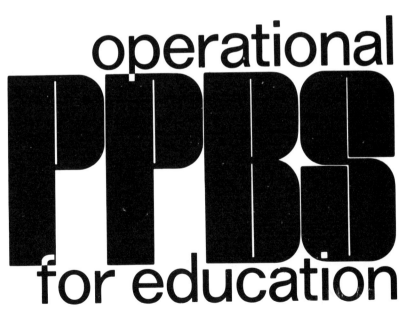

operational PPBS
for education

A PRACTICAL APPROACH TO EFFECTIVE DECISION MAKING

HARPER & ROW, PUBLISHERS
New York, Evanston,
San Francisco, London

to Beverly and Libby

operational PPBS for education

Copyright © 1971 by Robert F. Alioto and J. A. Jungherr

Harper & Row, Publishers, Inc.,   49 East 33rd Street, New York, N.Y. 10016.

Standard Book Number: 06-040203-2
LIBRARY OF CONGRESS CATALOG CARD NUMBER: 70-174519

106308

contents

v

LIST OF FIGURES

editor's introduction

PPBS is an idea whose time has come to education in the 1970s. In the short span of several years, Planning-Programming-Budgeting Systems have progressed from the stage of conceptual blueprint to operational implementation in school districts all across the country. Because of the unusually comprehensive nature of the PPBS mode of thinking, this concept has become perhaps the most talked about and least understood innovation in educational administration. This text clarifies what PPBS is and specifies how this process has been successfully applied to the earthy reality of local schools.

What distinguishes PPBS from other innovations is that its methods are not only *newer,* but *better.* Although there are many different ways to define PPBS, its basic purpose is to aid educators in: (1) identifying goals and defining objectives; (2) designing curricular programs to achieve objectives; (3) analyzing systematically the alternatives available; (4) providing decision makers with more and better data; (5) evaluating costs and effectiveness of competing programs; (6) extending the time span in planning; (7) allocating budget dollars to instructional programs; (8) identifying program priorities; (9) promoting innovative programs and methods; and (10) increasing public understanding of, and support for, the schools during the present Accountability Era.

This book satisfies an urgent need. It reveals how to *do* PPBS in an applied sense. Until now, the literature on PPBS has emphasized its conceptual-expository aspects, but has overlooked the operational-demonstrative facets. Alioto and Jungherr undertook the challenge to relate the theoretical properties of PPBS to the contemporary practice of education. They have demonstrated how decisional technologies associated with the "systems approach" can be used to humanize learning and improve educational services in an efficient manner. The results of their work are a major contribution to both management science and educational leadership.

Harry J. Hartley

preface

A key issue in American education is the drive for reform. The need for restructuring education has been dramatized by the critics who argue that most schools stifle, bore, oppress, confuse, and often fail to educate children. The authors believe that the Planning-Programming-Budgeting System approach can be a significant lever for educational change. Properly used, it will document, in detail, progress in moving toward accepted goals and will provide copious information for basic reforms in education.

Reflecting on the future of PPBS in schools, we feel that there is a need to achieve progress in two areas. First, we need to develop the analytical frameworks, forms, and procedures for implementing PPBS. A second major area is the development in school personnel of the habits of thought and the capacity for systematic analysis which are necessary to the operation of a PPB system. This latter task may turn out to be more difficult than the former. However, the development of procedures for implementing PPBS is a necessary prerequisite to the development of the analytical ability of school personnel.

The basic purpose of this book is to provide a practical approach for the introduction and installation of a PPB system. The PPBS concept is a simple one. What do you want to achieve? How can you achieve it? When will you achieve it? How will you know that you have achieved it?

Part One of the book describes the components that are necessary for an operationalized PPB system; it suggests methods of achieving those components; and it attempts to illustrate some of the risks and problems involved in the developmental process.

Part Two provides a comprehensive example, through a procedures manual and a display document, of how to collect, analyze, and display the necessary information for a viable PPB system. Both the manual and the document represent an initial effort and should not be construed as ideal models. They may serve, however, as a starting point for possible modification to meet local district needs for implementing PPBS.

Part Three includes representative samples of various forms and other materials that have been developed by school districts in order to facilitate the implementation of a PPB system.

The reader must recognize that the techniques, formats, procedures, and forms described in this book represent suggestions that should serve as a basis for modification, adaptation, or complete redevelopment to meet a particular school district's needs. A consistent attempt has been made to provide alternative starting points, methods, and strategies for the installation of a PPB system. This is in recognition of the fact that there is no one best way to proceed with the installation of PPBS in education.

There are several common threads which run throughout the book. These include stressing wide involvement of staff, community, and board members throughout the entire installation process. The second thread is that districts should begin with the information and procedures that already exist. Most school districts are presently involved, to some degree, in all of the components of a PPB system and by capitalizing on this involvement the transition to a PPB system can be more readily effected. Finally, we have attempted to alert practitioners to the necessity of being realistic in their expectations during the installation of a PPB system.

The writers recognize that PPBS is new to education and therefore its applications have not been fully explored. We further recognize that there are a number of risks and problems associated with the PPBS approach. We are, however, firmly convinced that the potential payoff in terms of benefits to the students and school district makes the adoption of PPBS imperative.

We would like to acknowledge the critical contributions offered by Joseph M. Cronin (Harvard University), James A. Kelly (Columbia University), and Harry J. Hartley (New York University). We are also indebted to Eugene Rude (Pearl River School District), Stanley Schainker (Pearl River School District), David M. Jones (Sayville, New York, School District), Don Kase (University of California, Santa Cruz), and Jack Sullivan (New England School Development Council). Finally, we wish to thank Hazel M. Adams for preparing the manuscript.

Robert F. Alioto
J. A. Jungherr

part
one

ppbs
for
education

... the stage is set for the most familiar confrontation of modern life—between people who demand change and institutions that resist it. The institutions alter, but never fast enough, and those who seek change are bitterly disappointed.

John Gardner ∗

No social institution finds itself in greater trouble today and none is less likely to finish this decade recognizably intact than the American public school system. Convulsed by every critical social problem from segregation to drug abuse, tied to shrinking tax bases in both city and suburb, staffed and administered by persons who honed their responses in an earlier and more placid age, the schools are now revealing themselves as consistently unable to react appropriately to legitimate public demand. Public schools are embroiled in a major overriding crisis; demands for educational services have escalated much faster than the system's ability and resources to meet them.

In the past decade the clamor for more extensive, more humane public schooling has thrust the public education system into the very center of American life. For example, Charles Silberman in his *Crisis in the Classroom* presents considerable evidence that schools are for the most part grim, joyless, oppressive places.[1] Citizens and their elected representatives are unhappier than ever before with the performance of educators. This is reflected throughout the nation by the refusal of voters to allocate tax monies for school purposes.[2] This problem is not unique to elementary and secondary schools. Junior colleges, colleges, and universi-

---

*The Recovery of Confidence, New York, Norton, 1970, p. 29.

[1] Charles E. Silberman, *Crisis in the Classroom: The Remaking of American Education,* New York, Random House, 1970, p. 10. ©Charles E. Silberman.

[2] John Herbers, "Survey Finds Voters Across the Nation Opposed Bonds or Taxes for Education," *The New York Times,* November 8, 1970, p. 85; Ralph E. Winter, "Desperate Educators," *The Wall Street Journal,* June 15, 1970, pp. 1, 13.

3

ties are struggling with limited financial resources.[3] Universities are focusing on the problem of how to cope with today's financial crisis "... with a minimum of damage to their essential performance and to the already touchy relationships among their faculties, students, and administrations, all of whom are bound to feel the pinch."[4]

Although it is recognized that spiraling inflation plays a major part in budget defeats, perhaps the most significant factor may be the displeasure of the voters with the schools themselves. The first question they ask is, "What are we getting?" It is followed by numerous subtle variations of a second question, "Why can't the schools serve us better?"

NEED FOR PPBS

The president of the National Education Association was asked in November 1969 to give evidence before the House Subcommittee on Education that education is better now than it was just before the federal government began pumping money into local schools in various ways twelve years ago. He replied with five points: (1) per-pupil expenditures nearly doubled in ten years; (2) the number of elementary teachers with bachelor's degrees rose 20 percent; (3) average teachers' salaries almost touched $8000 annually by 1968; (4) the dropout rate decreased; (5) the number of men failing Selective Service mental tests declined.[5] A number of congressmen expressed dismay with this presentation. Only points (4) and (5) even attempt to answer the question satisfactorily. What is the product emerging from the schools? Is he any better educated today than he was fifty years ago when female teachers were forbidden to marry, when several children shared a textbook, and when students were dismissed to help their fathers till the fields?

The idea of providing evidence of educational achievement received thoughtful expression in President Nixon's special education message to Congress in March 1970:

School administrators and school teachers alike are responsible for their performance, and it is in their interest as well as in the interest of their pupils that they be held accountable. Success should be measured not by some fixed national norm, but rather by the results achieved in relation to the actual situation of the particular school and the particular set of pupils. . . . We have, as a nation, too long avoided thinking of the productivity of schools.[6]

This shift in attitude has also been recognized by Leon Lessinger, who states:

[3]"How Colleges Cope with the Red Ink," *Business Week,* November 21, 1970, pp. 56-60.

[4]William McCleery, "One University's Response to Today's Financial Crisis," interview with William G. Bowen, *University: A Princeton Quarterly,* reprinted in *Princeton Alumni Weekly,* December 15, 1970.

[5]Ron Schwartz, "Accountability," *Nation's Schools, 85,* no. 6 (June 1970), 31, 32.

[6]"Excerpts from the President's Special Message to Congress on Education Reform," by *The New York Times Company,* March 4, 1970, p. 28. Reprinted by permission.

Seekers of educational funds have always talked in terms of books, staff, materials, equipment, and space to be acquired or used, together with students to be served and programs to be offered. Questioners in the past were content to listen to accounts of resources allocated. This has changed. Today the questions focus on results obtained for resources used. The questions are pointed, insistent, and abrasive. The public school system is being held accountable for results. Accountability is the coming sine qua non for education in the 1970's. How to engineer accountability for results in public education is the central problem for the education profession. [7]

Most educators seem to agree on the necessity for accountability, and simultaneously they acknowledge the absence of any real, systematic effort to judge school productivity. The day-to-day pressures of administering a school system are often given as the rationale for not evaluating student performance. School administrators, with considerable justification, also claim that society has articulated inconsistent expectations for the schools. Various factions within a community hold expectations that may be in direct conflict with each other. For instance, a part of a community demands that students be given the right of self-direction, while another part of the community expects the schools to establish control, discipline, and rigorous academic standards. In many cases there is a lack of consensus on the desired expectations; consequently, school personnel, lacking clear direction, are not held accountable for the performance of a school district.

The school administrator, the teacher, and the school board trustee are all faced with the job of turning the education establishment around to meet squarely the pressures of a sometimes tumultuous and unhappy citizenry. If the schools are not altered to accommodate the demands for change, no matter how poorly those demands are articulated, then various alternative approaches for the dismantling of public education will unquestionably find favor with the voters. One such alternative that is receiving increasing attention is the education voucher plan which is being promoted by the U.S. Office of Economic Opportunity. [8] Another alternative is the guaranteed student performance approach popularly referred to as performance contracting. [9] The quest for educational reform has reached the point where the question of whether or not public schools are obsolete is being examined. [10] The AASA brings this question into sharper focus in its

---

[7] Leon Lessinger, "Engineering Accountability for Results in Public Education," *Phi Delta Kappan, 52,* no. 4 (December 1970), 217-225.

[8] *Education Vouchers: A Preliminary Report on Financing Education by Payments to Parents,* Cambridge, Mass., Center for the Study of Public Policy, 1970.

[9] Education Turnkey Systems, *Performance Contracting in Education: The Guaranteed Student Performance Approach to Public School System Reform,* Champaign, Ill., Research Press, 1970.

[10] Christopher Jencks, "Is the Public School Obsolete?" *The Public Interest,* Winter 1966; Kenneth B. Clark, "Alternative Public School Systems," *Equal Educational Opportunity,* Cambridge, Mass., Harvard University Press, 1969; James S. Coleman, "Toward Open Schools," *The Public Interest,* Fall 1967; Milton Friedman, "The Role of Government in Education," *Capitalism and Freedom,* Chicago, University of Chicago Press, 1962; Henry M. Levin, "The Failure of the Public Schools and the Free Market," *The Urban Review,* June 1968.

publication "Instructional Technology and the School Administrator" as follows:

We come now to the most profound question of the entire discussion: Will the school as a formal institution disappear in a new era of totally cybernetic education? This query may not be as fanciful or irresponsible as it seems. One of the more knowledgeable observers of the new educational technology believes that, by combining mass instructional technology with individual instructional technology, it would be technically possible (but prohibitively expensive for some time) to eliminate not only the teacher but also the entire school system. According to some, totally automated education may be achievable almost immediately.[11]

The lack of clear expectations, increasing demands for educational services, limited financial resources, and pressure for establishing performance accountability are all interrelated problems facing educational leaders. The inability of educators to deal with these problems lies in part with the lack of a comprehensive management system. The existing system for preparing programs and developing budgets is totally inadequate. In most school systems educational planning is accomplished by the instructional staff without regard to the budget cycle and long-range fiscal impact. Program objectives and evaluative criteria are usually missing. Various alternatives for achieving stated objectives are not fully explored.

Under traditional budgeting procedures, it is difficult to use the budget as a tool for implementing educational program changes. The business administrator preparing a traditional budget assumes that existing programs will continue unchanged. Using the current year's budget as a base, he adds salary increases, increases mandated by law, and increases due to inflation for equipment and supplies. The aggregate of these items then become a new budget total. This process is termed incremental budgeting.[12]

In the process of building the traditional budget the major role normally is assumed by the school business administrator. The educators and lay citizens find only masses of detail that are of interest primarily to accountants. Although it is recognized that most school business administrators have trained in education rather than school business management, the very nature of their task forces them to focus on the business aspects of their job to the extent that they become so specialized in these areas that they often lose contact with the instructional program. The curriculum specialist has a limited opportunity to participate meaningfully during the construction of the budget. Normally his role is limited to ordering supplies and equipment. In fact, traditionally there is little if any relationship between program development and the preparation of the budget.

Not only is the process that creates a traditional budget somewhat deficient, it also is difficult to use for communication purposes. A budget

---

[11] Stephen Knezevich and Glen G. Eye, eds., *Instructional Technology and the School Administrator,* Washington, D.C., American Association of School Administrators, 1970, p. 144.

[12] Fremont J. Lyden and Ernest G. Miller, eds., *Planning Programming Budgeting: A Systems Approach to Management,* Chicago, Markham, 1967.

must be constructed to inform the staff and community of the school board's educational decisions and priorities. The budget serves as the basis for communicating the educational program to the community. The difficulty in locating board decisions in most school budgets is illustrated in the following news story:

The board questioning was led by Dr. David Sanchez, Dr. Laurel Glass, both of whom are educators holding Ph.D. degrees, and by Alan Nichols, an attorney. Despite their unusual qualifications the trio found administration budgeting unclear and at times misleading.

Many less trained people in the audience appeared to agree with a housewife who stood up to say that she was unable to follow what the board was talking about.

. . .

Nichols called the board's attention to one item which, without mentioning ROTC, provided for a $26,000 increase in spending for the program.

Nichols said that the information was buried and said that the board was facing an acute "information gap."

. . .

But what Drs. Glass and Sanchez were attempting to do was establish priorities in education—that is, if you budget $100,000 for one item, then it is not available for another.
They were hoping to use the budget as a tool for enforcing board decisions on what was most important.[13]

This problem is not unique to big-city school districts. A relatively wealthy suburban school district, the North Rockland School District, located in the New York metropolitan area, provides another example of the difficulty of using the traditional budget to communicate with the public:

The parents also became disconcerted when they learned from the assistant superintendent for finance, Dr. Joseph Phillips, that $50,000 of the defeated budget allocated to health education was actually to be used for narcotics education. They said they could not understand why this allocation had not been spelled out in the budget report released to the public and at the public hearing prior to the election.

Mrs. Ralph Everett, the outgoing president of the Council, said the apparent lack of information on the narcotics program was a "classic example of poor communication," which, she asserted, was a "factor in the defeat of the budget."[14]

Of all of the deficiencies that could be enumerated regarding the traditional budgeting process, the most important is that it is too limited in providing for a comprehensive approach to the planning and implementa-

---

[13] "School Board OKs $116 Million Budget, 73¢ Tax Hike," *The San Francisco Examiner,* August 6, 1969, p. 9.

[14] Walter J. Ford, "Revised North Rockland School Budget Discussed," *The Journal News,* May 13, 1970, p. 1.

tion of school instructional programs.[15] Thus, it is not surprising that those interested in education are beginning to explore alternative methods of dealing with the complex problems facing education today. The alternative that appears to hold the greatest promise for reducing or eliminating the deficiencies under which current educational programming and budgeting are accomplished is the Planning-Programming-Budgeting System (PPBS).

THE DEVELOPMENT OF PPBS

The probable beginning of the modern attempt to integrate movements in budgetary practice, management science, and computer technology was around 1950. At this time the RAND Corporation was particularly influential in translating the performance budget recommendations of the Hoover Commission into a new preliminary framework for "program" or output budgeting. Literature on program budgeting emerged, but this literature was largely concerned with noneducational topics. Donald M. Levine, in discussing the emergence of PPBS, reviewed the literature as follows:

Although the literature made it clear that applications of PPB in non-educational areas could not be applied easily to the educational domain, it did make important contributions to the theory of program budgeting.

. . . Many articles have been written on the value of PPB for education. For the most part, these articles have been expository pieces on the bare bones of the technique and do not take up more technical questions relating to the methodology of applying PPB to education.[16]

Administrators of public agencies are still trying to sort out the implications of an executive order announced by President Lyndon B. Johnson before a news conference on the morning of August 25, 1965. That morning, the President called in the national press and told them that he had just imposed PPBS on the federal bureaucracy under his control. He described PPBS as a "very revolutionary system of planning and programming and budgeting throughout the vast Federal Government, so that through the tools of modern management the full promise of a finer life can be brought to every American at the lowest possible cost." President Johnson continued:

---

[15] Sol Levin, "The Need for Budgeting Reform in Local Schools," in Harry J. Hartley, *Educational Planning-Programming-Budgeting: A Systems Approach,* Englewood Cliffs, N.J., Prentice-Hall, 1968, pp. 128-153.

[16] Donald M. Levine, "The Emergence of the Planning, Programming, Budgeting, Evaluation System (PPBES) as a Decision and Control Technique for Education," *Research Corporation of the Association of School Business Officials,* October 1969, p. 2.

This program is designed to achieve three major objectives: It will help us find new ways to do jobs faster, to do jobs better, and to do jobs less expensively. It will insure a much sounder judgment through more accurate information, pinpointing those things that we ought to do more, spot-lighting those things that we ought to do less. It will make our decision-making process as up-to-date, I think, as our space-exploring programs.[17]

Although there was a considerable lag in adapting PPBS to education, there have been some significant efforts made. PPBS was one of the chief issues at the fifty-sixth annual meeting of the Association of School Business Officials (ASBO) at Seattle. The 3300 conferees were told that nineteen states had mandated some type of program budgeting and nearly two-thirds of the states were eyeing similar moves.[18] The ASBO in cooperation with the Dade County, Florida, school district received a major three-year grant from the United States Office of Education to develop and disseminate a conceptual design for a PPB system. The New England School Development Council and the American Association of School Administrators, among others, have expended efforts on behalf of their organizations to develop PPBS for education. The adoption of legislation by the State of California establishing an advisory commission, whose purpose is to assist all school districts in the installation of PPBS, has promoted the application of PPBS to education. Perhaps the single greatest catalytic agent for PPBS in education has been Harry J. Hartley whose book, *Educational Planning-Programming-Budgeting: A Systems Approach,* was the first major work in the educational area.[19]

WHAT IS PPBS?

Planning-Programming-Budgeting System is an approach to decision making which systematically integrates all aspects of planning and implementation of programs. The activities involved in the process have been described as follows:

The Planning-Programming-Budgeting System is a framework for planning—a way of organizing information and analysis in a systematic fashion so that the consequences of particular choices can be seen as clearly as possible. It attempts to do three things:

1. To display information about the functioning of actual governmental programs so that it is possible to see easily what portion of Federal resources is being allocated to particular purposes, what is being accomplished by the programs, and how much they cost;

---

[17] David Novick, ed., *Program Budgeting: Program Analysis and the Federal Budget,* Cambridge, Mass., Harvard University Press, 1965, foreword, p. v.

[18] "PPBES (Planning, Programming, Budgeting, Evaluation System), Vandalism, and the Voucher Plan," *Education, USA,* National School Public Relations Association, November 2, 1970, p. 51.

[19] Hartley, op. cit.

2. To analyze the costs of alternative methods of achieving particular objectives so that it is possible to rank the alternatives in terms of their relative costs;

3. To evaluate the benefits of achieving objectives as comprehensively and quantitatively as possible in order to facilitate the setting of priorities among objectives.[20]

PPBS is not a package that you can buy. It is a process—a mode of thinking. The initials PPBS are not important. Many different acronyms are being used to identify the process.[21]

PPBS is essentially a tool; it is a framework within which the school community, teachers, board members, administrators, and citizens can bring about the integration of the uncoordinated, sometimes competing, usually confusing activities performed by teachers, planners, and financial experts. By displaying data in a comprehensive format, it assists educators to analyze and judge all the disparate activities of the school, not as separate entities but as an organized whole. PPBS assists the decision makers in allocating scarce resources to programs within the framework of an annual budget cycle.

The four components of a PPB system—planning, programming, budgeting, and evaluating—are described as follows:

Planning is directed toward keeping the school doing what it is supposed to do. That is, the process generates a series of objectives devoted primarily toward assisting the school system to meet its responsibility to society.

Programming is concerned with the generation of a series of alternative activities and the selection of a specific activity or a group of activities designed to bring about the achievement of an objective. Programming includes multi-year planning, program review, and the analysis of alternatives.

Budgeting is the allocation of financial resources to the activities selected according to established priorities.

Evaluating consists of a review of actual performance which provides evidence of whether or not the stated objectives have been obtained. Evaluation leads directly to a redesign of objectives, a reassessment of programs and priorities, and the allocation of resources. Therefore, the evaluation components of PPBS may provide for continuous renewal of the educational program.[22]

---

[20] William Gorham, "Notes of a Practitioner," *The Public Interest,* no. 8 (Summer 1967), © National Affairs 1967.

[21] For example: ERMD (Educational Resources Management Design), ERMS (Educational Resources Management System), RMS (Resource Management System), PPBES (Planning-Programming-Budgeting Evaluation System), and PB (Program Budgeting).

[22] *Report of the First National Conference on PPBES in Education,* Chicago, Research Corporation of the ASBO, June 10, 1969, p. 45.

BENEFITS OF PPBS

There are numerous benefits that may be gained through the use of a PPB system. However, because of the flexibility of PPBS it is difficult to determine specific benefits that may be gained by a particular school district's installing the system. Depending on its use, some districts will receive benefits that others will not. The use of the PPBS process and the resulting benefits depend upon what Harry Hartley has termed the "artistry of the user."

The following items represent the potential benefits that may be achieved by the various groups making up the school community. In order to place benefits into a specific group or category it was necessary to be somewhat arbitrary; therefore, it should be recognized that many of the benefits are not mutually exclusive but rather cut across two or more of the groups that have been listed.

students

☐ The articulation of the school district's expectations should facilitate a clearer understanding on the part of students, which in turn leads to improved learning. Stating the school district's objectives can help a student understand what is expected of him.

Until the thoughts, feelings, and behavior needing change are brought to the surface for the individual and made public to those helping him (in formal learning situations, the teacher and other members of the learning group), there is little likelihood of learning or change. Buried, they are blurred and indistinct for the learner, covered by misperceptions of adequacy, anxieties, defensiveness. Surfaced, they can be examined by learner, teacher, and learning group in the light of greater reality.

Until thoughts and behavior are revealed and exposed, there is little that the learner or his helpers can take hold of to bring about improvement or change.[23]

Three important conditions of learning are that the student must perceive his expectations as (1) relevant, (2) meaningful, and (3) achievable. PPB helps make the expectations visible and therefore subject to evaluation in terms of these criteria. The benefit to the student is the redefinition of expectations if they are faulty on any of these variables; this increases the likelihood that learning will occur.

teaching staff

☐ In many explicit and subtle ways, PPBS may reduce tensions among classroom teachers, principals, central office administrators, and other supervisors. Objectives and priorities established in a PPB system provide for the clarification of the district's conception of role expectations for teachers. The staff's anxieties, which are too often present in educational

---
[23] *Three Human Forces in Teaching and Learning,* Washington, D.C., NTL Institute for Applied Behavioral Science, 1961, p. 11.

institutions and which are dysfunctional to the achievement of the organization's objectives, may be relieved. The clarification of the teachers' role will make them less subject to the whims and arbitrary authority of school administrators.

The PPBS process offers a legitimate vehicle for teachers to participate in the decision making on priorities and objectives that they and the school system can reasonably expect to achieve. PPBS provides the possibility of joint decision making between teachers and administrators—one of the primary goals of the PPB system. Teachers also can be more deeply involved in the development of the instructional programs. In a position paper on PPBS for the California Teachers Association, Robert Stahl wrote:

Classroom teachers can reject teacher planning implications inherent in the PPBS system. If rejection occurs, then someone else will operate the planning and others removed from the classroom scene will continue to make teacher decisions about children and the program. Our literature is filled with generalities about teachers being placed in a decision-making capacity. Teachers can rise to new heights of professional competence and performance if they seize the opportunity afforded by PPBS.[24]

PPBS also serves teachers by promoting their professional freedom through the removal of noneducators from the methodology of teaching. The school board and the community are primarily interested in the objectives of the school system and in the performance of the staff in relation to those objectives. Given the objectives, there is less tendency to interfere or regulate the methods of achieving them. Thus, the manner of achieving those objectives is left to the teaching and administrative staff—the people who are most competent to make those decisions. PPBS provides for the evaluation of teachers on the basis of what children learn—not on their ability to keep discipline, write orderly lesson plans, or maintain a clean classroom.[25]

It may be argued that the PPBS approach will create a change in the items negotiated by teachers. Because the focus shifts to programs, curricular issues could be included at the bargaining table. Indeed, Robert Bhaerman, the American Federation of Teachers' Director of Research, argues, "If the resources which support curriculum programs are incorporated into the budget, then unavoidably curriculum matters will arise in negotiations. Isn't this what we have been seeking?"[26]

Curriculum issues are not the only negotiable items that could be affected by PPBS. The whole question of teacher salary and welfare demands may be subject to a completely different type of analysis. Instead of asking how salary demands compare with other districts in a given geographic

---

[24] Robert Stahl, "PPBS and the Teacher," *The Challenge of Planning-Programming-Budgeting Systems,* Supplementary Research Report No. 104, Burlingame, Calif., California Teachers Association, 1969, p. 14.

[25] The preoccupation of American educators with order and control has been described by Silberman in *Crisis in the Classroom,* op. cit., p. 122. ©Charles E. Silberman.

[26] Robert Bhaerman, "In Quest: The Danger of Program Budgeting," *American Teacher, 55,* no. 2 (October 1970), 23.

area, questions may be posed on the impact of salary and benefit demands on existing programs. For instance, what programs would receive increased support and which of the competing programs would have to be reduced or eliminated? Bhaerman recognizes that this is a legitimate question in PPBS. Furthermore, Bhaerman states:

It is not unlikely that specific salary schedules would be affected in another way. The single salary schedule, based upon the factors of education and experience, while not without its weaknesses, would be structured upon curriculum priorities. It would be a unique form of differentiated staffing. However, instead of the hierarchy of master-senior-staff teachers, the vertical ladder could be established on a hierarchy similar to this:

> *early childhood reading teachers*
> *high school science teachers*
> *high school math teachers*
> *junior high school social science teachers*

The pattern decided upon would depend on program priorities. While such a ladder obviously would not be easy to set up, it is the logical extension of PPBS. [27]

Because PPBS provides a basis for a whole new set of questions regarding collective bargaining it may give both teachers and boards of education a different set of alternatives and trade-offs which either side may use to resolve conflict.

administrative staff

☐ The school administrator profits from PPBS by having established, in consultation with the community and professional staff, a hierarchy of objectives which may serve as a master plan for future decision making. The administrator will possess a document with which to manage a district on a daily basis with the perspective of the district objectives and priorities. He will be able to make recommendations for the allocation of fiscal resources for specified programs. The administrator can utilize the data gathered in the PPBS process to ascertain the relevancy of the stated objectives and to modify them where necessary.

PPBS demands the integration of two disparate operations of the school district—instruction and business. These two activities have been historically autonomous and sometimes conflicting. It is evident that the power (whether perceived or real) will be shifted from the office of the business administrator to the instructional administrators where it more properly belongs.[28] This is not to say the school business administrator resists removal of the power from his office but, rather, he recognizes that in most cases he has been forced to assume greater responsibility than

---

[27] Ibid.

[28] David M. Jones, "PPBS—A Tool for Improving Instruction," *Educational Leadership,* Association for Supervision and Curriculum Development, *28,* no. 4 (January 1971), 405-409.

necessary for the preparation of the traditional budget because of the vacuum that instructional personnel have allowed to exist.

The essential executive functions as presented by Chester Barnard are " . . . first, to provide the system of communication; second, to promote the securing of essential efforts; and, third, to formulate and define purposes."[29]   PPBS, taken to full installation, will give the administrator an ideal network for internal communications. It is evident that the communication network established under a PPB system need not follow traditional communication lines such as from superintendent to assistant superintendent to building principal to staff. Thus, the system produces a number of alternatives for communication between staff members. Communication in a PPB system is not limited to the sending of memoranda or administrative bulletins but, rather, refers to the level of communication described by John Gardner: "Communications in a healthy society must be more than a flow of messages; it must be a means of conflict resolution, a means of cutting through the rigidities that divide and paralyze a community."[30]   The joint establishment of objectives and determination of programs under the PPBS approach requires staff involvement. If the administrators' aspirations are for total staff involvement in the decision-making process it can be accomplished most reasonably and effectively through the systematic PPBS approach.

Finally, program data generated as a part of the PPBS process will increase the adminstration's knowledge of the education program. Rodney Wells, superintendent of schools of the Portland, Maine, City School System, stated:

I consider this one of the wisest decisions which I have made as a superintendent. Although it is a very time-consuming responsibility I have learned more about the programs in our system—their weaknesses and strengths—than I ever thought was possible. I have more intimate knowledge about these programs and the dollars required to meet program objectives in a city of our size than I did as a superintendent in a much smaller community with a line item budget.[31]

school board

☐ PPBS can augment the school board's ability to influence the quality of education in its school district. The statement of objectives and priorities resulting from a PPBS process can serve as a precise expression of board policy. This is important to the board for two reasons: (1) it helps hold top administrators accountable for achieving specific objectives; and (2) it allows the board to bend the organization to its collective will.

Information gathered by program rather than on the traditional function-object basis gives the board more useful information for making crucial fiscal and program decisions. If the budget must be cut, the program format allows the board to do so without affecting the major or

---

[29] Chester I. Barnard, *The Functions of the Executive,* Cambridge, Mass., Harvard University Press, 1966, p. 217.

[30] Gardner, op. cit., p. 59.

[31] Rodney Wells, in a letter to Robert F. Alioto, dated January 15, 1971.

top priority areas. It eliminates random percentage cuts and substitutes selective program cuts. Similarly, the program budget permits school boards to achieve an objective more quickly by allocating additional resources to activities leading to the achievement of that objective.

PPBS also increases the school board's capacity to respond rationally to political pressures. Most citizens who appear at board meetings express concern about specific programs; they want the establishment of a black studies program, a better reading program, or a modern math program for accelerated students. The data generated as a result of the installation of a PPB system can be utilized by boards of education in providing a rationale for either accepting or rejecting such pleas. The school board can also utilize this data to isolate community resistance through linking special-interest groups to specific programs that have been established as part of the educational plan. Further, if the priorities have been established in conjunction with the professional staff and members of the community, there will be greater support for the board of education decisions affecting the special-interest groups.

community

☐ As citizens become more suspicious of their educators, less satisfied with the system, and more willing to withhold their tax money, it is evident that substantial reform as well as some new communications mechanism is sorely needed. A PPB system can clearly help the public to understand what is going on in its schools as well as to heighten public control of education through appointed or elected school boards. The two elements which the PPB system stresses—objectives and results—are precisely the most nebulous items in the public mind.

Although the PPBS approach provides no simple answer to this compelling problem, it does provide a framework through which dialogue can take place with the community. The potential benefits of utilizing PPBS as a tool for communicating with the community cannot be overestimated. The lack of clear, understandable information about the schools has become of increasing concern to those interested in public education. A Gallup poll of national opinions of our schools concluded that the stagnation of public education could be blamed in part on public ignorance. This study concluded: "The public is so uninformed about innovations and so lacking in objective ways of judging school achievement that little, if any, pressure is exerted by them to make improvements. . . ."[32]

Once a school system orients itself toward a PPBS approach, the community and its board of education have a far greater opportunity for becoming full partners in the educational enterprise. PPBS provides the framework for a community to become involved in stating its aspirations and its expectations for the children in the school system at a level of specificity that is not possible without this systematic approach.[33]

---

[32] George Gallup, "How the Nation Views the Public Schools: A Study of the Public Schools of the United States," Princeton, N.J., *Gallup International* as sponsored by CFK, Ltd., Fall 1969, p. 25.

[33] It is interesting to note that the authors have received numerous requests regarding PPBS from a number of chapters of the League of Women Voters across the country.

PPBS puts the problem-solving process in an arena where the defensiveness of educators can be diluted by sharing with the community acceptance of partial responsibility for the achievement of the aspirations and expectations for the children. Recognizing the necessity for educational accountability, Barry R. McGhan, writing for the American Federation of Teachers, argues that there should be some sort of mutual accountability so that the public cannot accuse teachers of failing to do their jobs, while at the same time it fails to provide adequate funds, thereby causing many of the teachers' problems.

To be fair, this concept of mutuality should be extended to a kind of interlocking accountability which includes teachers, students, administrators, paraprofessionals, school boards, parents, and the public at large. This would require enforceable guarantees that each group meet its responsibilities to each of the others, and would tend to eliminate such possibilities as administrators trying to make teachers the scapegoats for education's inadequacies.[34]

PPBS also enhances the stability and continuity of the district's programs if there is turnover in top-level administration or if school board members are replaced. Having a comprehensive statement of objectives, priorities, and programs as a basis for initial analysis of the school district, the new superintendent or new school board member is not greeted by mass confusion when assuming office.

This same information should help the school districts in hiring administrators who best fit its programs. School board candidates may ultimately be required by the community to run on platforms containing specific instructional programs under which they have identified and articulated support. That is, board candidates will be pressed beyond simple statements of pro- or anti-school spending to specify which school programs they support and are willing to expend additional resources on and which programs they want modified, reduced, or eliminated.

Finally for those school systems required by law to have their budgets adopted by municipal authorities or through a public referendum, the PPBS document can be utilized to communicate the school board's rationale for its recommended budget.[35]

MISCONCEPTIONS
OF PPBS

Although PPBS is a systematic approach for collecting data for decision making, it will not resolve all of the financial and program problems of a school district. In fact, the process itself may lead to the discovery of new

[34] Barry R. McGhan, "Accountability as a Negative Reinforcer," *American Teacher,* *55,* no. 3 (November 1970), 13.

[35] Robert F. Alioto and J. A. Jungherr, "Using PPBS to Overcome Taxpayers' Resistance," *Phi Delta Kappan, 51* (November 1969), 138.

problems. Because it is a system that relies on human judgment for making decisions, it does not guarantee "correct" decisions. PPBS is not synonymous with a computer-centered organization. It is not making decisions by computer and it does not eliminate intuition in decision making.

School costs are neither increased nor decreased as a result of the utilization of PPBS. On this question, PPBS is neutral. It can be used as a vehicle to justify increased costs in order to meet community expectations or it can be used to reduce costs through the elimination of services or programs that the community is unwilling or unable to support.[36]

PPBS does not require that all the objectives of an organization be quantified and measured. "If you can't count it, it doesn't count" is not the guiding philosophy for a PPB system. For example, objectives dealing with student attitudes may be adopted under a PPB system and evaluated subjectively.

CONSTRAINTS IN INSTALLING A PPB SYSTEM

The move to PPBS is a major policy decision in itself; it leaves no one unaffected. Because of its potential for affecting the total school community, operationalizing a PPB system will lead to the emergence of innumerable problems. Some are inherent in any bureaucratic change of PPBS's magnitude. Other problems might be unique to only one school system.

Problems emanating from the activities leading to the installation of a PPB system will become restraining forces for the installation of the system and need to be considered. The constraints that have provided a resistance to implementing PPBS are discussed below. This discussion is not intended to be all-inclusive. It represents the major constraints that have been identified by those attempting to install a PPB system.

inherent conservatism of the schools

☐ Schools are among the most stable and conservative of our social institutions.[37] To a great extent, the men who staff and administer them have themselves been schooled in a limited concept of the "proper role" of public education. H. Thomas James, former dean of Stanford University School of Eucation, has given the problem authoritative expression: "It is no wonder that school officials find PPBS disturbing; given lifelong exposure to the conservative climate of the school . . .they find it difficult to cope with the potential for change inherent in this new budget procedure."[38]

[36] Hartley, op. cit., p. 75.

[37] Reprinted with permission of the publisher. From Matthew B. Miles, *Innovation in Education*, New York, Teachers College Press. © 1964.

[38] H. Thomas James, Horace Mann Lecture, 1968, *The New Cult of Efficiency and Education*, Pittsburgh, University of Pittsburgh Press, 1969, p. 41.

School districts tend to reward those individuals who support and maintain the status quo, and therefore those who attempt to install a new program will be running contrary to the established norm.[39] PPBS is particularly threatening because it questions the status quo. It requires an assessment and justification of existing educational programs as well as proposed programs. That is, existing educational practices will be subjected to rigorous, systematic scrutiny in terms of effectiveness in reaching objectives. Peter A. Pyhrr has referred to this concept as "zero-base budgeting."

Traditionally, problems like this boil down to one question: How should the company shift its allocations around? Rather than tinker endlessly with its existing budget, Texas Instruments prefers to start from base zero, view all its activities and priorities afresh, and create a new and better set of allocations for the upcoming budget year.[40]

Historically, in education, monies expended for a program during the previous budget year are assumed and the only undetermined factor is how much more will be allocated for the ensuing year. Those who have vested interests in particular programs naturally resist any new process which forces them to compete for limited resources.

**threat of
accountability**

☐ Not every school administrator and school board member wants to open his educational system to public scrutiny. "Why," some ask, "bring the walls down on ourselves?" Also, organized teachers view with some skepticism efforts to link their profession with measured productivity.

"You can lead a horse to water, but you can't make him drink." This adage seems to capture the spirit of one of the principles of education. Namely, that no matter how much effort is expended by the teacher, students will not learn unless they have an inner motivation to learn. If this is true, then of the two individuals engaged in the teaching/learning act, the student has the more important role for the act to be successful: thus, teacher accountability places the emphasis on the wrong person.[41]

Accountability raises the specter of evaluation and all of its concomitant inadequacies and potential misuses. Resistance to exposing deficiencies is considerable, primarily because one of the end results of such exposure is threatened job security. The concept of accountability has also been resisted by some administrators, although several schemes have been tried in an effort to increase administrative accountability.[42]

---

[39] Miles, op. cit., p. 76.

[40] Peter A. Pyhrr, "Zero-Base Budgeting," *Harvard Business Review, 48,* no. 6 (November-December 1970), 111.

[41] McGhan, loc. cit.

[42] Kenneth E. Underwood, "Just What Will You Be Accountable For?" *The American School Board Journal, 58,* no. 3 (September 1970), 32-33.

☐ Taken separately, each of the four components of a PPB system—planning, programming, budgeting, and evaluation—has been dealt with in education, some with greater success and greater understanding than others. However, because PPBS attempts to integrate these four components the complexity is greatly increased. It can be argued that the whole is greater than the parts. Educators have not been trained to think in terms of an integrated, comprehensive systems approach. The integration of a wide variety of competing activities represents one of the most difficult tasks facing those attempting to install a PPB system.

complexity of PPBS

The present limitations for obtaining reliable evaluative data lead to considerable difficulty in determining whether or not certain objectives have been achieved. The subjective nature of some of the evaluative data leads to overinterpretation, rationalization, and/or outright rejection. Because of the limitations of the evaluative data, the whole dimension of effectiveness is difficult to determine.

There is a complete taxonomy of terms which have been utilized in describing a PPB system.[43] These terms, such as output, input, program structure, program accounting, needs identification, system analysis, and cost-benefit ratio, have not enjoyed popular usage in the field of education. The lack of familiarity with these terms sometimes leads to misinterpretation, apprehension, and confusion.

The task of reaching consensus on all of the school district's objectives is exceedingly difficult. The differing backgrounds and the wide range of value systems of individuals involved in reaching consensus bring to the surface many complex issues that must be resolved. Recognizing the potential conflict of values in defining objectives, Silberman states " . . . deciding an organization's objectives—a business firm's no less than a school system's—involves value judgments, which means that the decisions are political in the most fundamental sense of that much-abused term."[44]

image

☐ In one school district attempting to provide in-service training to members of its professional staff on PPBS, a classroom teacher sent the superintendent the following note: "I will not be taking part in this workshop as I refuse to contribute to the further dehumanization of this school system. You may deal with 'outputs' but I work with children and hope to continue to do so."

Because PPBS contains an aura of computers, a set of routines, analytical tools, and systematic analysis, it is easily perceived to be mechanistic in nature. In addition, because of the central role of the business administrator in the development of a budget, PPBS is interpreted as emanating from the business office. This perception can be supported because, on a national scale, the leadership was initially assumed by the Association of School Business Officials. The widespread misconception that PPBS is merely some newfangled bookkeeping system has been further supported

[43] Hartley, op. cit., p. 253.
[44] Silberman, op. cit., p. 507.

in countless districts where the PPBS assignment has been dumped into the lap of the school business official.[45] Some professionals fear that PPBS will lead to a regimentation of educational programs that will focus primarily on efficiency and productivity rather than on students as human beings. Those perceiving PPBS in this manner provide considerable resistance to its installation.

legal

☐ The U.S. Office of Education, *Handbook II, Financial Accounting for Local and State School Systems,* recommends a function-object system of accounting.[46] In many cases, this recommendation has been modified and adopted at the state level. Most states require the submission of financial reports conforming with its reporting format, and this may result in a duplication of effort by the school district in order to meet state reporting requirements. In addition, there may be local requirements contained in municipal charters or regulations that prescribe procedures for financial accounting and budget preparation that are not consistent with the PPBS approach.

The remaining chapters of the book will suggest strategies to overcome these constraints in order to install, in a reasonable period of time, a fully operationalized PPB system.

SUMMARY

The traditional methods for preparing programs and developing objectives are totally inadequate. Those interested in improving education are beginning to explore PPBS as an alternative method for dealing with the complex problems education is now facing. Planning-Programming-Budgeting System (PPBS) is an approach to decision making that systematically integrates all aspects of planning and implementation of programs. PPBS is a process or mode of thinking about curriculum programs.

Misconceptions regarding PPBS include fears that decisions will be made by a computer, that decisions emanating from the process are infallible, and that all objectives must be quantified and objectively measured. There are numerous constraints to operationalizing a PPB system, some of which may be found in any bureaucratic change and some of which are unique to PPBS.

[45] "PPBS—A Communication Jack-in-the-Box," *Trends,* National School Public Relations Association, December 15, 1970, p.1.

[46] *Financial Accounting for Local and State School Systems, Handbook II,* Bulletin No. 4, Washington, D.C., State Educational Records and Report Series, U.S. Office of Education, 1957.

By displaying data in a comprehensive format PPBS assists the decision maker in analyzing and judging all the disparate activities of the school system as an organized whole. Benefits to the entire school community may be gained through the use of PPBS. The potential benefits of PPBS to school officials, teachers, pupils, families, and taxpayers through more efficient and effective use of limited resources make PPBS worth the considerable effort required in establishing it.

initiating:
how to introduce a
ppb system

The installation of an innovation in a system is not a mechanical process, but a developmental one, in which both the innovation and the accepting system are altered . . . . Matthew B. Miles ▪

A PPB system will assist those individuals who are action-oriented and who desire to bring about changes in education in order to make schools more responsive to society. The problem is, "How does one go about introducing the system?" There are a number of factors that must be considered in order to insure the likelihood of a successful installation. First: What resources will be needed to install and operate a PPB system? Resources fall into three major categories: personnel, equipment and materials, and their related costs. Consideration should be given to both professional personnel and secretarial support requirements. Second: How much time will be required to accomplish the necessary tasks? Third: What specific strategy or steps for installing the system need to be considered?

RESOURCES FOR
INSTALLING PPBS

**professional
staff resources**

☐ Most school districts—city, suburban, and rural—possess the professional staff resources necessary to install a PPB system. There has been some debate regarding the necessity for providing additional staff in order to install and operate the system. At the AASA National Academy for School Executives, Dr. Stephen J. Knezevich argued that most school districts have

*Reprinted by permission of the publisher. From Matthew B. Miles, *Innovation in Education,* New York, Teachers College Press, © 1964, p. 647.

barely enough administrative staff to maintain status quo, and therefore the staff must be increased in order to implement a PPB system. He stated that it would take more than a dedicated and retrained administrative staff to make PPBS work.[1]

Experience has shown, however, that a district is capable of implementing PPBS without the addition of professional personnel. Darien, Connecticut, Skokie, Illinois, and Pearl River, New York, have successfully initiated PPBS using only existing professional staff. One of the arguments of this book is that the existing workload of the staff already encompasses work required for operationalizing the components of a PPB system. The school budget is now being completed, financial reports submitted, program changes suggested, and some districts are currently developing objectives. The program analysis component is probably the only area of a PPB system that receives little or no attention at the local school district level.

Moreover, consideration could be given to the elimination of certain tasks currently being completed by the professional staff and the reallocation of the time saved to the PPBS effort. In the Portland, Maine, School District the duties of an administrative assistant were reduced and he was assigned major responsibility for installing PPBS by the superintendent of schools. School districts might consider replacing existing efforts on rewriting curriculum guides with the development of educational objectives.

The activities performed for the traditional budget are consistent with the requirements of a PPB system. There is no change in the responsibility of the business office for consolidating material and equipment requests, estimating salary and fringe benefits for personnel, preparing worksheets, and balancing projected revenues with estimated expenditures. The only change for the business office is the manner in which the information is gathered and displayed.

Through careful redesign in the business area, the integration of program budgeting and accounting with the existing accounting system will result in a negligible workload increase. Chapters 5 and 6 contain some suggestions for accomplishing this integration.

The size of the school district may not be a significant factor for determining the number of professional personnel required in the installation of a PPB system. A study for installing PPBS in New York State school districts found that in a small district there is the benefit of greater flexibility and responsiveness and shorter lines of communication, although a large district has the ability to commit more personnel to the program analysis and other required tasks.[2]

---

[1]Stephen J. Knezevich, *Symposium on Organization and Resource Allocations Required by School Systems Desiring to Implement PPBS,* speech at AASA National Academy for School Executives at Lake Tahoe, Nevada, August 1969.

[2]*Planning, Programming, Budgeting System Implementation in Two New York State School Districts: Spring Valley Public Schools, Pearl River Public Schools,* New York, Peat, Marwick, Mitchell & Co., June 1970.

The addition of new professional personnel could lead to the speeding up of the implementation schedule. However, the so-called speed-up is limited because of the necessity for involving the total school community in the process and for relating the effort to the existing budget cycle. Thus, the need for adding professional staff in order to install PPBS has not been demonstrated. Indeed, Harry J. Hartley has argued that by being opportunistic, that is, by taking advantage of the activities in which a district is currently engaged, the installation of the system can be accomplished without additional personnel.[3]

**secretarial
support resources**

□ The second major personnel consideration is in the area of secretarial support services. The arguments discussed regarding the necessity for additional professional staff may be extended to the assessment of the existing secretarial staff and the need for additional resources in this area. It is clear that because of the requirements for statements of objectives, descriptions of existing programs and program changes create the need for extensive secretarial support. The alternatives open to the district include adding secretaries, reallocating the workload of existing staff, and/or updating office equipment. It appears that the annual addition of up to two full-time secretaries for approximately three months will provide all the secretarial support required to install PPBS. However, it should be noted that in some school districts no additional secretarial support was required.

**equipment
resources**

□ Equipment should be provided for dictation, typing, and rapid reproduction services. The availability of adequate office equipment will reduce the necessity for adding secretarial staff. The provision of appropriate office equipment such as dictation units will greatly enhance the efforts of the professional staff in meeting the information requirements of a PPB system. The use of advanced typing equipment that captures the typed material on magnetic or paper tape allows the material to be updated rapidly, and it will considerably increase both typing capacity and efficiency.[4]

It will be necessary to reproduce a number of documents for wide distribution and reaction. Equipment should be available for reproduction of short-run materials and also for the final documents which will require long-run reproduction capability. Short-run reproduction capability can be best achieved through one of the new types of copy machines. Long-run capabilities can be achieved through high-speed mimeograph or photo

---

[3]Harry J. Hartley in a speech, "PPBS History, Rationale, and Theory," at the New England School Development Council Information Conference on PPBES, Nashua, N.H., February 1970.

[4]Several different types of automatic typewriters are available. IBM has a magnetic tape selectric typewriter (MTST) that has a typing speed of 175 words per minute and can be used with one or two magnetic tapes. The Editype 200 uses an IBM Selectric typewriter connected with the Edityper 200. This unit uses folded paper tape. The Itel word processor 852 is a self-contained unit and uses punched paper tape.

offset equipment.[5] This type of equipment can be obtained through rental, lease-purchase, or purchase. In order to minimize equipment costs, the rental or leasing of such equipment might be limited to the period when the program documents are actually being prepared.

The use of computer equipment can be of value to the business office in producing program-oriented financial reports. This can be done through the redesign of the existing system so that the program reports will become a byproduct of the regular computerized accounting system. Computer services can also be utilized to record and display data on a program basis. However, computer equipment is not required for the installation of a PPB system. Small districts can utilize worksheets and standard adding machines to develop program budget data. Worksheets of the type that can be used by districts without computer capability are discussed in Chapters 5 and 6.

resource costs

□ An important consideration of the human and material resources necessary for installing PPBS is the cost factor. Any substantive diagnosis of the personnel costs will depend on whether the work is performed on purely a voluntary basis, in lieu of other assignments, or with additional pay as required by a contractual agreement. The number of hours required to complete the job will also depend on several variables such as the size of the district, the rate of installation, the degree of staff competency, the number of staff participating, and the office and data processing equipment available.

Because districts are currently doing most of the tasks required for a PPB system it can be argued that the shift from traditional curriculum building and budget processes to the PPB approach can be accomplished with little or no additional expense.

In analyzing the district's ability to provide the resources necessary for installing PPBS, school districts may find cost savings by working on a cooperative basis, i.e., with another district on a county or regional level. Computer services, consultants, and long-run reproduction equipment lend themselves to this type of cooperative effort. Districts may also work on a cooperative basis in in-service training or on a specific component of PPBS such as developing evaluative criteria.

TIME REQUIRED TO OPERATIONALIZE PPBS

The speed with which a PPB system can be initiated within a school system will depend upon the backing and active interest of the board of education and central administration and on the quality and number of

---

[5] There are several copying processes available on the market. The most popular is the xerographic method. Second is the electrostatic method, followed by Thermal. There are also three basic duplicating processes available: (1) offset, (2) stencil, and (3) spirit.

personnel assigned to specific tasks. In governmental agencies it was found that the achievement of a smoothly running PPBS system could not be expected in one or two years.[6] A considerable amount of time, perhaps three to five years, will be required in order to install all of the components of a PPB system. According to Harold McNally, chairman of educational administration and supervision at the University of Wisconsin at Milwaukee, one of the biggest mistakes educators make in introducing changes into schools is to underestimate the amount of time needed. It takes from one to five years to plan and implement a significant change, he indicated, because that length of time is needed to reduce the insecurity of administrators and to bring along support groups, teacher organizations, and the community.[7] However, with a concerted effort it is definitely possible to achieve the installation of a PPB system within a shorter time frame. Through the use of sufficient manpower and time commitment it might be possible to operationalize a PPB system in less than three years. The change to a PPB system is of such magnitude that it would be virtually impossible to install the complete system in a one-year time frame.

However, the school community may enjoy some of the positive benefits of a PPB system far sooner than designers of theoretical models have previously suggested. PPBS is divisible, that is, the components can be initiated on a partial basis; therefore, the district has considerable latitude in choosing a starting point. The initial benefits that a school district can achieve will depend on both the starting point selected and the effort devoted to activities leading to the installation of a PPB system.

STRATEGIES FOR
THE INTRODUCTION
OF A PPB SYSTEM

administrative
endorsement

☐ The assessment and final determination of the strategies to be utilized in installing PPBS might be made following a review of the literature on bringing about innovation in education.[8] It is clear, for instance, that administrators, as authority figures, are crucial in introducing innovations, particularly those involving instructional change. Because institutions are

[6]Harry P. Hatry and John F. Cotton, *Program Planning for State County City,* State-Local Finances Project, Washington, D.C., The George Washington University, January 1967, p. 34.

[7]As reported in *New York State School Boards Assoc. Newsletter, 12,* no. 2 (November, 1970).

[8]For a more detailed review of the problems of change, see Goodwin Watson, ed., *Concepts for Social Change,* Washington, D.C., National Training Laboratories, NEA, 1967; Warren G. Bennis, Kenneth D. Benne, and Robert Chin, eds., *The Planning of Change: Readings in the Applied Behavorial Sciences,* New York, Holt, Rinehart & Winston, 1962; Goodwin Watson, ed., *Change in School Systems,* Washington, D.C., National Training Laboratories, NEA, 1967; Ronald Lippett, Jeanne Watson, and Bruce Westley, *The Dynamics of Planned Change,* New York, Harcourt Brace Jovanovich, 1958; and Richard O. Carlson et al., *Change Processes in the Public Schools,* Eugene, Oregon, University of Oregon Press, 1965.

hierarchical, administrators have more power and thus they can handle the problems associated with the introduction of innovations more effectively than others.[9] The implications of the literature for bringing about innovation in education demonstrates the need for attaining a commitment from the top-level administrators. Without their commitment PPBS will probably not be successfully installed in a school district.

school board
support

☐ The administration is naturally preoccupied with the successful operation of existing educational programs and therefore pressure for innovation must also come from the school board and public. Miles has stated " . . . In most cases the initiation for change in an educational system appears to come from outside."[10] Thus, a formal resolution endorsing the concepts of PPBS should be passed by the board of education as a visible manifestation of its commitment to the installation of the system.

PPBS task team

☐ The resolution by the board of education approving the concept of PPBS and sanctioning its installation leads to the consideration of strategy to be utilized in order to operationalize PPBS. In order to bring about any change in a bureaucratic organization there must be persons willing and able to make decisions on activities necessary for effecting the change. Unilateral and arbitrary decision making by a single individual, usually the chief executive officer, does take place in some organizations. In most organizations decisions regarding change are made on both a formal and informal group basis.[11] However, the installation of a PPB system should not be left to an informal group process. While the power of communications in decision making by informal groups has to be recognized, the installation of PPBS can best be accomplished on a systematic and formalized basis. Because the components of a PPB system cut across all activities and the organizational structure of a school system, the systematic linkage of all the components is an absolute necessity for a fully operationalized PPB system.

In order to formalize the decision-making process and to guarantee the systematic linkage of the components, a group of ten to fifteen persons should be assigned the overall responsibility for the installation of the PPB system. In the private sector, attempts are being made to provide flexible organization arrangements that purposefully seek new and innovative ways to solve problems. For example, rather than assign responsibility to a single manager, one firm designates a task force to "solve knotty problems that transcend divisional boundaries, project teams to handle more complex jobs involving practically every part of the organization, and ad hoc problem-solving groups to resolve immediate issues such as a major

---

[9] Miles, op. cit., p. 64.

[10] Miles, op. cit., p. 640.

[11] Chester I. Barnard, *The Functions of the Executive,* Cambridge, Harvard University Press, 1966, pp. 185-186.

customer service problem."[12] A number of organizational arrangements are, of course, possible. Some type of a central planning-programming-budgeting group reporting directly to the superintendent of schools is required to initiate and develop the system. Such a central group might be referred to as a PPBS task team.

Appointment of a PPBS Task Team

The members of the task team should include a broad cross-section of the professional staff with two representatives from the community and one from the board of education. No one segment, e.g., administrators, should dominate.

Although the school business administrator could be a member of the task team, consideration for the image of PPBS as strictly a business enterprise should preclude him from the chairman's role. While the task team may or may not have representation from the business office, the assistant superintendent for instruction, or someone who has major responsibility in the curriculum area, should be a member of the task team. If PPBS is to be used for improving instruction, and if it is going to be perceived by the staff in that manner, then obviously a key person from the curriculum area must have an active role on the task team.

If the members of the task team have high status their recommendations are more likely to be accepted, particularly if the task team has been strongly legitimized.[13] Thus, the task team should be appointed by the board of education upon recommendation of the superintendent of schools. Officers of the teachers' organization or union as well as informal status leaders from the professional staff should be selected. The importance of using informal status leaders has been recognized by Campbell, Cunningham, and McPhee, who stated, "Informal group leaders are important opinion leaders. . . . A deliberate movement of an informal leader into a formal position of leadership is an example of the formal organization affecting the informal structure."[14]

Purpose of the Task Team

The task team should serve as an ongoing committee with the authority to elect its own chairman. It should also have the authority to establish subcommittees on an ad hoc basis.

The task team should serve as a catalytic agent for the introduction of the system. It will be responsible for gathering data, formulating plans, determining strategies, determining a starting point, and providing recommendations to the superintendent of schools on the various elements that may be required to be developed in order to establish PPBS. The task team

---

[12] "Group Approach Harnesses Youth's Creativity," *Management in Practice,* American Management Association, October 1970, p. 3. Reprinted by permission of the publisher from *Management in Practice,* October 1970, © 1970 by the American Management Association, Inc.

[13] Miles, op. cit., p. 643.

[14] Roald F. Campbell, Luvern L. Cunningham, Roderick F. McPhee, *The Organization and Control of American Schools,* Columbus, Charles E. Merrill, 1965, p. 283.

should meet regularly with the superintendent of schools to keep him abreast of the progress, problems, and recommendations.

106308

ACTIVITIES NECESSARY FOR THE INSTALLATION OF PPBS

In order to achieve the installation of the PPB system, the task team must assume responsibility for the accomplishment of the following activities:

1. Task team orientation
2. Consideration of alternative resources
3. Preparation of the detailed installation plan
4. Design of the program structure
5. Preparation of objectives, establishment of priorities, and evaluation of achievement
6. Preparation of the program budget
7. Design of the program accounting system
8. Programming: Providing for multi-year planning, program review, and analysis of alternatives
9. Preparation of the PPBS document.

The organization of the task team is shown below, and a flow chart of the task team implementation activities is shown in the chart on pages 30 and 31.

TASK TEAM ORGANIZATION CHART

Superintendent of Schools

PPBS Task Team

Responsibilities

1. Consider alternative resources
2. Prepare installation plan
3. Design program structure
4. Monitor preparation of objectives
5. Assist in establishing priorities

6. Assist in evaluating achievement
7. Assist in preparing program budget
8. Review program accounting system
9. Programming
10. Assist in preparation of PPBS document

Objective Subcommittee (one or more)

Program Analysis Sub-committee (one or more)

School Business Administrator

Program Budget Accounting

Communications

Public relations

Personnel

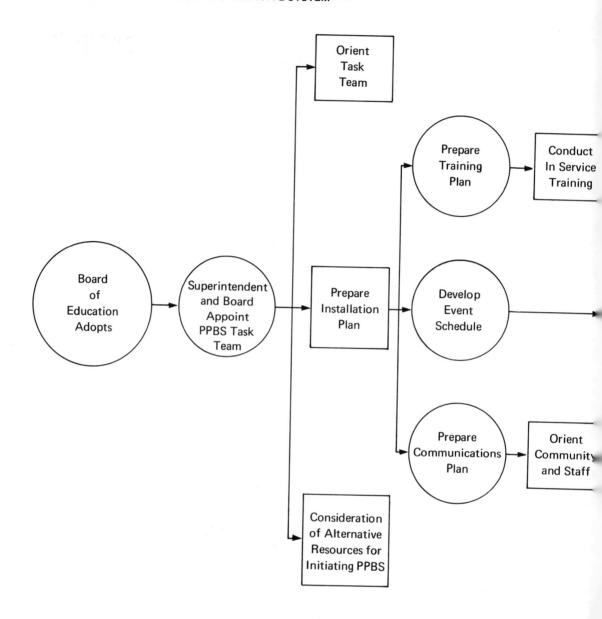

task team orientation

☐ The purpose of the orientation should be to have members of the task team reach a common understanding of the meaning and implications of a PPB system. In order to accomplish this, the task team members might review the literature dealing with PPBS.[15] The task team may also find

---

[15] See David Novick, ed., *Program Budgeting: Program Analysis and the Federal Budget,* Cambridge, Mass., Harvard University Press, 1965; Harry J. Hartley, *Educational Planning-Programming-Budgeting: A Systems Approach,* Englewood Cliffs, N. J., Prentice-Hall, 1968; *Report of the First National Conference on PPBES in Education,* Chicago, Research Corp. of the ASBO, 1969; Stephen J. Knezevich, ed., *Administrative Technology and the School Executive,* Washington, D.C., American Association of School Administrators, 1969; S. A. Haggart, et al., *Program Budgeting for School Planning: Concepts and Applications,* Englewood Cliffs, N. J., Educational Technology Publications, 1971.

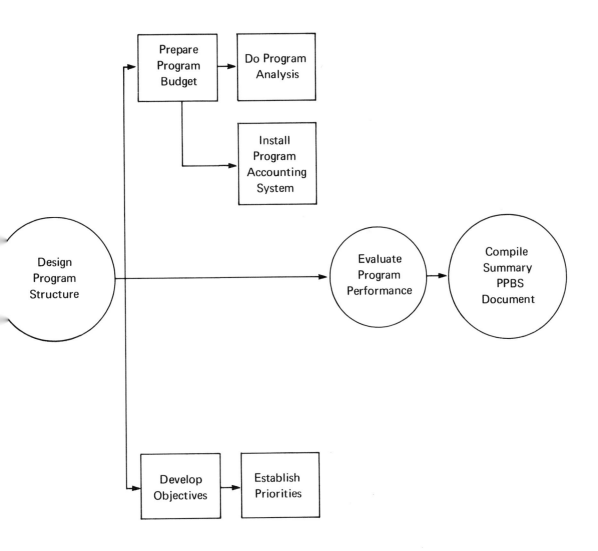

value in studying model systems such as those developed by the Association of School Business Officials,[16] the California State Department of Education Advisory Commission,[17] and the Western New York State Study Council,[18] as well as those developed by various commercial consulting firms.

---

[16] *Report of First National Conference on PPBES in Education,* ASBO, op. cit.

[17] *Conceptual Design for a Planning, Programming, Budgeting System for California School Districts,* Advisory Commission on School District Budgeting and Accounting, August 1969.

[18] *An Operational Model for the Application of Planning-Programming-Budgeting Systems in Local School Districts,* Pre-Pilot Test Version, Williamsville, N.Y., Western N.Y. School Development Council, 1970.

It may be advisable to have members of the task team attend state and national conferences dealing with this topic. For those states in which there has been vigorous leadership at the state level for PPBS, a representative of the State Education Department could be contacted for assistance in the orientation of the task team. Finally, if the district is willing to expend the necessary funds, an outside consultant may be secured for this purpose.

consideration of alternative resources

☐ There are innumerable options for approaching the installation of a PPB system that should be considered by the task team. It would appear, however, that the following three alternatives are the most frequently employed: (1) utilizing existing staff, (2) employing an outside consultant, or (3) purchasing a packaged program. There are a number of advantages and disadvantages that may be realized through the exclusive use of any one of these alternative approaches. The function of a task team is to determine the advantages and the disadvantages of each of the basic approaches in relation to the problems of their particular school systems. The table shown below illustrates some of the advantages and disadvantages of each of the three approaches for installing a PPB system that may be applicable to a school district.

ADVANTAGES AND DISADVANTAGES OF THREE APPROACHES TO INSTALLING A PPB SYSTEM

Use of existing members of the school district staff for the development and installation of PPBS

Advantages	Disadvantages
It encourages maximum involvement and thus strengthens commitment.	It is time-consuming and could lead to considerable frustration.
It broadens the professional staff's knowledge of their jobs.	The staff generally lacks expertise on PPBS, particularly in writing behavioral objectives.
It promotes teamwork through the use of compromise and consensus.	
It results in instructional objectives that will be relevant to the local community.	There is a risk for the duplicating of work which has already been completed in other school districts—the so-called "reinventing the wheel."
It may be accomplished at little or no additional expense.	This approach can be extremely costly if teacher contracts require overtime pay for any work performed other than actual classroom teaching.

The use of outside consultants

Advantages	Disadvantages
They provide proven expertise and up-to-date knowledge of PPBS.	Outside experts can be costly.
They may serve as catalytic agents to insure continuous progress on installation.	They may lack knowledge of the problems and expectations of the school district.

The use of outside consultants (continued)

Advantages	Disadvantages
They are not bound by existing traditions of the school system. They are able to effect a more rapid movement toward change.	The professional staff sometimes regards outside consultants merely as pawns for imposing new schemes.

The packaged program approach

Advantages	Disadvantages
Model program structures, model objectives, and evaluative criteria which have been professionally prepared are immediately available. They provide a shortcut and reduce frustration and the benefits of the district can accrue more quickly. They make the task of developing objectives in accordance with a program structure much more manageable. The cost is normally exceptionally low. There is avoidance of the risk in a district that duplicate work has already been successfully completed in other school districts.	It inhibits local creativity. It increases the likelihood that the staff might not develop a commitment to PPBS. The design may not be relevant to local needs and may require extensive adaptation. The packaged objectives are subject to misinterpretation. Nationally promoted packaged programs raise the fears of national assessment. There is no one package that contains all the components of a PPB system.

A task team may employ a combination of two or more of the alternative approaches in establishing a PPB system. Although a district may have the expertise and time to install all the components of the system, many short-cuts and time-saving devices can be achieved through the use of an outside consultant or a packaged program. As shown above, each of the three alternative approaches has both merit and potential drawbacks. By attempting to realize some of the advantages contained under each of the alternatives, the school district may be able to overcome many of the installation problems in an effective manner. The combining of the approaches is perhaps the most appropriate method for initiating PPBS.

The decision to be made by the task team is a relatively simple one—how can these approaches be mixed to utilize internal and external resources in achieving the installation of the PPB system? In making a final determination on which internal and external resources will be used the task team must keep in mind that the crux of a successful installation lies in professional staff commitment. The social scientists recognize that staff commitment is obtained through staff involvement. In this sense, every approach must be, to some extent, an internal one. Outside consultants and packaged programs should be evaluated in terms of their potential for facilitating internal commitments. The task team should be constantly alert to the fact that in the final analysis it is the local district personnel that must actually complete the tasks necessary for installing and operating the PPB system.

**preparation
of the detailed
installation plan**

☐ Because innovations with built-in implementation support are more rapidly accepted than those not so supported, a detailed implementation plan for PPBS must be prepared. The value of such a plan has been recognized by Matthew B. Miles, who stated:

This process obviously requires continuing technical attention. Yet for various reasons—perhaps connecting with existing educational ideology— deliberate planning of change is more often than not slighted, rejected as "manipulative," or ignored completely. Often, much more attention is put on constructing the innovation itself than on planning and carrying out the strategy for gaining its adoption. . . .

Yet it seems very clear that for almost all innovations the process of implementation itself needs careful study, planning, and experimental work . . . This is true both in general and for specific situations . . . And when a particular programmed learning device is introduced to a particular target system, much energy is required to shepherd its adoption and continued use. The understanding—and management—of change efforts thus becomes important to the success of any innovative effort.[19]

Thus, one role of a task team will be to develop an implementation plan that will bring together all of the factors necessary to install a PPB system successfully.

The plan should incorporate the assignment of resources and personnel, the selection of specific activities, the establishment of a time frame under which the activities will be completed, and the procedures for monitoring progress. Questions dealing with the initial starting point, a training program, and communications activities should also be examined and accounted for as a part of an implementation plan.

Event Schedule

The organization of the activities required to install PPBS, along with the assignment of personnel to carry out these activities and the target dates for completion, can be displayed in an event schedule. An event schedule provides a means for operationalizing the implementation plan and serves as a way of monitoring progress during the period of installation. Work plans, flow charts, or more sophisticated techniques such as program evaluation and review techniques (PERT) can be used to display this information.[20] Alternative schemes for displaying this data are shown in Figures 1, 2, and 3.

The event schedule must be coordinated with all the scheduled activities of the school system, such as board, budget, PTA, curriculum, or community

---

[19] Miles, op. cit., pp. 647-648.

[20] W. Hartman et al., *Management Information Systems Handbook: Analysis-Requirements Determination-Design and Development-Implementation and Evaluation,* New York, McGraw-Hill, 1968; Desmond L. Cook, *Program Evaluation and Review Technique: Applications in Education,* OE-12024, Coop. Research Monograph, No. 17, U.S. Dept. Health, Educ. and Welfare, 1966; Frank Greenwood, *Managing the Systems Analysis Function,* New York, American Management Association, 1968.

**FIGURES 1-3
PAGES 213-216**

meetings. Once the task team has prepared the event schedule, it should be submitted to the superintendent for review and approval. This approval is particularly important because it legitimizes the meetings to be held by the task team with members of the staff.

In preparing the event schedule the task team might be advised to request each individual who has specific responsibilities to submit his suggestions in terms of a time schedule that he would need to accomplish the activities that have been assigned to him. The role of the task team, then, would be to submit a compendium of all of the suggested time schedules, coordinate each and request modification where the time frame recommended appears to be inappropriate or in conflict.

To monitor progress and bring additional support or pressure on those individuals who are not meeting expectations, the event schedule might be displayed on a large wall chart. This chart can be mounted in the room which is used most frequently for the task team meetings. This technique has proven to be of value both to members of the task team and to members of the administrative staff who may not serve on the task team but who may have responsibility for completion of the activities described on the event chart. It will also provide the superintendent with a quick overview of progress at any given time. In order to take full advantage of this technique, the chart must be continually updated.

Staff Training Program

As part of the implementation plan, a program for training members of the staff should be developed. A team may assume responsibility for the preparation of the in-service training program. When the program has been fully developed, it should be included as a part of the event schedule. The in-service training program should consider the following:

= Who should be trained?
= What is the training need?
= When should training be given?
= Who should provide the training?

In determining who should be trained, the task team should consider the necessity for widespread staff involvement in order to secure commitment for the installation of PPBS. Some attention must be given to familiarizing all members of the staff with the concepts of PPBS. However, care should be taken to reduce significant overlap of training and to refrain from informing members of the staff about components for which they have no responsibility or interest. For instance, the techniques of program accounting will be of little, if any, value to classroom teachers. Interest in PPBS may be retained if the training program is operated on the principle of "need to know." Thus, although a general overview of the system should be given to the total staff, groups should not be forced to listen to details of jobs that others must perform.

The need for training will be based on the degree of sophistication that the staff already possesses regarding the various components of PPBS. If district personnel have spent time developing behavioral objectives then obviously the need for training in this area is greatly reduced, if not totally eliminated. The timing of the in-service training will depend upon the speed, as reflected in the event schedule, with which the district plans to install the system. In-service training should be given as the task team prepares to initiate work on a particular component. Training should take place as close as practical to the actual work to be performed. For example, the staff should not be exposed to program analysis until the task team is actually prepared to use that concept. Therefore, the training program should be used as a continuing activity that would be extended throughout the entire installation process.

Finally, the timing of the in-service training program may be affected by teacher contracts which may preclude the use of after-school time unless there is remuneration. There are a number of strategies that may be used to overcome this problem, such as released time, use of preparation periods, or in-service training credit for salary purposes. If the staff is convinced that PPBS will assist them to reshape educational programs for students, they may be willing to participate on a voluntary basis. In any case, every effort should be given to minimizing after-school time requirements and maximizing in-service training through the use of brief, clearly written training materials.

Ideally, members of the task team should conduct the in-service programs. If the district finds it is necessary to use an outside consultant, then members of the task team should provide for his orientation and introduction to the remainder of the staff. See Figure 4 for a training program schedule.

Communications Plan

Immediately following the development of the training program, a communications plan should be prepared by the task team. A communications plan is merely a schedule of the dates for informing the various groups regarding the concepts and progress of the installation of the system. This plan should become a part of the event schedule.

It may be advisable for the task team to secure the assistance and recommendations of other members of the staff who have the expertise and responsibility for the district's public relations program. The task team must not overlook the fact that its members can be a valuable aid for informal communications, particularly because it establishes a basis for credibility.[21]

design of the program structure

☐ Possibly the most important decision that the task team may make during the installation of a PPB system will be the determination of the program structure that will be adopted. The program structure is defined as the framework that groups the school district's activities according to the objective each activity serves. It provides the basis for preparing,

---

[21] Miles, op. cit., p. 652.

FIGURE 4
PAGE 217

assembling, organizing, analyzing, and displaying information. A more complete discussion of program structure will be found in Chapter 3, page 41.

In order to develop a program structure, the task team should consider the recommendations of the building principal, curriculum coordinator, central office personnel responsible for curriculum, and the business administrator. The development of the program structure is the responsibility of the task team and should not be delegated to a subcommittee or other members of the organization.

preparation of objectives, establishment of priorities, and evaluation of achievement

☐ The element of a PPB system that will require the greatest amount of time and effort to accomplish is the program planning element: the development of objectives, evaluative criteria, and the establishment of priorities for program areas. If the task team attempts to assume major responsibility in these areas, then their efforts to install a PPB system will be greatly diminished. Therefore, the task team should establish a subcommittee, or a number of subcommittees, composed of staff members and community residents to undertake this effort. In order to maintain some consistency or quality control over the objectives and evaluative criteria prepared by the subcommittees, the task team should review and recommend their adoption to the superintendent and the board of education. If the task team delegates the responsibility for developing these elements to only one subcommittee, then it should select the program area for the initial work of the subcommittee. The objectives may be philosophical, instructional, or supportive in nature. Philosophical objectives are statements of general educational aims or goals, while the instructional objectives are statements of behavioral change to be accomplished through the educational programs. Support objectives represent statements of the purposes of the supporting services and their relationship to the instructional program. The establishment of priorities is the assignment of relative importance to the program objectives. Evaluation of achievement is defined as generating evidence that can be used to determine whether or not, or to what extent, an objective has been accomplished. Chapter 4 deals with procedures for program planning.

preparation of the program budget

☐ Because of the unique nature of the program budget, the responsibility of the task team should be limited to coordinating the time schedule suggested by the business administrator for the budget process. The program budget represents the budget element of PPBS. It is the displaying of cost data according to the program structure that has been adopted. The activities to be accomplished in order to prepare this budget must be the responsibility of the business office. It is quite possible, however, for the task team to play a supportive role in the dissemination of instructions to the staff for the preparation of the program budget document. Chapter 5 is devoted to the program budget.

design of the program accounting system

☐ Similarly, the development of a program accounting system should be considered the sole responsibility of the business administrator. The role of the task team is to insure that the accounting system adopted provides the necessary information for decision making and meets the time requirements as described in the event schedule. Program accounting is the process of recording, classifying, and summarizing financial transactions of school districts based upon the adopted program structure. It displays both the actual and budgeted revenues and expenditures on a program basis. Chapter 6 is devoted to program accounting.

programming: providing for multi-year planning, program reviews, and analysis of alternatives

☐ Programming represents the process which provides information about the benefits and full cost implications of program alternatives that have been proposed for achieving each objective. Multi-year planning is a part of programming because it represents an attempt to predict the long-term consequences of program decisions. Again, the task team should delegate the program analysis activity to a subcommittee. Once the task team has determined the program area to be analyzed and appointed a subcommittee to do this analysis, its responsibility should be to monitor the progress of the subcommittee in relation to the adopted event schedule. Chapter 7 discusses programming.

preparation of the PPBS document

☐ The preparation of the PPBS document should be the responsibility of the superintendent of schools. The task team should serve in an advisory capacity to the superintendent, particularly in the area of the format of the document. The PPBS document organizes and integrates all of the information related to the various components of a PPB system. The techniques for preparing a PPBS document are described in Chapter 8.

SELECTION OF THE COMPONENT TO BEGIN THE ACTUAL INSTALLATION OF THE PPB SYSTEM

An important question that the task team must face will be the decision regarding which component of the system will serve as the starting point. Once the orientation of the task team has been completed the decision must be made on where to begin the actual implementation of the system. There are a number of components from which a district may select a starting point. The generally accepted components for starting the installation of the PPB system are:

= preparation of objectives
= preparation of program structure

= program analysis
= program budget

It has also been argued that the starting point need not be one of the elements of PPBS but rather it can be the assessment of the needs of a school district.[22]

Among school districts attempting to install PPBS, there is no consensus as to which starting point is the most effective. The starting point is important when the district is concerned with the nature of the initial benefits that it desires to achieve. If, for instance, the school district wants to communicate the school's aims to its professional staff and community, then a comprehensive statement of objectives may serve that purpose. The Westport, Connecticut, School District, in cooperation with its community, developed a statement of goals (objectives) on PPBS as its first step in installing PPBS.[23]   Thus, Westport started with the development of. objectives in an attempt to improve school-community communications. On the other hand, in the Milford, New Hampshire, School District a need was expressed for analyzing expenditures within and between the various programs offered.[24] By using the existing program as the program structure, costs were allocated to the various programs and analyzed on a program basis. The board of education was then able to allocate resources by program.

The basic starting points for installing the system are not mutually exclusive. In the Portland, Maine, School District both the objectives and program structure were started concurrently. This approach is feasible if the district's commitment is high and resources in terms of staff are available.

The task team must examine alternatives for starting the installation of PPBS in relation to the resources it has available. It must consider the sophistication of staff in dealing with the systems approach, the receptivity of the staff and community for a major change in programming and budgeting procedures, and the particular benefits it wishes to achieve most rapidly.

Although the initial component selected by the task team will depend on its diagnosis of the factors previously mentioned, the argument must be offered that the one starting point that will increase the possibility of a successful installation is the preparation of the program structure. This argument is made because the program structure provides an overall framework for the development of all of the other components of the PPB system. Once the program structure has been determined, objectives can be developed in a hierarchical manner within the parameter of the adopted

---

[22] Roy Sweigert, Jr., and Donald Kase, *Assessing Educational Needs of California: A Progress Report,* a paper prepared for the Region III Conference on Title III of ESEA, Denver, Colorado, March 1969.

[23] *Report of the Advisory Committee on School Goals to the Board of Education,* Westport, Connecticut, June 1969.

[24] Richard M. Durstine and Robert A. Howell, *Toward PPBS: Program Budgeting in a Small School District.* Boston. New England School Development Council, 1970.

program structure. Thus, the objectives can be organized, displayed, and assigned a priority in an orderly fashion. Financial data can also be displayed on a program basis in accordance with the program structure. In other words, the program structure provides the basis for the rational development and integration of all the other components of a PPB system.

Furthermore, if a district begins the installation of the system with objectives, it will run the risk of getting bogged down or wearing out its staff before any significant benefits can be achieved. However, if a district starts with the program budget or program analysis activity it will run the risk of having PPBS being perceived as a mechanistic, business office procedure.

The final decision on the first step for the installation of a PPB system should be made by the task team after consultation with the superintendent. The task team should also tentatively agree on the sequence for installing the remaining components.

SUMMARY

There are a number of factors to be considered in installing PPBS, including personnel and equipment resources, time requirements, and the various strategies for introducing the system.

In most school systems, the existing workload of the staff encompasses the components necessary for a complete PPBS. By capitalizing on the work already being accomplished and through the reallocation of tasks currently being completed by the staff, PPBS may be installed at little or no additional cost to the school district. Three to five years has been estimated as the time necessary for complete installation of the system.

The introduction of PPBS might best be accomplished by a task team representing a broad cross-section of the staff and community. The task team must assume responsibility for training the staff, analyzing resources available for the initiation of the system, and preparing the various plans of action recommended for an orderly installation of PPBS. Further, the task team must delegate responsibility for the completion of specific activities to various subcommittees. Finally, the task team must select the initial component for the actual installation of the system.

The task team must analyze the alternative starting point in terms of the resources it has available and the initial benefit it wishes to achieve. However, the program structure component should receive major consideration because it provides a basic framework for the development of the remaining components.

structuring:
how to design the
program structure

We need to seek a broader interpretation of education that discards rigid structuring for a freer adaption to differing needs, timing, and goals . . .   James E. Allen, Jr. ∗

The program structure provides the basis for generating, assembling, organizing, analyzing, and displaying information about the activities of the school district. The program structure may be utilized for the systematic analysis of the activities of the school district. The relationships of these activities to their attendant costs and to the objectives they are intended to achieve may also be examined through the use of the program structure.

The program structure provides for the integration of all the components of a PPB system. It is the basis for displaying objectives and evaluation data by program area. It also provides for the grouping of activities to which costs can be assigned. The analysis within a particular group of activities or between groupings of activities can be accomplished as a result of the program structure. Thus, the program structure furnishes the framework for unifying all of the components of a PPB system.

The purposes of the program structure are: (1) to display information that will be meaningful to administrators and usable in decision making, and (2) to provide a base of information that will support subsequent efforts at systems analysis.

Each of these purposes can be accomplished by establishing a classification scheme that groups the organization's activities according to the objective that each activity serves. Within the resulting taxonomic framework, information can be brought together on resource requirements, cost,

---

*James E. Allen, Jr., "Preparing the Way for a New Era of Advancement in Education," in *1969-70 AASA Report,* Washington, D.C., American Association of School Administrators, 1970, p. 9.

outputs, and benefits of all the activities carried on by the organization. The array of categories used to represent the activities of the organization and their interrelationships is known as a program structure.[1]

Thus, the development of a program structure is important for the successful installation of PPBS. Because the program structure produces a concise, schematic description of the district's total program, it is one of the major components of the system. "The very heart of the PPBS concept is the program structure, for it makes the outputs of a school district visible and identifies the resources required to yield these outputs."[2]

CRITERIA FOR DESIGNING A PROGRAM STRUCTURE

In developing a program structure it is not necessary to follow the school district's established organizational hierarchy. It may cut across existing lines of authority and program areas. As a result, the different types of program structures that can be adopted are unlimited.

However, there are two general characteristics applicable to all program structures:

It must embrace all the activities of the school district.
It must provide a hierarchical classification scheme.

It is necessary for the program structure to account for all of the activities in the district. This means the program categories must provide for instructional activities, administrative activities, and supporting services such as the operation and maintenance of facilities, bus transportation, or school lunch programs. In addition, the structure should make provision for activities that are funded by various state, federal, and private grant or aid programs. Before decisions can be made regarding a particular program area, information must be obtained not only on that program but on all programs. In other words, in order to diagnose the total district's efforts in one area, such as reading, all of the major activities dealing with this area must be accounted for in the program structure. For instance, if a district's regular reading program is supplemented by a federally funded special reading program and/or a summer school reading program, then all this information should be related in one comprehensive program area for diagnosis. It should be noted that the source of income for each of these activities within the reading program is different, but this should not preclude the relating of these activities in the program structure for the analysis of the district's total reading effort.

[1]S.A. Haggart et al., *Program Budgeting for School Planning: Concepts and Applications,* Englewood Cliffs, N. J., Educational Technology Publications, 1971.

[2]Harry J. Hartley, *Educational Planning-Programming-Budgeting: A Systems Approach,* Englewood Cliffs, N. J., Prentice-Hall, 1968, p. 154.

In order to understand and analyze the district's activities a hierarchical classification scheme should be provided. This scheme should be the framework for organizing district activities into a relatively small number of programs that can be subdivided into more narrowly defined levels. The first level of program structure should be general in nature and move through levels two, three, four, etc., with the activities under each level becoming more narrowly specified. The following table illustrates a hierarchical program structure with five levels.

Program structure may have as many levels as needed by the district to display the data necessary for analysis and resource allocation. Although the program levels can be extended further downward, a program structure with up to six levels will adequately serve most school districts. Extension of the levels beyond six may tend to become dysfunctional and not worth the effort.

Program Level	Program Description
I	District
II	Instruction
III	Regular Instruction
IV	Social Studies, grades K-12
V	American History, grade 12

The two general characteristics embracing all activities and a hierarchical classification scheme should serve as a reference point during the preparation of the program structure. There are several additional criteria that should be considered in designing a program structure. A program structure should:

1. Be structured using categories and elements that are as mutually exclusive as possible.
2. Facilitate the transition from currently used procedures to corresponding procedures in an integrated PPB system.
3. Provide decision makers with relevant information required to determine priorities among objectives, select educational program alternatives, and develop long-run plans.
4. Be usable downward through the organizational structure of the educational system in which it is to be made operative.[3]

The program structure should use categories that are, for the most part, mutually exclusive. It is recognized that some degree of arbitrary decision making will occur in order to place the various activities in program categories in the program structure. To the extent that the program structure has classifications to which activities can be readily assigned, the necessity for making arbitrary decisions on the placement of activities will be greatly reduced. Therefore, when developing the program categories it

[3] For other criteria on developing program structures, the reader is referred to Donald R. Miller, *An Introduction to Planning-Programming-Budgeting Systems,* Operation PEP, March 1969; Haggart, op. cit.; Hartley, op. cit.; *Conceptual Design for a Planning, Programming, Budgeting System for California School Districts,* Advisory Commission on School District Budgeting and Accounting, 1969.

is important to minimize the confusion as to which activities relate to a specific program classification. Assigning activities to a specific classification is complex because certain activities may contribute to more than one objective and therefore may be placed in more than one category. This problem has been identified by S.M. Barro, who provides the following example:

> ... Certain music and art courses may be of value to most students primarily as sources of cultural enrichment and means of nonvocational self-expression, while for other students they may constitute training for future artistic careers. Similarly, certain shop or craft courses may constitute vocational training for some students, while they may provide avocational or recreational skills for others.[4]

For this reason it is important to note that it is possible for certain activities to contribute to the achievement of several objectives although assigned to only one program category. Thus, in making decisions regarding the assignment of activities to program categories it may be necessary to assign the activity to that category to which it is most closely related. The teaching of citizenship may take place in a music classroom, a math class, or even on the physical education field. However, if the social studies program has the primary responsibilty for the achievement of this objective, then the activities in the citizenship education area should be assigned to the social studies program category.

In order to accommodate those activities that cannot be assigned to a program, a category entitled "unclassified activities" or "non-program activities" should be added to the program structure as a device for accounting for all of the activities of a school system. Thus, an expenditure such as refund of property taxes due to over-assessment can be accounted for even though such an expenditure can not be properly placed in a regular program category.

Another criteria in designing the program structure is that it should facilitate the transition from traditional programming and budgeting procedures to the integrated PPB system. This can be accomplished by designing, at least at the outset, a program structure which follows existing educational and supporting services programs. As discussed on page 42 there is virtually an unlimited number of structures that one may devise. While it is possible to develop an entire program structure around a single concept such as creativity, it would be extremely difficult, if not totally impossible, to provide the relevant data—including cost information—that would be necessary in order to operationalize the PPB system. Using the principle of "starting where you are" the task team is cautioned to develop a program structure that can be supported by the existing system. This is not to say that the program structure should serve as an inhibiting force for the creative development of new educational programs. It merely recognizes the necessity for building on what already exists.

---

[4]Haggart, op. cit., p. 27.

The program structure must also be designed to provide the information required for determining priorities among objectives, selecting educational program alternatives, and developing long-range plans. The structure should facilitate the production of the data necessary for the assessment and analysis of program objectives and educational program alternatives, both within a particular program area and between other major program categories. The long-range planning activities of a school system can be supported through the data displayed by the program structure. These criteria should be considered both during the initial design and in subsequent years, as the structure is modified or updated.

PROCESS FOR
DESIGNING A
PROGRAM STRUCTURE

In determining a program structure, consideration must be given not only to the design criteria but also to the component that has been selected as the starting point for the installation of a PPB system. If the district has elected to install PPBS by starting with the development of a program structure, then the process would include grouping the existing activities of the school district according to apparent similarity of purpose. Once the activities have been brought together according to purpose, then the groups may be assembled into larger program aggregates. This process involves starting at the lower levels of the hierarchy with the more specific activities and working them through a regrouping process into the higher levels of the program structure.

However, if the district has decided to begin the installation of PPBS by stating its objectives, then the basis for establishing the program structure should be the groupings of objectives that have been specified and agreed upon. The objectives can be subcategorized into more specific objectives that in turn provide the various levels of hierarchy for the program structure.

These two basic approaches have been characterized as prescriptive and descriptive.[5] The prescriptive approach defines programs according to a conception of what schools ought to be doing. The descriptive approach identifies programs and objectives inductively from relationships among actual, ongoing activities. Thus, a program structure based on existing activities would be descriptive, while the structure developed around objectives would be prescriptive.

Regardless of which approach the school district adopts, experience has shown that the process itself, apart from the determination of the actual program structure, is valuable because of the incentive it provides for reexamination of established activities. As a result of organizing the

---

[5] Ibid.

district's activities into a program structure, the Portland, Maine, School District discovered many inconsistencies and unnecessary duplications in existing programs. The program structure in and of itself will not resolve these problems; however, the process of developing the program structure can highlight such problems and display data that will assist in their resolution.

activity

Four techniques to provide assistance for determining a program structure are described here. First, a program structure may be constructed by describing each major activity of the school district on a separate index card and then displaying the card in a hierarchical relationship on a large wall chart. Those activities that are deemed most important should be placed at the top and any related activities should be placed in order of importance directly below. The process of rearranging, consolidating, and eliminating will produce a tentative program structure which can be prepared in a smaller chart form for distribution to key staff for review and reaction.

org. chart

Another technique for developing a program structure is to use the existing school district organization chart. By substituting a description of the major activities for the names or position of each individual listed on the chart, a natural hierarchical grouping of activities may be determined. Once the activities have been stated, they may be shifted within or between organizational classifications. As previously stated, the program structure is not required to follow traditional organizational lines. These groupings of activities may serve as the basis for an initial draft of the program structure which can be sent to the staff for review.

obj

A third technique for developing a program structure is to state on index cards the major objectives of the school system. Once the school system's objectives have been arranged in hierarchical order, with the most specific at the lower levels and the broad or general objectives at the higher levels, a program structure can be determined for staff review. A program structure developed around the objectives of the school system would be based on a prescriptive approach.

model

Finally, a program structure can be developed by selecting a model structure that has been suggested or used by another school district or by an outside organization and then adapting it to fit local requirements. As a result of the activities across the nation on PPBS, a number of different program structures have been developed by states, universities, and private consulting agencies. The State of California has adopted a uniform statewide program structure.

To date, many of the program structures that have been developed are based on subject area, building, or grade level, or some combination of these three. However, there appears to be a strong argument for encouraging each school district to develop a program structure in accordance with its own needs. The program structure must account for the differences between school districts, whether or not the district has based its program structure on existing activities (descriptive) or on proposed objectives (prescriptive).

A program structure should be developed for the entire school system. However, in large city school districts, particularly those that are decentralized, a separate program structure may be developed for each of the decentralized units. Although this may not prove to be the ideal program structure, at least in terms of reaching the citywide objectives, it will allow the staff and community in each of the decentralized units to establish its own program priorities.

The following alternative methods of grouping instructional activities may serve as the basis for developing a program structure:

1. Subject area—major subject disciplines such as mathematics, foreign language, English on a district-wide (kindergarten through grade 12) basis. (Figure 5)
2. Target group—target population such as gifted, disadvantaged, non-English speaking. (Figure 6)
3. Grade level—preschool, kindergarten through grade 12 on an individual grade basis. (Figure 7)
4. Grade span—preschool, elementary, middle, and secondary. (Figure 8)
5. Building—on an individual building basis. (Figure 9)
6. Objectives—by grouping educational objectives such as cognitive, affective, and psychomotor. (Figure 10)
7. Hybrid—any combination, such as subject area and grade level. (Figure 11)

The district's choice of program structure is not limited to the alternative groupings that have been listed. Depending upon the expertise and creativity of the staff, consideration may be given to entirely new or different approaches for developing a program structure, such as:

1. Develop a program structure around the individual learner concept—a separate program for each child.
2. Develop a program structure that encompasses all aspects of the child's learning environment—church, youth groups, special federal programs, mass media, welfare, mental health, probation, and any other agencies that serve the community.
3. Develop a program structure around priority areas of identified learning needs—self-concept, inquiry, special interests, survival requirements or specific cross-discipline curricular areas.

Again, each district must develop or adapt a program structure to suit its own particular purposes and there is no one best program structure applicable to all school districts.

There are advantages and disadvantages for each of the four techniques for determining a program structure. Obviously, constructing a program structure around a group of objectives will be an extremely time-consuming and complex process. The modification and adoption of a "model" program structure will be somewhat less time-consuming; however, it may be difficult to modify it to meet the district's needs. The use of the district's organization chart for establishing a program structure will be a limited, or even a useless, technique if the chart has not been kept current. This technique however, does provide the advantage of an established hierarchical order of activities. Furthermore, the program structure evolving from the organization chart may be the one most

FIGURES 5-11

PAGES 218-227

readily accepted by staff. The technique of using existing activities for determining a program structure has the advantage of capitalizing on established and accepted practices.

The time required for developing a program structure may be well spent in terms of acquiring greater commitment for the PPBS process from the staff. The importance of allowing sufficient time to determine a program structure has been illustrated in a report of the city of Dayton, Ohio, which stated:

In retrospect, this has been the major failing in the entire process to date. . . . Hindsight now shows us that we apparently spent an inordinate amount of time on developing our program analysis abilities . . . in proportion to the time spent on some of the basic cornerstones of the PPBS process—namely, the program structure.[6]

Whether the program structure is developed internally or adapted, the important dimension is the review and recommendation of key staff members. For instance, the instructional specialists must be given the opportunity to respond to the implications that the program structure may have for the development and planning of their instructional programs. The business administrator must be given an opportunity to indicate whether or not he can produce the fiscal data necessary to support the suggested program structure. After the review of the recommendations and comments of key staff leaders, the program structure should be recommended by the task team for approval by the superintendent.

NEED FOR REVISING PROGRAM STRUCTURE

It must be recognized that the program structure adopted should not represent the "final" program structure. Provisions must be made to allow the district's personnel the opportunity to recycle objectives and activities continually and this will result in some regrouping and restructuring of the structure. The program structure must be viewed as a dynamic, flexible framework. In order to avoid perpetuating the status quo, the adoption of any program structure should be viewed as tentative and, therefore, subject to change. For example, the Skokie, Illinois, School District found that their subject-oriented program structure was inadequate because early work with the district's Goal Committee indicated a concern for the whole child, a child's personality, and social and academic development. Furthermore, they found that managing programs by subject would have

[6]*PPBS Pilot Project Reports from the Participating 5 States, 5 Counties, and 5 Cities,* State-Local Finances Project, The George Washington University, February 1969, p. 107.

demanded too much reorganization. Thus, Skokie switched from a subject-oriented array of programs to a school and grade level program structure.[7]

The program structure will also affect the decision makers' perspective, depending on the manner in which the program categories were selected. For example, a program structure designed to emphasize target groups will tend to focus the attention of the decision makers and to limit their analysis of data to the problems and accomplishments of specific types of student groups. This will serve the purpose for which this particular program structure was established. Indeed, the target area perspective may be a legitimate one. As Burkhead has indicated, an area approach to budget allocation within a large city may be desirable.[8] However, to the extent that one analyzes data solely on the basis of the program structure adopted, his perspective will be limited, particularly in generating alternatives.

It may well be that one of the inherent problems of adopting a program structure is that it may inhibit the district's creative potential in resolving critical educational problems identified in the planning process. Therefore, it is important that the task team be aware of this possibility and that they continually provide for the reassessment and restructuring of the adopted program structure. If subsequent analysis indicates that restructuring is necessary, such restructuring should occur in conjunction with the annual budget cycle. The rationale for this is to provide the time necessary for the reorientation of the staff, the generation of new information, and the relation of resources to the revised program structure. The flexibility for instituting new programs or reallocating resources during the budget year that a school district possesses under a traditional function-object budgeting system should be retained under the PPB system. Although new programs may be instituted in order to respond to an unanticipated educational problem, the program structure should probably remain unchanged for a complete budget cycle.

Thus, although the program structure is one of the more important decisions to be made, it need not and indeed should not be allowed to become a stagnant, inflexible framework for developing programs and allocating resources. The identification and articulation of new objectives, new problems, and new information should lead to an ongoing reassessment of the adequacy of the adopted program structure. Every program structure will contain potential problems and inadequacies. However, despite its limitations, it is the heart of a PPB system because it unifies all of the activities of the school district and provides a basis for systematic analysis and decision making. No longer can separate staffs for planning, programming, and budgeting act apart from one another.

---

[7]Arthur E. Kent and Wesley F. Gibbs, "Why Skokie Switched to PPBS Grade Level Array," *Nation's Schools,* January 1970, p. 44.

[8]Jesse Burkhead, "The Theory and Application of Program Budgeting to Education," Proceedings of *National Education Association School Finance Conference,* April 6, 1966, p. 13.

SUMMARY

The program structure provides the framework for generating, assembling, organizing, analyzing, and displaying information about the activities of the school district. Through the program structure a classification scheme may be established for grouping the district's activities according to the objectives that each serves.

A program structure must embrace all the activities of the school district and it must provide a hierarchical classification scheme. The criteria for designing a program structure include: developing mutually exclusive categories, ease of transition, provision for relevant data, and being usable downward through the school district's organizational structure.

A program structure may be determined by (1) describing existing activities, (2) redefining the district's organization chart, (3) grouping and ranking objectives, and (4) adapting an existing model. Regardless of the technique used to determine a program structure, it should be recognized that there is no one best program structure applicable to all districts. Therefore, each district must develop or adapt a program structure to suit its own particular purposes.

In order to avoid perpetuating the status quo the program structure should be viewed as a dynamic, flexible framework that is subject to change.

planning: how to develop program objectives, establish priorities, and evaluate achievement

It is quite plain, I think, that the task of improving the American schools is not simply one of technique—however comforting it would be to some professional educators to think so. What is at issue, rather, is a deeper problem, one that is more philosophical than psychological or technological in scope. Let me put it in all innocence. What do we conceive to be the end product of our educational effort? I cannot help but feel that this rather overly simplified question has become obscured in cant.   Jerome S. Bruner *

Do the staff, students, and community know what the programs are meant to accomplish during any given period of time? Do they feel that any desired accomplishment is more important than another? Do they know whether or not they have accomplished that which they sought? Too often people associated with educational organizations have not even asked these questions, let alone attempted to answer them. Charles E. Silberman, in *Crisis in the Classroom*, brings this criticism into sharp focus when he recognized that the most important single cause of educational failure has been that the managers—principals and superintendents—have not asked what the organizational goals are and have not made sure that the question was studied and answered.[1]

The fundamental intent of the planning component is to provide a vehicle for asking and answering these essential questions. The planning component should encompass all the activities that lead to the development of objectives, ranking those objectives in order of importance, and evaluating the progress made in obtaining those objectives. In a PPB system statements

---

*Jerome S. Bruner, "Learning and Thinking," in Alice and Lester D. Crow, eds., *Vital Issues in American Education,* New York, Bantam Books, 1964, p. 191.

[1] Charles E. Silberman, *Crisis in the Classroom: The Remaking of American Education,* New York, Random House, 1970, p. 507. ©Charles E. Silberman.

of objectives provide guidelines for both planning and evaluation. Objectives may serve to facilitate the setting of priorities because they provide the specific expectations on which judgments of relative importance are made.

The primary strength of PPB as a system is the integrative nature of its components; this is particularly true of the planning component because its elements—establishing objectives, priorities, and evaluative criteria—are interdependent. The establishment of objectives without the assignment of priorities reduces their effectiveness and they must be evaluated or they will be rendered meaningless. Priorities cannot be established without a statement of specific objectives. Furthermore, the evaluation of progress made toward the attainment of the objectives provides the base for the revision of priorities. Evaluation is based upon the expectations reflected in the statement of objectives. Finally, the emphasis of the evaluation effort is determined by the established priorities. The relationship between the elements of program planning is displayed in the following model:

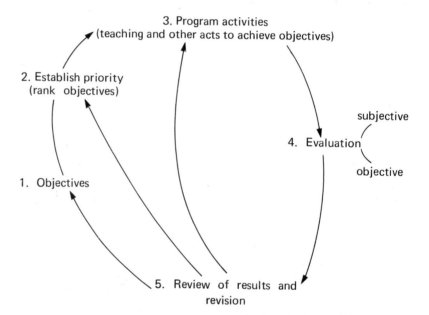

Thus, the crucial challenge facing those interested in improving education today is to establish meaningful objectives, to determine priorities among them, and to evaluate progress toward their achievement. "It is not possible to manage, in other words, unless one first has a goal. It is not even possible to design the structure of an organization unless one knows what it is supposed to be doing and how to measure whether it is doing it." [2]

Techniques for establishing objectives, priorities, and evaluative criteria in a PPB system are discussed in the remainder of this chapter.

---

[2] Peter F. Drucker, *The Age of Discontinuity,* New York, Harper & Row, 1969, p. 190.

DETERMINING
OBJECTIVES

An objective may be defined as something toward which effort is directed, an aim or end of action. An objective attempts to describe the intent of a particular program or activity and it may be framed in terms of desired performance or behavioral expectation. The program structure developed as a part of the PPB system provides a framework for systematizing and displaying the multitude of objectives that a district can generate. This should lead to a greater understanding of the relationships of the various objectives within a particular program and between other programs as well.

Also, PPBS gives meaning to objectives by providing a vehicle which the school district can use to allocate their limited resources to its stated priorities. Historically, it has been extremely difficult to operationalize them partly because resources have not been directly applied in order to bring about their achievement. The allocation of resources, on a priority basis, to the adopted objectives should minimize the risk that they will become, as has occurred so often in the past, meaningless platitudes or embalmed in curriculum guides and forgotten in the pressure of new demands.

types of objectives

☐ It is useful to conceive of objectives as existing at several levels reflecting varying degrees of abstraction. The most abstract level consists of broad general statements which may be useful for determining long-range educational plans. At the most concrete level of the hierarchy are found the lesson plan objectives of the teachers and the desired outcomes of the students stated in behavioral terms.

Under a PPB system each level may have its own set of objectives which should be related through the program structure. Therefore, a hierarchical relationship of objectives is established. The objectives become more specific, behavioral, observable, and measurable as one proceeds through the various levels of the program structure. Stated another way, "The smaller the unit within an organization for which one is planning, the statements of objectives become more specific; the target date for accomplishment of the objectives become more precise; and resource requirements are easier to identify."[3]

In order to facilitate the development of objectives under a PPB system, it will be helpful to classify objectives into three basic types. This classification will assist in minimizing semantic confusion and communication problems that may exist in developing objectives. The three basic types of objectives are given below.

---

[3]*An Operational Model for the Application of Planning-Programming-Budgeting Systems in Local School Districts, Pre-Pilot Test Version,* Williamsville, New York, The Western New York School Development Council, Part IV, 1970, pp. 2, 3.

1. Philosophical Objectives

These are statements of general educational aims, such as school board policies that are philosophical in nature. They are usually based on an assessment of the general expectations of community, student, and professional staff. Philosophical objectives by definition are general and timeless. They are helpful to the extent that they provide overall direction for the development of more specific objectives. Referring to the program structure, philosophical objectives may be developed for levels one, two, and possibly three. Philosophical objectives are synonymous with goals as defined by Hartley and others.[4] For an example of philosophical objectives, see Figure 12.

2. Instructional Program Objectives

Instructional program objectives are statements of anticipated behavioral change to be accomplished in a particular instructional program area. Instructional objectives are prescriptions for change. They describe what is to be learned, when the information or skills will be learned, and the circumstances under which the learner will be evaluated. An instructional program objective describes the educational intent of the instructional program rather than the teaching method for achieving it. Further, it describes the conditions under which the behavior will occur and establishes criteria for judging acceptable performance. An instructional program objective differs from a philosophical objective because it requires a specific time frame and evaluative criteria. Refer to Figure 13 for an illustration of an instructional program objective.

3. Support Service Program Objectives

Support service program objectives are statements of the purpose of these services and their relationship to the overall instructional program. Examples of supporting service program areas are transportation, school cafeteria, and plant operation and maintenance. Support service objectives should be designed using the same criteria as the instructional program objectives. That is, they should include a statement of the purpose of the supporting service, the time frame under which it is to be accomplished, and the criteria that will be used for determining whether or not it has been accomplished. See Figure 14 for examples of support service objectives.

Both instructional program objectives and support service program objectives will be found at the lowest levels of the program structure of a school system as previously discussed.

Because PPBS is a system, the relationship among the three types of objectives—philosophical, instructional, and support service—is important. Much of the benefit accrued from PPBS approach is the fact that these relationships can be spelled out. The instructional program objectives—the

---

[4] Harry J. Hartley, *Educational Planning-Programming-Budgeting: A Systems Approach,* Englewood Cliffs, N.J., Prentice-Hall, 1968, p. 155; *Conceptual Design for a Planning, Programming, Budgeting System for California School Districts,* Advisory Commission on School District Budgeting and Accounting, 1969.

FIGURES 12-14

PAGES 228-231

most numerous and difficult to determine—are related to the philosophical objectives. Support service program objectives can be justified and evaluated primarily in terms of their contribution to the instructional program. The PPB system links the three types of objectives into a functioning whole. This facilitates the gathering and analysis of data on all the programs that make up the school system.

problems in determining objectives

☐ The process by which objectives are developed or selected is extremely time-consuming and complex. There are many reasons for this. First, the process invites the clash of value systems and is even further complicated because most of the professional staff have not, in the past, identified or attempted to reach consensus on their values. Also, personal needs often conflict with organizational needs and the difficulty is to accommodate personal needs without sacrificing organizational ones in determining objectives. Further, the plurality and complexity of educational demands cannot be readily reduced to specific objectives.

It has been recommended that the installation of PPBS involve a large number of people—both staff and members of the community. This recommendation is particularly applicable in the development of objectives. However, it must be recognized that to the extent people are involved, the amount of time required to complete the task will be greatly increased as will the frustrations of those involved. Further, the status differences of the people that need to be involved also lead to complications.

Finally, the emphasis on measurable results often gives rise to the controversial and threatening aspects of accountability and this leads to resistance to development of evaluation criteria that are necessary to operationalize objectives. The potential for hostility, conflict, and emotional reaction on the part of staff that can be generated around the areas of evaluation-assessment-accountability cannot be overstated.

responding to the problems of determining objectives

☐ Those responsible for developing objectives must face up squarely to the issue of consensus and commitment at the very beginning of the process. Their primary intention should be to improve instruction by guiding the school community toward a rigorous emphasis on the objectives of education and the result to be achieved. This probably will not occur if objectives are imposed or if the staff perceives them as capricious, arbitrary, or otherwise contrary to their personal and professional interests.

Staff and students must perceive that the statement of objectives will assist them in attaining what they see as their legitimate ends rather than as static, restrictive, exclusive statements of someone else's interests that will be used to pressure them into compliance. The more opportunity they have to influence the development of the objectives, the more likely they are to perceive them as being not only helpful, but vital to the accomplishment of the stated ends.

In terms of the personal needs vs. organizational needs, the leadership must accept the reality of personal objectives existing in the midst of organizational ones.

If a man's most powerful driving force is comprised of his need, wishes, and personal aspirations, combined with the compelling wish to look good in his own eyes for meeting those deeply held personal goals, then management by objectives should begin with his objectives.[5]

While it is not suggested that it is necessary to begin with each individual's objectives in developing a school system's objectives, care should be taken to accommodate the personal aspirations of the staff.[6] They may be dealt with through utilization of some of the basic concepts contained in human relations theory for reducing resistance to change such as:

Resistance will be less if administrators, teachers, board members, and community leaders feel that the project is their own—not one devised and operated by outsiders.

Resistance will be less if the project clearly has wholehearted support from top officials of the system. . . .

Resistance will be less if participants see the change as reducing rather than increasing their present burdens. . . .

Resistance will be less if the program offers the kind of new *experience which interests participants. . . .*

Resistance will be less if participants have joined in diagnostic efforts leading them to agree on the basic problem and to feel its importance.

Resistance will be less if the project is adopted by consensual group decision. . . .

Resistance will be reduced if it is recognized that innovations are likely to be misunderstood and misinterpreted, and if provision is made for feedback of perceptions of the project and for further clarification as needed. . . .

Resistance will be reduced if the project is kept open to revision and reconsideration if experience indicates that changes would be desirable. . . .[7]

In addition to this listing, further insights and recommendations for reducing resistance to change may be found in Herbert Thelen's *Dynamics of Groups at Work.*[8] Thelen, who advocates the use of small subgroups to accomplish change, recommends a number of specific techniques for making such groups effective.

---

[5] Harry Levinson, "Management by Whose Objectives?" *Harvard Business Review,* July-August 1970, p. 129.

[6] H. Richard Wald, "Reconciling Organizations and Personal Goals," *Personnel Journal,* January 1970.

[7] Goodwin Watson, ed., "Resistance to Change," *Concepts for Social Change,* Washington, D.C., NTL Institute for Applied Behavioral Science, 1967, pp. 22, 23.

[8] Herbert Thelen, *Dynamics of Groups at Work,* Chicago, University of Chicago Press, 1954.

School systems, particularly large ones which are bureaucratic in nature, have been characterized as incapable of change. However, Peter Blau in *The Dynamics of Bureaucracy*[9] has documented the fact that bureaucratic organizations can establish a climate for change.

Indeed, he presents a strong argument against the prevailing view that bureaucratic organizations are structurally static. Therefore, with appropriate planning a change of the magnitude of PPBS can be attained in a school system.

subcommittee for determining objectives

☐ Again, determining objectives is a complex, time-consuming task. Because the task team must devote its energies to the installation of the total PPB system, it should not assume responsibility for developing objectives. Rather, the task team should establish one or more sub-committees for this purpose. The role of the task team should be limited to appointing the subcommittee, to monitoring its progress, and to reviewing its recommendations.

The subcommittee should be composed of community representatives and staff members. Consideration should also be given by the task team to including some student representatives on the subcommittee. Reasonableness in terms of the size of the group for effective communication purposes will be a determining factor on the actual number of participants. However, in no case should the group be overloaded with either administrators, teachers, citizens, or students. The rationale for this recommendation relates to one of the basic premises in installing PPBS which is to broaden the base of involvement in all phases of decision making affecting the school district.

The role of the subcommittee should include the following:

1. Selecting a target program area or areas for which objectives will be determined.

2. Deciding where to start the process of writing objectives.

3. Deciding the techniques for writing the objectives for the target program area.

4. Soliciting comments on the objectives and reviewing, revising, and recommending the objectives for the program area selected.

selection of target program areas

☐ A decision must be made either to develop objectives for the entire school system or to select one or more program areas for the initial effort. In subsequent years this effort may be expanded to the development of objectives in the remaining programs. A decision may also be made to write philosophical objectives for the upper levels of the program structure and to write instructional program objectives for one target program area.

---

[9] Peter Blau, *The Dynamics of Bureaucracy: A Study of Interpersonal Relations in Two Government Agencies,* Rev. Ed., Chicago, University of Chicago Press, 1955.

Obviously the simultaneous development of objectives for all programs will require a major effort by the district. Not only must the district provide considerable staff support, but it will also probably find it necessary to establish several subcommittees involving a greater number of community and/or student participants. While this approach broadens the base of involvement, it may lead to a great deal of confusion and wasted effort. Under this approach, the information required and the amount of data to be analyzed would be considerable, and the top-level decision makers may find themselves overwhelmed as a result. The development of objectives for all program areas may only be realistic for those school districts already possessing a sophisticated information retrieval system.[10] Such a system must possess the necessary data for the development of objectives as well as the capability for accommodating new information generated as a result of that development. However, due to the complexity of determining objectives, the development of instructional program objectives for all areas is not a realistic alternative, even with an information retrieval system.

An advantage to starting more slowly, that is, in one program area, is that those participating in the development process would be given the opportunity for increasing their familiarity with the concepts and techniques for stating objectives before moving to other program areas. By starting with a target program an opportunity to select a particular program area that will not pose all the difficult problems in determining objectives will be provided. This would also give the staff the chance to become more sophisticated in the techniques of developing objectives before attempting more complex program areas.

There are several limitations to determining objectives in a program-by-program approach. First, this approach requires that a selection be made of a particular program area. This may cause some consternation for the staff in both the program area that is selected and in those that are excluded. The former will ask, "Why are you picking on us?" The latter may wonder, "Why aren't we being given the same opportunity?" Of course, more than one program may be selected, but as the number of programs increase, the advantages of this approach are diminished.

Furthermore, the program-to-program approach limits the number of staff, students, and community participants working on developing objectives—the one element in the installation of a PPB system in which participation may be most relevant. Finally, the selection of this approach may extend the determination of objectives over so many years that the full impact of a PPB system will not be realized as readily as the staff and community may desire.

---

[10] For definitive works on information systems, see Enoch Haga, ed., *Automated Educational Systems,* Elmhurst, Ill., The Business Press, 1967; *Educational Technology, 9,* no. 6 (June 1969); Harvard Business Review, ed., *New Decision-Making Tools for Managers,* Cambridge, Mass., Harvard College, 1963; W. Hartman et al., *Management Information Systems Handbook: Analysis-Requirements Determination-Design and Development-Implementation and Evaluation,* New York, McGraw-Hill, 1968.

Should the decision be made to adopt this approach, the selection of a target program in the instruction area would be well advised. This would underscore the educational value for installing a PPB system and may minimize the perception that it is only a business management tool.

A third alternative is to develop objectives for all program areas at the upper levels of the program structure and at the same time to select one target area for the comprehensive determination of program objectives. This would provide the school system with a set of philosophical objectives for all program areas, along with a set of program objectives for one target area. The value of this approach would be that a large number of persons can be involved in reviewing philosophical objectives, while a small subgroup can concentrate in an intensive effort to develop objectives in a target program area. Philosophical objectives will serve to encourage those who are especially interested in their operationalization to get involved in the development of instructional program objectives. Also, philosophical objectives will give general direction to programs while the development of instructional and support service objectives is accomplished for the remainder of the program areas. (See Figure 15.)

**deciding where
to start the process
of writing objectives**

☐ Once a determination has been made regarding the scope of the initial effort for developing objectives, consideration must be given to the alternatives for starting the writing process. The following three options should be considered:

1. Needs Assessment Survey

One basic starting point for developing objectives would be to conduct an extensive needs assessment survey. Such a survey would envision communicating directly with the community to determine its expectations for the school system. By comparing the existing program with community expectations, the discrepancy that results is termed needs. The needs assessment survey should not be limited to the local community but should consider others, such as potential employers of students, college admissions officers, and college placement officers.

The advantages of starting with a needs assessment survey would include the determination, on a current basis, of the expectations of the groups mentioned as well as the creation of an awareness and commitment to the district objectives. A major disadvantage to a needs survey includes the time commitment necessary to do an adequate assessment. Such a survey would require the use of research experts in order to insure that the data received did not become outdated before programs could be developed to meet the stated expectations. Costs involved for an extensive survey of this nature might also be considerable.[11]

---

[11] Roy Sweigert, Jr., and Donald Kase, *Assessing Educational Needs of California: A Progress Report,* a paper prepared for the Region III Conference on Title III of ESEA, Denver, Colorado, March 1969.

FIGURE 15
PAGES 232-233

2. Utilizing Existing Data

Those participating in the determination of instructional objectives may wish to begin with data that already exists. For example, if the staff has recently produced a curriculum guide it already possesses data with which to begin the development of objectives. Board of education policy statements are another source of basic information, as are existing test data or even statements of course requirements.

By starting with existing material, the district may save considerable time. The risk of this method is that the status quo may be perpetuated and the information may be faulty or misleading. This risk may be minimized through an awareness of the problems of using this method and by testing the assumptions on which the data were built.

3. Brainstorming Objectives

All existing data and community expectations may be disregarded and completely new objectives created. The development of such objectives would tend to focus on the prescriptive—what one wants to accomplish—as opposed to the descriptive, in which existing practices and expectations are described. These objectives may be determined through a process of so-called brainstorming and they would undoubtedly reflect the advantages and disadvantages inherent in this approach.

The persons participating in this approach would be free to develop new ideas based on their experience and expertise. They would not be hindered by tradition or existing problems. The risk involved in utilizing this approach would be that the end product may not be relevant to the community's expectations for the schools—in fact, they might be in direct conflict with them.

techniques for writing objectives

☐ Following the decision on where to start the process for determining objectives, consideration should be given to the writing process. Separate sets of criteria should be recognized for each of the types of objectives previously identified. They are as follows:

1. Philosophical objectives:
    = are general and provide overall direction
    = have a time frame that should be indefinite
    = must be related to program structure
2. Instructional program objectives:
    = describe what is to be learned in behavioral terms
    = indicate when the information or skill will be learned
    = specify the circumstances under which the learner's performance will be evaluated
3. Support service program objectives:
    = include a statement of the purpose of the service
    = define their relationship to the overall instructional program, if one exists
    = establishes the time frame under which it is to be accomplished
    = specifies the criteria that will serve as the basis for determining whether or not it has been accomplished

As each objective is developed the criteria should be used to determine its adequacy. This will provide for consistency in the statement of objectives and also some quality control of their content. The utilization of a standard set of criteria for stating objectives will enhance both their meaning and their value for analysis purposes.

The criteria discussed above are particularly important because most educators seem to base objectives on the process of teaching—that is, on teacher behavior, materials used, classroom environment, and so forth. They focus on what the teacher does or on the activities and materials he uses rather than on the desired behavioral change expected of students. This observation has been supported by Dr. Herbert Hite, Director of Teacher Training at Washington State University, who has stated:

I know that when I look at my own past as a teacher, I have often acted as if the object of teaching were classification of the pupils, or to have so many seats filled for so many timed periods, at the end of which we had "educated" people. . . . Inasmuch as we teach, we have purpose, and without that purpose behind it, you don't have teaching. The object, then, is for the teachers to define the evidence that they'll accept as proof that this learning has taken place, and then to arrange matters so that the individual learner does demonstrate this evidence.[12]

This emphasis on student learning rather than on teaching methods serves as the basis for the work of Bloom and others whose classification of instructional objectives has received wide acceptance in the educational field.[13] They have classified instructional objectives into three separate domains, as follows:

1. Cognitive. Objectives which emphasize remembering or reproducing something which has presumably been learned, as well as objectives which involve the solving of some intellective task for which the individual has to determine the essential problem and then reorder given material or combine it with ideas, methods, or procedures previously learned. . . .

2. Affective. Objectives which emphasize a feeling, tone, an emotion, or a degree of acceptance or rejection. . . .

3. Psychomotor. Objectives which emphasize some muscular or motor skill, some manipulation of material and objects, or some act which requires a neuromuscular coordination.[14]

The use of Bloom's three types of basic objectives may be helpful but they are not essential for the preparation of objectives in a PPB system. What may be of more value to those persons actually charged with the responsibility of writing objectives would be participating in an in-service training program devoted to techniques of writing objectives. An in-service

[12] Herbert Hite, "A Model for Performance Certification," in Robert C. Burkhart, editor, *The Assessment Revolution: New Viewpoints for Teacher Evaluation*, National Symposium on Evaluation in Education, undated, pp. 196-197.

[13] David R. Krathwohl et al., *Taxonomy of Educational Objectives: The Classification of Educational Goals, Handbook II: Affective Domain*, New York, McKay, 1964.

[14] Ibid., pp. 6, 7.

training program need not be an extensive or expensive undertaking. Experience in the Portland, Maine, School District has shown that approximately six hours of instruction is sufficient to train staff in how to write objectives.

There are several texts available that provide considerable detail on writing objectives. Robert F. Mager's book, *Preparing Instructional Objectives,* is the most popular book in this area primarily because it is easy to read and understand, and it provides an individual with sufficient content in a programmed learning format to teach himself to write objectives.[15] Another source designed for programmed learning on how to write objectives is, *A Systematic Approach to Developing and Writing Behavioral Objectives.*[16]

Other resources available to assist those developing objectives include securing the services of an outside consultant or purchasing a pre-packaged set of objectives from which selections can be made. The advantages and disadvantages of each of these alternative resources have been discussed in Chapter 2, pages 32 and 33.

The availability and quality of outside consultants depend upon the demands, resources, and geographic location of the school system. If a decision has been made to use consultants, their credentials should be checked. This can be accomplished by checking with school districts that have used their services recently and by reviewing samples of their work. Consultants in the field of writing objectives may be available from certain state departments of education, county or regional educational centers, colleges and universities, private nonprofit organizations, and private industries.

The development of packaged objectives has been given some attention by both university educators and private educational enterprises. At the university level, the major work to date has been accomplished by the Center for the Study of Evaluation at the University of California at Los Angeles. Under the direction of Marvin C. Alkin, an Instructional Objectives Exchange (IOX) has been established. The purpose of this exchange is to make it easier for the teacher or administrator to select from among a number of objectives than it would be for him to formulate an entire set of behavioral objectives and measurement criteria. Its proponents claim that there is no attempt to dictate curriculum through this service. Rather, the goal of the Exchange is:

. . . To expedite the user's selection of his own objectives.

The user may select from among these objectives those which are consistent with his own curricular goals, since, in many cases, there will be more objectives contained within each Collection than an individual teacher or district will wish to use in a particular instructional situation. In

[15] Robert F. Mager, *Preparing Instructional Objectives,* Palo Alto, Calif., Fearon, 1962.

[16] D. Robert Armstrong, *A Systematic Approach to Developing and Writing Behavioral Objectives,* Tucson, Ariz., Educational Innovation Press, 1968.

addition, he may generate objectives to fill gaps which he perceives to exist within the set of objectives as they have been developed.[17]

Thirty-five separate collections of objectives are available from the IOX covering a wide range of subjects in grades K-12. Many of these objectives are accompanied by test items which may be used to measure whether the objectives have been achieved. A sample of several objectives developed by IOX are shown in Figure 16.

Private educational enterprises have also prepared objectives and evaluative criteria. For instance, the Litton Educational Publishers, Inc., have prepared a compilation of behavioral objectives for The Read System, a reading series produced by the American Book Company. In their compilation the learners' behavior is measured by the task undertaken on check-up tests. The items measuring a particular objective are indicated ahead of the objective. An example from the compilation of behavioral objectives is contained in Figure 17.

The use of packaged objectives will have value in terms of reducing the workload of those responsible for preparing objectives. Problems of modifying them to fit a local district's situation are very real. However, given the appropriate staff and community involvement this problem can be overcome. If this is true, then this approach for determining objectives becomes very attractive.

Regardless of the resources or methods used in determining objectives, the crux of a successful effort lies in (1) professional staff commitment, and (2) the reasonableness of the initial effort. Professional staff commitment is obtained through meaningful involvement and therefore every strategy for determining objectives must be an internal one, to some extent. Thus, consultants or packaged objectives should not only be used for their expertise and time-saving features but, more importantly, to facilitate internal staff commitment.

The initial effort in developing objectives should reflect a strong measure of reasonableness. During the initial phase of writing the objectives, there should be no expectation of meeting the ideal model. In fact, the first set of objectives may be crude in nature and fall short of the criteria established. Recognition should be given to the fact that objectives will evolve over a period of time. The quality of the statement of the objectives may be expected to improve with each subsequent writing. Figure 18 shows the evolution of objectives for a diagnostic reading clinic.

soliciting comments, reviewing, revising, and recommending objectives

☐ As objectives are prepared by the subcommittee, they should be transmitted to the task team and staff for reaction. A uniform format should be developed for this purpose. (See Figure 19.)

[17] *Social Science K-9,* Instructional Objectives Exchange, a Project of the Center for the Study of Evaluation, Los Angeles, UCLA Graduate School of Education, undated, p. I.

FIGURES 16-19
PAGES 234-237

After objectives for a target program area have been reviewed by the subcommittee they should be recommended to the superintendent of schools for his reaction or approval. Once reviewed and recommended by the superintendent, they should be submitted to the board of education for consideration and adoption. Upon receipt of the final approval by the board, the program objectives will be implemented in accordance with the time schedule established as part of the implementation plan contained in the PPB system.

ESTABLISHING PRIORITIES

Society's demands on the school system seem to be unlimited. Among other things, educators are being asked to solve the drug problem, insure a healthy sex life, promote racial harmony, and develop individualism and creativity. Educators are expected to teach reading, writing, arithmetic, and aesthetic perception and to give more attention to the humanities, physics, auto repair, and French conversation. They are expected to do all this more quickly and efficiently than in the past. Obviously, some of these demands conflict, but, even if they didn't, it is impossible to give them all equal attention in terms of time, financial support, and emphasis. Harold Howe, former U. S. Commissioner of Education stated:

In effect, the idea of critical mass says to us educators: "Select your priority problems, those you must solve first in order to avoid disaster. Concentrate your resources upon them and be willing to let other matters go if necessary, while you focus on the most pressing needs." [18]

Therefore, in addition to developing objectives, one of the overriding tasks facing the pluralistic school community is to determine priorities among the many objectives.

The establishment of priorities—the assignment of relative importance of objectives—is an indispensable element of a PPB system. The allocation of resources on a priority basis to the adopted objectives is a major factor in insuring that an attempt will be made to achieve them. Again, objectives may remain meaningless unless there has been a commitment of district resources to them. The establishment of priorities is important to the decision makers in the planning process because it allows an actual commitment of resources to be made.

The establishment of priorities should probably be made on a districtwide basis. The ranking of objectives in order of importance will serve not only for the allocation of resources but also as a direction for the efforts of the staff. Day-to-day operational decisions will be affected by the established priorities.

---

[18] Harold Howe II, "The Frustrations of Progress," in *1967-68 AASA Official Report,* Washington, D.C., American Association of School Administrators, p. 150.

In those school districts in which objectives have been developed for decentralized units, priorities should be established in relation to the objectives developed within that unit. However, a separate statement of objectives need not be developed in order to determine priorities within a decentralized unit or any other unit within a school system. That is, given a school system's statement of objectives, it is conceivable that they may be ranked in different orders of importance, depending upon the geographic area served or the needs of a particular pupil population. Therefore, priorities may be established on a districtwide level, at a subdistrict level, or even at the school building level. Most suburban school systems—especially those which are homogeneous in nature—should establish priorities for their entire school system. In most city or urban type school districts priorities should be decentralized, that is, established to reflect the aspirations and needs of the various groups served by the system.

Whether priorities are established on a districtwide or subdistrict level, the relative importance of objectives must be determined both within and among program areas. Consideration should be given to the relative importance of objectives within, for example, the mathematics program, and among the mathematics program, the physical science program, the social studies program, and so forth. By ranking objectives in terms of their priority, the decision makers will have a basis for allocating resources. This will allow for an analysis within a particular program area as well as among the various programs.

barriers to establishing priorities

□ Although the concept of establishing priorities is not new to education it has not, historically, been effectively utilized. In fact, more often than not, all programs have been supported equally. In order to establish priorities, educators must become accustomed to ranking certain objectives and programs as less desirable or important than others. Thus, it can be anticipated that there will be some resistance to establishing priorities because it is much easier and less threatening to pay lip service to all programs.

Another barrier is that once it becomes clear that resources will be applied in relation to priorities, vested interest groups will actively compete for a higher ranking of their objectives. This does not mean that such groups are not competing now. However, the parameters of existing competition seldom include the elimination of one program (low priority) while at the same time significantly increasing support for another program (high priority).

Finally, because of differing perspectives on what is important, both within the staff and the community, the ranking of objectives is difficult to achieve. The legitimization of the established priorities will depend on broad-based support. However, because of conflicting values, consensus may require a number of compromises. This, of course, will not be true in a school system plagued by major visible deficiencies.

These factors may inhibit the determination of priorities. Priorities must be written within an environment of reality. Therefore, techniques for dealing with these barriers should be considered.

techniques for establishing priorities

☐   Once the importance of establishing priorities is accepted, then the question of how to establish them emerges. There are a number of sophisticated techniques that have been identified in the literature for assigning relative importance to objectives. The Churchman-Ackoff method and the Delphi method represent the two most widely used approaches for ranking objectives.[19] The Churchman-Ackoff method forces an individual or group to consider and reconsider the relative importance of objectives both singularly and in combination. The individual or group is expected to generate a set of internally consistent assignments of importance to each objective. The Delphi method essentially is designed for group judgments and it arrives at consensus by using a series of steps. In each step subjects are told the results of judgments made at the end of the previous step. Those people who maintain extreme judgments are required to justify their positions for others to evaluate. Through this procedure, consensus is ultimately achieved.[20] In fact, the hypothesis that this technique can be used to mold opinion as well as collect it has been supported.[21]

Techniques to determine the relative importance of objectives need not be highly sophisticated. A school district may legitimately determine priorities by the use of information obtained through the use of simplified questionnaires. Inputs regarding priorities can also be obtained through the use of committees, advisory councils, or public forums. For instance, in Torrance, California, a special committee drafted a proposed statement of existing goals of the school system which was circulated to all teachers, the PTA, the Chamber of Commerce, and a 250-member citizens group, the Educational Council of Torrance. "This document was rewritten three times as a result of feedback of the staff members and members of the community in terms of what they thought the goals of the Torrance district really were," said Assistant Superintendent Frank Mattox. "And the final document was not the same as the one we started with."[22] If

---

[19] Stanford Temkin, "An Evaluation of Comprehensive Planning Literature with an Annotated Bibliography," *Research for Better Schools, Inc.,* Philadelphia, Pa., 1970, pp. 4, 5.

[20] For additional information on the methods discussed, see Russell L. Ackoff, "Towards a Quantitative Evaluation of Urban Services," *Public Expenditure Decisions in the Urban Community,* Washington, D.C., Resources for the Future, Inc., 1962; William J. Baumol, "Neumann Morgenstern Cardinal Utility," *Economic Theory and Operations Analysis,* Englewood Cliffs, N.J., Prentice-Hall, 1961, pp. 331-346; C. West Churchman et al., "Weighting Objectives," *Introduction to Operations Research,* New York, Wiley, 1957, pp. 136-154; Nicholas Rescher, *Delphi and Values,* Santa Monica, Calif., The Rand Corporation, September 1969.

[21] Frederick R. Cyphert and Walter L. Gant, "The Delphi Technique: A Case Study," *Phi Delta Kappan, 52,* no. 5 (January 1971), 273.

[22] Frank Mattox, "Setting New Education Communication Priorities," as quoted in *Trends,* National School Public Relations Association, December 15, 1970.

there is wide involvement of individuals and groups regarding their preferences for objectives, computer processing of data would undoubtedly be required.

Although inputs from a wide cross-section of the community are desirable, final determination of priorities should not necessarily be left to a popular vote. The superintendent and board of education should, because of their responsibility and in-depth knowledge of problem areas, make the final determination on the relative importance of objectives.

The establishment of priorities must occur prior to the assignment of monies and therefore this activity should take place in relationship to the budget cycle. In this way priorities would be established prior to the allocation of resources so that the allocations may reflect these priorities.

EVALUATING
PROGRESS TOWARD
THE ATTAINMENT OF
STATED OBJECTIVES

Evaluation is the third element of the planning component of a PPB system. Its relationship to the other two elements—determining objectives and priorities—has been illustrated on page 52. Evaluation has probably received more attention, criticism, and resistance than any other element in a PPB system.

resistance to evaluation

☐ Historically, educators have been reluctant to plan programs that include, as an integral part, evaluative criteria. Because the integration of evaluation with planning is an essential part of a PPB system, there is considerable resistance to the installation of the system, especially the evaluation element. For instance, Miles Myers, senior vice-president of the California Federation of Teachers, in an article entitled "The Unholy Marriage—Accountants and Curriculum Makers," characterized this activity as "stultifying," a "bizarre joke," and "enshrining trivia."[23] It is such a highly controversial topic that Hartley advises:

If supervisors, administrators, and curriculum specialists disagree as to appropriate evaluative criteria, it is obvious that the program budgeting specialist and systems analyst who seek identifiable results would be well advised to tread lightly in this context.[24]

Professional staff resistance to evaluation is, to some extent, legitimate. The existing limitations of testing methodology and assessment criteria

[23] Miles Myers, "The Unholy Marriage—Accountants and Curriculum Makers," *American Teacher, 55,* no. 3 (November 1970), 14-16.

[24] Hartley, op cit., p. 242.

have been recognized in the literature. Coleman[25] and others point out that education is a multifaceted process encompassing a number of dimensions and therefore does not easily lend itself to evaluation. Aside from the sheer number of dimensions to evaluate, there is real concern by many educators of their inability to apply evaluative devices to those objectives within the affective domain. The first point seems to be concerned with the difficulty of articulating, in terms of objectives, the type of educational program these educators are envisioning. The second point is evidently concerned with the inadequate state of evaluative methodology. Both positions are grounded in valid arguments and should not be ignored.

Another contributing factor to the resistance to evaluation has been the recognition of the implications of evaluation for accountability—job security, rewards, or sanctions. Resistance for this reason may be legitimate if individuals are held responsible and accountable for areas over which they lack adequate control or influence.

Although the constraints and limitations on evaluation of educational programs are substantial, it does not follow that efforts at assessing and evaluating programs should be abandoned.

need for evaluation in PPBS

□ John Gardner in *The Recovery of Confidence*, stressed the importance of program evaluation when he stated:

...that government officials must be required to be specific about goals—that is, about outcomes that would have to be achieved to count a given activity successful; they must develop measures to determine whether those outcomes have occurred; and they must apply the measures systematically to performance—all to the end that they can say of any program, "It worked" or "It didn't work."[26]

As previously stated, evaluation represents one of the most important elements of a PPB system. If one accepts that the primary purpose of any evaluation of an institution is to aid in decision making, then the role of evaluation in PPBS should be clear, as the mission of the system is to obtain better information with which to make decisions.

The evaluation dimension of a PPB system allows the decision maker to focus on the question, "Where are we now?" Although there are definite limits to evaluation that must be kept in mind, the contribution of evaluative data to a PPB system can be described as follows:

1. It generates information to determine whether or not, or to what extent, objectives have been accomplished.

2. It provides information for planning and management of the system.

---

[25] James S. Coleman et al., *Quality of Educational Opportunity*, Washington, D.C., Office of Education, 1966.

[26] John W. Gardner, *The Recovery of Confidence*, New York, W. W. Norton, 1970, pp. 40-41.

3. It allows for the analysis of the validity, importance (priority) and/or relevance of the objectives, and the determination of the obsolescence of objectives, thus insuring the process of self-renewal of the organization.

Thus, another difficult task facing those installing a PPB system is to develop an evaluation system that will generate the data necessary to determine the success of the various educational programs. Although it may be more natural for a school district to attempt to install a comprehensive evaluation system, it may be more realistic to begin with the data on hand.

the evaluation process

☐ In determining how to evaluate progress toward the attainment of stated objectives the following points should be considered:

= use of available evaluative information
= use of university or commercially prepared evaluative instruments
= when evaluation should take place
= who should conduct the evaluation program.

The whole evaluation process should focus on the question, "What evidence is acceptable to demonstrate that an objective has been accomplished?" The issue of whether to use existing data or to develop new evaluative techniques may be resolved by continually asking the question of the staff and community, "What evidence are you willing to accept to show that an objective has been accomplished or that a program has been successful?"

Use of Existing Evaluative Data

Most school systems administer a wide variety of tests and collect a considerable amount of information regarding student performance. The linking of this information to a compilation of objectives as contained in a given program area will assist in the evaluation of the effectiveness of the program. For instance, through the use of item analysis techniques on a standardized test, a determination might be made regarding the achievement of a specific program objective.

Predictably, some members of the staff will resist the use of existing student performance data. While their concerns may have merit, it would be unconscionable for professionals to turn away from information which already exists in the district. Indeed, given weekly quizzes, semester exams, oral exams, final exams, departmental exams, statewide exams, interest inventories, IQ exams, and attitudinal exams, it is not unusual for a student to spend fully one day per week, or approximately one-fifth of the school year, engaged in assessment activity. Yet most school districts are failing to use test results in educational decision making. Richard M. Jaeger, chief of evaluation methodology, U.S. Office of Education, said his experience shows that districts tend to pay little attention to annual test results. However, he said, "Research conducted this past year leads me to suggest that many institutional decisions can be based upon test results for as few as 5% of the children in a school system . . . ."[27]

Galen Saylor, professor of the Department of Secondary Education at the University of Nebraska, points out that there is not only a great deal of evaluative data available, but in fact programs have been developed using such information. As Saylor has insightfully pointed out:

It should not be forgotten that we do have a great deal of knowledge about educational achievement in the schools. Our pupils are the most tested human beings in the world; and we know a vast amount about the nature of their educational attainments. Many of our existing programs have been developed on the basis of an intelligent use of such evidence.[28]

A major advantage of PPBS might be to provide for the gathering, displaying, and relating of existing test data with which to make decisions. Thus, if the available standardized test information demonstrates the proficiency of students in French and this is an objective of the program, then it should be used for that purpose. If the objective deals with attitudes toward French and there is no current data dealing with that objective, then a new test must be adopted or a different technique devised for measuring that objective.

Use of University or Commercially Prepared Evaluative Instruments

A school system does not need to rely solely on its present evaluative program. Although it has been argued that available assessment data be used for certain objectives, it may be necessary to consider other sources of information, such as commercially or university prepared evaluative instruments.

The increasing emphasis on objectives and their evaluation has resulted in the development of a number of resources available for use by school districts. For example, the Center for the Study of Evaluation, University of California at Los Angeles, under a contract with the U.S. Office of Education, has developed an elementary school evaluation kit. They have outlined 145 goals for elementary school education and assigned tests measuring each specific educational objective.[29] An illustration of this approach is shown in Figure 20.

The employment of evaluative instruments or techniques developed by experts in the field of tests and measurements can increase the likelihood of having a school system's evaluation data meet the requirements of a good assessment program. However, without attempting to diminish the importance of the contributions of the experts in tests and measurements,

---

[27] Richard M. Jaeger, as quoted in "Testing Policies, School Span Under Fire," *Education, USA,* National School Public Relations Association, November 9, 1970, p. 57.

[28] Galen Saylor, "National Assessment: Pro and Con," *The Record,* Teachers College, Columbia University, *71,* no. 4 (May 1970), 593.

[29] Ralph Hoepfner et al., *CSE Elementary School Test Evaluations,* Los Angeles, Center for the Study of Evaluation, UCLA Graduate School of Education, 1970.

FIGURE 20
PAGE 238

the evaluation process in a PPB system must recognize the need and importance of personal judgment. Assessment data can be of value in making decisions without meeting all of the criteria for research and design espoused by educational psychologists. Nor is there a need for a complex statistical analysis of the data. Common sense as applied to the question, "What minimal evidence will you accept that an objective has been achieved?" should be the determining guide in evaluating progress.

Time Frame for Evaluating Progress

Evaluation activities should be performed on an ongoing basis; that is, progress should be monitored throughout the year so that adjustments can be made in a program area as the necessity arises. For PPBS purposes, the major evaluation efforts should be tied into the budget cycle because decisions on objectives and programming are implemented through the budget. The evaluation activities must be accomplished in time for the appropriate analysis of the data for program change purposes.

Who Should Conduct the Evaluation Program?

A school system may use its PPBS task team in an evaluator capacity in an effort to provide for program evaluation. However, the demands of time would prohibit any substantial effort for evaluation by the task team. Further, because of the inherent critical dimension of evaluation, such a role would affect the task team's ability to install a PPB system. Finally, the direct use of the task team in the evaluation process raises the problem of objectivity. Herbert J. Walberg, professor at the University of Wisconsin, has identified the problem of an evaluator's allegiance—he may be biased and unable to see all the weak points of his work. "An evaluator on a project staff may have conflict of interest which bias his judgment. Since he is paid by the project, his job or even the project may be at stake if he publishes an uncomplimentary report."[30]

Hartley, in discussing the installation of PPBS itself, recognized that it may be doomed to success. " . . . That is, if evaluation of this concept is made by the same administrators who introduce it into a school district (as is the case with many innovations) it is unlikely that they will claim that it is anything less than a smashing success."[31]

Because evaluation for program development purposes should be strongly supported by personal judgment, the problem of objectivity is a crucial one. Faulty and misleading evaluation information may result in improper decisions. Several possible methods of avoiding this problem have been suggested. For example, Richard M. Durstine of the Harvard University Graduate School of Education has developed the idea of an accountability information system. He recommends the creation of an "office of accountability information." This office would be responsible for

---

[30] Herbert J. Walberg, "Curriculum Evaluation: Problems and Guidelines," *The Record,* op. cit., p. 568.

[31] Hartley, loc. cit.

collecting, keeping, processing, and using information about accountability measures. He has developed a number of specific steps for the establishment of such an office.[32]

In further support for a separate department of evaluation, Howard O. Merriman, Director of Evaluation Research, Columbus, Ohio, City Schools, states:

. . . if the evaluator is established separately, if he has an identity which is not linked too closely to any one audience, he will be capable of being more objective, or at least broader, in perspective. Evaluators must be able to relate across many different groups of people which may have quite divergent views.[33]

Finally, Leon Lessinger, professor at Georgia State University, has recommended an Independent Educational Accomplishments Audit (IEAA) similar to that used in a fiscal audit, with the emphasis, however, on student performance.[34]

The employment of one of the approaches recommended by Lessinger, Merriman, or Durstine would reduce, if not totally eliminate, the problem of providing for objectivity in assessment. However, the evaluation process viewed within the PPBS context should encompass the philosophy of broadly based involvement. There is no reason why a multitude of resources cannot be used to provide for the assessment of progress toward the attainment of objectives. Administrators, subject supervisors, parents, employers, and even students can make a contribution. The approaches to evaluation that have been suggested are not mutually exclusive. Certainly it has not been proven that any one approach is best. Therefore, some combination of approaches appears to make the most sense. Regardless of which approach is adopted for providing assessment information, a review of the problems of developing an effective evaluation system suggests that evaluation be a cooperative effort.

SUMMARY

Objectives, priorities, and evaluative criteria are the interdependent elements of the planning component of a PPB system. Establishing meaningful objectives, determining priorities among them, and evaluating progress toward their achievement is one of the crucial challenges in education today.

---

[32] Richard M. Durstine, "An Accountability Information System," *Phi Delta Kappan, 52,* no. 4 (December 1970), 236-239.

[33] Howard O. Merriman, "Profile of a School District's Department of Evaluation—Present and Future," as printed in *Educational Evaluation: Official Proceedings of a Conference,* Columbus, Ohio, Ohio Department of Education, 1969, p. 85.

[34] Leon Lessinger, "Engineering Accountability for Results in Public Education," *Phi Delta Kappan, 52,* no. 4 (December 1970), 222.

To facilitate the development of objectives, they may be classified into three basic types: (1) philosophical objectives—the statements of general educational aims; (2) instructional program objectives—the statements of behavioral change to be accomplished in a program area; and (3) support service program objectives—the statements of the purpose of these services and their relationship to the instructional program.

Because of the many problems, time requirements, and the need for involvement for the development of objectives, the task should be delegated to a subcommittee. The role of the subcommittee would include selecting a target program for which objectives will be determined and deciding where to start the process of writing them. The subcommittee should also consider alternative techniques for writing the objectives. Finally, they should determine the procedures for soliciting comments and reviewing, revising, and recommending the objectives that have been developed. The crux of a successful effort in determining objectives lies in securing professional staff commitment and in the reasonableness of the initial effort.

The establishment of priorities—the assignment of relative importance to objectives—provides a basis for allocating resources and insures that an attempt will be made to achieve them. Priorities should be established on a districtwide level; however, in city districts they may be determined for decentralized units.

There are a number of factors that may inhibit the development of priorities; therefore, techniques for establishing them should be considered. Although sophisticated techniques may be utilized for assigning relative importance to objectives, priorities may be legitimately determined through the use of information derived from questionnaires, committees, advisory councils, or public forums.

Staff resistance to evaluation has long been recognized. This resistance is, to some extent, legitimate because of the limitations of existing evaluative programs. It does not follow, however, that an attempt should not be made to determine the success of various educational programs.

The whole evaluation process should focus on the question, "What evidence is acceptable to demonstrate that an objective has been accomplished?" Consideration should be given to using available evaluative data and to using university or commercially prepared evaluative instruments.

For PPBS purposes, the major evaluation efforts should be tied into the budget cycle because decisions on objectives and programming are implemented through the budget.

Finally, because evaluation for program development purposes should be strongly supported by personal judgment, the problem of objectivity should receive considerable attention. The establishment of some type of separate office or audit for evaluation has been suggested, but it may be that the most successful evaluation program will be based on a cooperative effort.

budgeting:
how to prepare a
program budget

The schools of the future will eliminate uneconomic procedures so that available funds can go further.... Expenditures will be applied to the more functional and important type of learning. Relatively unimportant school activities must qualify after honest appraisal of their values.   J. Lloyd Trump *

The program budget is a tool which shows how cost information relates to the categories in the school system's adopted program structure. The program budget represents the budget element of PPBS.

The distinction between the function-object budget and the program budget is important. The major difference between the two approaches is that the program budget displays costs on a program-by-program basis whereas the function-object budget shows cost by the type of item purchased. For example, a function-object budget would show salaries for teaching, while a program budget would display salaries for teaching for a particular program, e.g., mathematics, or social studies, or grade four. Figure 21 shows a comparison of the same budget on a program basis and on a function basis.

Preparing a program budget as part of the installation of the PPB system is important for the following reasons:

= It provides a format for decision makers to begin the important task of program analysis.
= It provides a basis for examining the adequacy of the program structure.

---

*J. Lloyd Trump, "Focus on Change: Guide to Better Schools," in Alice and Lester D. Crow, eds., *Vital Issues in American Education,* New York, Bantam Books, 1964, p. 222.

= It provides the decision makers a framework for allocating resources on a programmatic basis.
= It can be accomplished in a one year budget cycle, thus providing immediate benefits.

One of the risks involved in preparing the program budget during the first year of the PPBS effort is that some districts may consider the program budget the full payoff of a PPB system and will not install the other important components. It should be recognized that the greatest impact on a school district's educational program will come from the installation of the complete PPB system. However, it is clear that school districts can use the program budget as an interim step and can achieve some immediate benefits as discussed in Chapter 2.

Another problem in the preparation of a program budget is that it emphasizes and focuses on the role of the school business administrator. It may serve, therefore, to reinforce the perception that PPBS is merely an alternative budgeting system. Without minimizing the importance of the business administrator's efforts during the program budgeting phase, the task force team should attempt to seize opportunities to insure a visible role for the curriculum-oriented staff members.

ALTERNATIVE APPROACHES TO PROGRAM BUDGETING

School systems can prepare the program budget in at least two different ways. The first alternative is to have principals, instructional specialists, and classroom teachers submit budget requests in accordance with the newly adopted program structure. For example, proposed expenditures for teaching supplies would be identified and coded in accordance with specific program areas, such as physically handicapped, mathematics, or grade level, depending on the program structure that has been adopted by the district. The budget data submitted to the business office must already be cast in programmatic terms. The problem with this approach is that the staff will be unfamiliar with the new coding system and they may require considerable training before they will be able to prepare budget requests according to the appropriate program category.

The second alternative is to utilize the traditional function-object budget categories during the initial stage of the program budget cycle. Under this method, the staff would submit budget requests in exactly the same manner as in previous years under the function-object budgeting approach. The task of the school business administrator would then be to translate and code these budget requests into the new program structure categories. This approach would save the staff considerable time; however, the problem with this method is that the school business administrator may not have the expertise to accurately classify cost data with the appropriate

FIGURE 21

PAGE 240

instructional program categories. If business administrators are left with the sole responsibility of judging cost allocations to instructional programs, their potential miscalculations will reduce the reliability and usefulness of the resulting data. Business administrators do not have the knowledge to do this by themselves, just as most teachers do not have the knowlege to prepare a comprehensive budget.

The second method of building a program budget is easily used, but the most persuasive argument is for the first alternative because it contributes to the implementation of the PPB system and it provides the most accurate data. If teachers and administrators submit budget requests by program, then the staff will begin thinking in program terms. This will help prepare them for the subsequent stages of the system—the generation of objectives, evaluation criteria, and alternatives.

The first step in the process of building a program budget is to develop a program coding system that can be used to identify budget requests with specific program categories.

PROGRAM CODING

The program coding system, based on the school district's program structure, should be developed by the school business administrator. The business administrator should assume this responsibility because the coding system must be correlated to the accounting, data processing, and financial reporting functions. The program code created by the business administrator must permit the district to draw program cost information from the accounting system. The coding procedures established for the program budget must also be designed so that the reporting requirements of state and federal agencies can be met without the necessity of maintaining two different budget designs. The school business administrator can establish a set of codes to obtain more than one report from the same base of information through the use of a coding system.

The extent of a district program coding system will depend upon the amount of detail necessary to meet the financial data needs of the school district. It is recognized that information needs are not the same for all school systems. Most school districts have some form of coding systems for reporting revenues and expenditures. The program coding system should be built around the district's existing coding system.

The following illustrations demonstrate techniques for expanding the traditional function-object coding system to a program coding system for both expenditure and revenue accounts.

expenditure codes

☐ The account code format for teaching supplies in the traditional function-object format is:

Fund	Function	Object
General	Instruction—Teaching	Supplies
A	220	300

By adding two to four digits to the standard function-object code format, provision can be made for coding the various programs contained in the program structure. A program code—for example, "60"—to represent a science program could be added to the existing function-object code as follows:

Fund	Program	Function	Object
General	Science, K-12	Instruction—Teaching	Supplies
A	60	220	300

This code embraces both the district's program structure and the function-object reporting requirements. The part of the code, A-220-300, meets legal and traditional financial reporting requirements for teaching supplies. The complete code, A-60-220-300, would provide the costs of supplies for the science program.

The traditional function-object code could also be expanded by four or more digits in order to provide for coding of the various levels within a program structure. Figure 22 illustrates a five-level program structure with a six-digit program code. Based on this figure the third-grade science program would be coded:

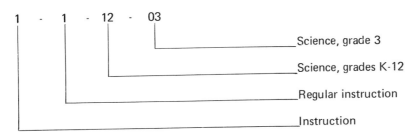

By expanding the traditional function-object code by six digits the following would be the code for third-grade science program supplies:

Fund	Program	Function	Object
General	Science, Third Grade	Instruction—Teaching	Supplies
A	111203	220	300

Computer availability for preparing program reports allows a district to utilize program coding for generating reports at each program level in the program structure. A manual accounting system could use a four-digit code such as "1203" to designate science, grade 3, or two-digit code, "12"

FIGURE 22
PAGE 241

could be used to designate only the science area. A three-digit program code is illustrated in Figure 23. Using this format, the elementary science program could be coded as follows:

20   E

Elementary, grades K-5

Science, grades K-12

By using code 20-E supplies for the elementary science program could be shown:

Fund	Program	Function	Object
General	Science, Elementary	Instruction—Teaching	Supplies
A	20 E	220	300

The program code can also show expenditures by facility or school building. Each building could be assigned a separate code. For example, using the program codes in Figure 24 and assigning code "30" to represent West High School and code "40" to represent East High School, high school science supplies would be coded as follows:

Fund	Program	Facility	Function	Object
General	Science, High School	West High School	Instruction—Teaching	Supplies
A	20 H	30	220	300

Fund	Program	Facility	Function	Object
General	Science, High School	East High School	Instruction—Teaching	Supplies
A	20 H	40	220	300

Certain types of expenditures cannot be readily assigned to a specific program because of the general nature of these expenditures. For example, legal judgments awarded against the school district may not be identified with a particular program. This type of expenditure can be coded "00," or nonprogram. The listing of an "00" nonprogram code is shown in both Figures 22 and 23.

The U.S. Office of Education has developed a revision of their widely used Financial Accounting Handbook.[1] This handbook recommends an expenditure coding structure which is compatible with the various

[1] *Financial Accounting: Definition, Classification, and Codes for Local and State School Systems (Handbook II, Revised),* Washington, D.C., National Center for Educational Statistics, U.S. Office of Education, 1970.

FIGURES 23-24
PAGES 242-243

program coding schemes discussed in this chapter. The Office of Education's handbook does not constrain a local district from developing program codes based on its own program structure.

Once a program coding system has been developed, the business administrator should modify all purchasing forms to reflect the new program coding system. Forms, such as purchase requisition, voucher, purchase order, and payment, should show the full expenditure account code. A purchase order with various expenditure codes is shown in Figure 24.

revenue codes

□ Similarly, revenue codes can be expanded to provide for program coding. Classification of revenues by program is probably useful only in large school districts where a wide variety of revenue sources (including specially funded state and federal aid programs) is received.

One possible format for revenue coding that makes provision for identifying both programs and specific projects is shown below:

Fund	Program	Project	Source
General	Science, K-12	Elementary and Secondary Education Act Title I, Project 01	ESEA, Title I
A	60	01	4100

Revenues can also be classified by school building. This might be useful for school lunch or for a specialized facility such as a swimming pool. An example of a revenue code including a facility identification would be:

Fund	Program	Project	Facility	Source
General	School lunch	none	West High School	Type "A" lunch sales
A	80	00	30	1420

PREPARATION OF
AN INSTRUCTIONAL
MANUAL FOR THE
PROGRAM BUDGET

The development of a comprehensive, detailed set of budget instructions is the next phase in the preparation of the program budget. The development and use of such a manual may prove particularly useful in those districts involving a large number of their staff in the budget-building process. This manual can be prepared by the school business administrator. However, in order to overcome resistance to the installation of PPBS as discussed in Chapter 1, it may be advantageous to have the task team explain the program budget instructions to the staff.

The business administrator, starting with existing budget instructions, should develop the entire manual. He may also choose to adapt those instructions which have been used in other school districts.

In developing the budget instruction manual, the business administrator might consider developing a comprehensive set of instructions that can easily be divided into separate instruction booklets for distribution to the staff in accordance with their area of responsibility. The distribution of booklets should follow the "need to know" principle. For example, a classroom teacher need not know the rationale for the description of program coding or the method of proration of staff and fringe benefits. Similarly, individuals responsible for buildings and grounds would not need to receive budget instructions dealing with budget requests for instructional programs. The rationale for this approach would be to eliminate possible confusion caused by issuing instructions to individuals who do not have responsibility for a particular segment of the program budget.

This is not to indicate that separate instruction booklets must be prepared for every staff group. Rather, a comprehensive set of instructions should be devised that can be broken down into separate booklets for purposes of distribution. In order to accomplish this, the overall or comprehensive set should touch on the following subjects:

= A general but brief description of PPBS, including the relationship of program budgeting to a total PPB system.
= A statement of commitment to the concept of PPBS endorsed by the board of education and the superintendent and his chief deputies.
= A statement of the philosophy for the preparation of the educational program.
= The specific assignment of tasks for the preparation of the program budget: professional staff, supporting service staff, board of education, and citizen advisory committees.
= A description and supporting rationale for the adopted program structure.
= A description of the program coding procedures.
= Budget forms: how to prepare them, the number of copies to be submitted, and how they will be processed.
= A budget calendar outlining target dates for submission and review of budget request.
= Student enrollment projections for a one-year period in order to provide the staff with data for projecting certain costs for the budget.

The school business administrator must also prepare a set of detailed instructions that are applicable only to the business office. These instructions should be incorporated into the manual of program budget instructions. The business administrator should provide directions for the following: (1) use of standard supply lists, (2) direct charges to program categories, (3) staff allocation by program categories, (4) allocation of support service costs, (5) allocation of employee benefits, and (6) preparation of revenue budget.

☐ Standard supply lists of office and classroom supplies are normally developed as part of the traditional budget process. These lists may still be used in preparing the program budget. The business administrator will need to develop a procedure for allocating the estimated costs of supplies on these lists to the various program categories. This allocation can be based on estimated percentages for the use of the supplies. Estimates should be prepared by the business administrator after consultation with staff members. These figures will only be approximate; however, they will give budget data that is accurate enough for analysis purposes.

In order to obtain more exact budget estimates, a considerable amount of staff time would have to be expended in analyzing the data. If the dollar amounts involved are not substantial, then the additional staff effort is questionable. Therefore, the business administrator should not be concerned with providing figures on the utilization of supplies for a particular program, such as the amount of paper to be consumed for the language arts program or the mathematics program. This would be difficult, particularly in those schools organized around a self-contained classroom concept. Staff estimates on usage can reasonably be considered to be within plus or minus ten percent of the actual figure. Figures 25 and 26 illustrate the technique for allocation of standard supply list costs to program categories.

use of standard supply lists

direct charges to program categories

☐ The program budget instructions should be written so that budget requests can be identified directly with a particular program. For example, the cost of renting a bus to take students to a theater performance should not be charged to the transportation program but should be charged to the language arts program or the English program, or the humanities program, or whatever program has been developed within the program structure framework that would account for this activity. Equipment should also be charged directly to the program where it is being used. Equipment shared by two or more programs may be budgeted to the various programs on a percentage of use basis. It may also reasonably be budgeted under the program where it is used the majority of the time. The determining factor should be whether or not the costs involved in the particular piece of equipment under consideration are substantial enough to warrant the additional effort to prorate them.

staff allocation to program categories

☐ Another task that the school business administrator must accomplish is the allocation of staff time and salaries—both teaching and support—in conformity with the program structure. The problems associated with prorating of staff depend on the particular program structure adopted. For example, in a subject area type of program structure, prorating will be complex because elementary school teachers customarily teach several subjects. Also, a secretary might handle the paperwork for a variety of teachers who are all attached to different programs. The task is complicated even further by the employment of part-time and seasonal

FIGURES 25-26
PAGES 244-245

staff members. The importance of this task is demonstrated by the fact that in most school districts staff salaries constitute 70 to 80 percent of the total budget. Suggested techniques for prorating staff are given below.

The three steps for allocating the number of staff and staff salaries by program categories are: (1) determine the total number of staff, (2) prorate estimated staff time for the various program categories, and (3) compute the salary budget for each program category.

The total number of staff may be determined by taking an actual count or by computing a full-time equivalency (FTE). Counting staff members in relation to the program that they serve, such as fifteen science teachers, thirteen special education teachers, and so forth, is easily and quickly accomplished. However, the total number of staff for each program category will be misleading if part-time, shared time, or seasonal employees are utilized. For example, the total count of staff for science can be fifteen, but because three staff members only work half time, the total number of hours of science instruction will be somewhat less than one might expect from a staff of fifteen full-time science teachers. Thus, the concept of FTE should be used to allocate more accurately staff time to program category. (See Figure 27.) This concept involves the establishment of a standard work year for the various categories of employees. Once the standard work year has been established for each of the groups, it serves as a basis for computing the full-time equivalency of each staff member in his respective category. See Figure 28 for an example.

The next step is to allocate the staff time to the program structure in terms of FTE. This allocation is based on the amount of time spent by each staff member on activities related to each program category. Consultation with the immediate supervisor or the staff member himself will furnish the approximate amount of time spent in each program area. Also, the allocation of time by program for staff members operating in a departmental set-up could be based on the daily schedule for that staff member. The amount of time spent on each program area should be determined so that FTEs can be calculated on a uniform basis. For example, a middle school organized on a modular schedule could have modules of different time lengths, such as twenty minutes or thirty minutes. It would be important to allocate FTEs on the basis of total time related to each program regardless of the number of modules involved. The same practice would be applicable to other schools in the district that may be organized on a different time or period basis. In this way uniform information could be received and comparisons between schools can be made.

Another method for prorating FTEs to program categories is to use a single staff member to serve as a prototype for all staff members in that employee group. For example, a separate time analysis could be prepared for one staff member at each elementary grade level and then applied to all the teachers at that level. The business administrator would then have a formula for allocating teacher time at each level according to program. Figure 29 shows the allocation of fourth-grade staff members by program.

This method has value in that it can be completed very quickly, but it will be somewhat less accurate than would be the analysis of each individual teacher's schedule. In a school district with a staff of 200 or more, this shortcut will provide data that ought to be accurate enough for meaningful analysis.

The final step in the allocation of staff to program categories is to compute salaries based on the FTE assigned to each program category. This can be achieved by taking the budgeted salary for each individual and relating it to his FTE breakout. This procedure is illustrated in Figure 30. This approach will give the most accurate cost information. However, the second approach would be to take the total amount budgeted for salaries and divide it by the total number of FTEs; the computation would be the average salary per FTE. The FTEs could then be multiplied by this average salary figure in order to obtain the total estimated salary costs by program categories. This method is illustrated in Figure 31.

In most instances, the first approach for computing salaries is preferred because it will display salary data that may be unique to a particular program category. For example, if a program category such as music has a disproportionate number of Ph.D.'s with many years of service credits, the salaries in that program would be higher than a program that, due to a high rate of staff turnover, had a number of beginning teachers. Thus, the fiscal information is highlighted so that it can be analyzed in terms of the instructional program.

allocation of support service costs

☐ Various instructional support service costs should not be allocated to the instructional program. Some argue that the cost of building management, plant maintenance and operations, and other support functions contribute directly to the various instructional programs and therefore should be prorated to the instruction categories.

However, the business administrator is better advised not to attempt to allocate or prorate general support costs. The problem is that perfectly sound rules of proration applied to identical circumstances can lead to very different results. For example, building management costs—school principal, clerical, and related costs—could be prorated by the number of students in the building or by the number of teachers served. Each would be logical, but programs with a high pupil-teacher ratio would appear to cost more under the first rule than under the second, even though the actual costs don't change.

Furthermore, proration of some support services—particularly administrative support service costs—is not politically justifiable. For instance, a principal may spend twenty percent of his time assisting teachers in the area of reading, and his salary might be prorated to the program category that accounts for this activity. However, because of public sensitivity to administrative costs, such a proration, defensible in terms of the application of the concept of program budgeting, would only serve to raise suspicion and undermine the confidence of the public in the PPBS approach.

FIGURES 30-31
PAGES 249-250

Therefore, the appropriateness of prorating the support service costs into program categories is questionable, particularly in the following areas:

= General administration—central office.
= Maintenance and operation of plant (utilities, cleaning and maintenance of buildings).
= School lunch programs.
= Transportation to and from school.
= Debt service.
= Pupil personnel service—guidance, health, and psychological service.
= Library and audiovisual services.

It should be noted that hidden in some support functions are costs that can and should be related directly to specific program categories. For instance, staff overtime costs and other costs required to prepare for a football game should be charged to the program category relating to interscholastic athletics, not to maintenance and operation of plant.

**allocation of
employee benefits**

☐ Employee benefits include costs for retirement plans, social security, health insurance, dental insurance, workmen's compensation insurance, and other employee benefits for which the district is responsible. Employee benefit costs may be allocated to specific program areas because these costs are directly traceable to salaries and, in fact, constitute additional employee costs for that program.

Employee benefits can be assigned to each program by multiplying salary costs for that program by the employee benefits percentage. The employee benefits percentage is computed by taking the total costs of employee benefits and dividing it by the total salary costs. This computation is illustrated in Figure 32. Separate calculations of employee benefits percentage should be made for each group of employees if their benefits differ.

The shortcoming of this method is that it assumes that every employee within a given group has identical benefits. This may not be true because such qualifications for benefits as "head of household" or years of service may directly affect the total benefit package an employee can receive. In order to overcome this problem, the business administrator may use the actual fringe benefit package associated with each individual employee. The time-consuming nature of this task is evident and it may not be worth doing.

A suggested worksheet for allocating employee benefits to each program is shown in Figure 33.

**preparation of
revenue budget**

☐ Revenue estimates should be submitted according to program categories along with budget requests. Examples would be: admission fees to sports events, federally aided programs, play tickets for the drama society, overdue library fees, and specially aided programs. This information can be used to generate a net cost for programs that have offsetting revenues and it will facilitate the analysis of such programs.

PROGRAM BUDGET
PROCESS

The school business administrator should assume responsibility for the preparation of a plan for processing the budget data and building the program budget document. His plan should include consideration of the roles of staff and community in the program budget process. No attempt will be made here to cover all of the personnel who might be involved in the budget process. However, the groups listed below should have a role in this process.

teachers

☐ The teacher's role primarily should be to recommend program changes and to prepare requisitions for supplies and materials for his particular program. He can also be involved in reviewing recommendations for program changes made by department chairmen, curriculum coordinators, administrators, or other teacher groups such as a faculty council.

principals

☐ Principals should review budget requests before they are submitted to the central office. They ought to consider program requests from the point of view of an administrator supervising many programs and try to balance them according to their sense of priority. They should prepare, with the assistance of their teaching staff, the estimated costs of the recommended programs.

central administration

☐ The successful preparation of a program budget requires the full support and participation of all the major administrators in the school district central office. One of the keys to success is the cooperation between the curricular and business administrators under the aegis of the superintendent. One man should assume operational control over the organization and flow of completed budget forms. This role should logically be assigned to the business administrator.

The business administrator—or whoever assumes this task—must maintain a well-organized filing and index system to cope with the financial data that will exceed, by a considerable amount, the data generated under the traditional function-object budget approach. One suggestion that might facilitate the organization of this data is the use of a separate loose-leaf notebook for each major program category according to the adopted program structure. In this way, all budget forms, supporting documents, and back-up materials can be filed together for easy reference.

The following steps are recommended as part of the central office's review of the program budget. They follow a chronological sequence:

Responsibility	Action
Business administrator	1. Receives all budget materials. 2. Checks forms for completeness. 3. Verifies totals submitted on forms. 4. Prepares summary worksheet by program for each account code (see Figure 34 for a suggested format for this worksheet). 5. Organizes and files materials. 6. Prepares and distributes to central office staff the first estimate of program budget.
Central office administrators	7. Reviews proposed budget in preparation for step 8. 8. Conducts a budget conference for each program area with the staff member responsible for preparing that budget attending. The scheduled conference should be open to other interested staff members. The purpose of these conferences will be to provide for a review of budget requests and allow for detailed exploration where necessary.
Superintendent of schools	9. Determines tentative budget expenditures. His decisions should be recorded on the budget forms. 10. Feedback conference on each program area. Same staff who attended budget conference may be present. Superintendent communicates his tentative decisions and solicits staff reaction. 11. Determines final budget to be recommended to board of education.
Business administrator	12. Prepares final detailed program budget document in accordance with superintendent's directions for submission to the board of education.

**budget
advisory committee**

□ A vital and necessary facet of PPBS is community involvement; therefore, a budget advisory committee ought to be established to review all budget requests and program changes and to recommend a budget to the board of education. The budget advisory committee should be composed of volunteers from the community and appointed by the board of education. The board must insure that a representative cross-section of the community is selected. The influence of status members of the

FIGURE 34
PAGE 253

community should not be overlooked in selecting a budget advisory committee. The committee should have access to all the information possessed by the district's administration. The involvement of a citizens' budget advisory committee in the preparation of the program budget can be an important vehicle for communications as well as a sincere acknowledgment of the principle of public control of public education.

board of education

□ The board of education reviews and determines the final program budget. This review should include the superintendent's recommended budget, the citizens' advisory committee's recommended budget, and the board's own assessment of the needs of the school system and the community. The board of education has the responsibility for communicating its decision to the staff and to the citizens' budget advisory committee prior to formal adoption of the program budget. The board also has responsibility for meeting legal requirements, such as municipal government or voter approval.

PREPARATION OF
PROGRAM BUDGET
DOCUMENT

The last step is the preparation of the actual program budget document for distribution to the staff, board, and community. The purpose of this document is to communicate the school district's fiscal plan for the ensuing year.

Program budget data that has been compiled should be displayed in accordance with the adopted program structure. Summary tables can be broken out according to levels of the program structure. The function-object comparison of the proposed budget to actual expenditure of previous years should also be prepared, at least in summary form. The presentation of the function-object budget summaries will demonstrate that the new program budget is not an attempt to hide budget information by using a different format. These summaries provide comparable figures of actual costs of previous years on the function-object coding along with the current proposed program budget.

In addition to the summary tables contained in a program budget document, personnel requirements and detailed cost projections for each program ought to be displayed. This is illustrated in Figure 35.

Again, the preparation of the detailed program tables and general summary tables is properly the task of the school business administrator. He may develop a set of worksheets designed to facilitate preparation of these tables. These worksheets may also be used to provide display data by program categories and by function-object categories to insure that they balance. The worksheets ought to be designed to whatever level of detail is planned for present action in the program budget. The amount allocated

FIGURE 35
PAGE 254

to each program must equal the various totals under the function-object codes. An illustration of a program budget worksheet is shown in Figure 36. These worksheets will provide the basis for establishing the program accounting system for the ensuing year. Program accounting techniques are discussed in Chapter 6.

SUMMARY

The program budget relates cost information to the categories in the program structure. The program budget displays costs on a program-by-program basis, while the traditional function-object budget shows costs by the type of item purchased.

A program budget may be prepared by having the staff submit budget requests in accordance with the program structure. Another alternative for preparing a program budget is to have budget requests submitted in exactly the same manner as in previous years and then have the business administrator translate and code these requests into the various program categories.

The program code procedures established for the program budget must be correlated with accounting, data processing, and financial reporting functions. It may be built around the existing system by expanding the function-object codes.

A detailed set of instructions for program budgeting should be prepared by the business administrator. These instructions must make provisions for the use of standard supply lists, direct charges, and staff allocations to program categories, as well as the allocation of support service costs and employee benefits. The revenue budget should also be prepared on a program basis.

The school business administrator should assume responsibility for the preparation of a plan for processing the budget data. His plan should describe the role of the staff and community in the budget process.

The final step in the program budgeting process is the preparation of the program budget document. The purpose of this document is to communicate the school district's fiscal plan for the ensuing year. Personnel requirements, detailed cost projections, and summary tables for each program area should be displayed in the program budget document.

FIGURE 36

PAGE 255

accounting:
how to install a
program accounting system

A good budget won't make a shaky institution strong but a bad budget, in times like these, can make a strong institution shaky and destroy a shaky one.

William G. Bowen ■

The program accounting system must be developed to meet all of the accounting requirements necessary to support a PPB system. Program accounting is the process of recording, classifying, and summarizing the financial transactions of a school district based upon the adopted program structure. It focuses on both the actual and budgeted revenues and expenditures by program area. This data is necessary for budget control purposes in order to insure that expenditures do not exceed budgeted amounts and to keep abreast of receipts. Program analysis and the preparation of multi-year fiscal plans hinge on the program accounting system. It provides the cost data for analysis of alternative ways to achieve the school district's objectives.

Accounting systems currently used in school districts do not provide the information needed for decision making within a PPBS framework. Most accounting systems are founded on the traditional function-object requirements made by the various state departments of education. Like the line item function-object budgets themselves, existing accounting systems display cost information on very broad and nondescript categories. They are, for the most part, little more than control mechanisms intended to insure that the school district does not exceed budgeted revenues.

---

*William McCleery, "One University's Response to Today's Financial Crisis," Interview with William G. Bowen, *University: A Princeton Quarterly,* Winter 1970-71. ©Princeton University

Program accounting in PPBS differs from function-object accounting in that it is structured to account for revenues and expenditures by each program in the program structure. The necessary legal and administrative functions of an accounting system are also performed in a program accounting system.

Although a program accounting system must be installed, this does not mean that a school district should discontinue its present accounting practices in order to install a completely new accounting system. Rather, the program accounting system ought to be incorporated within the existing system. The objective is to provide the financial data to operate a PPB system without the necessity of maintaining two separate accounting systems.

FACTORS
TO BE CONSIDERED IN
DESIGNING A PROGRAM
ACCOUNTING SYSTEM

The effectiveness of the program accounting system will, of course, depend on its design. It is important, therefore, to give consideration to the variables that might affect the composition of a program accounting system. The following represents those factors which may have a significant impact on the design of a program accounting system.

PPBS components

☐ A program accounting system cannot be developed without regard to the other components of a PPB system. For instance, the program structure and the program budget coding system that have been produced must be applied to the program accounting system. The system must be consistent with the program budget in terminology and in prorating and allocating procedures. This is necessary to insure that actual costs are accounted for in the manner in which they were budgeted.

legal requirements

☐ The program accounting system established must retain the capability to yield function-object data to meet state education department and other reporting requirements. This can be accomplished through the expansion of the account code as discussed in Chapter 5.

size of district

☐ The size of the school district is a major factor in the development of a program accounting system. As a school district increases in size, demands made upon the financial reporting system and the complexity of the contents of these reports may be expected to increase. This would suggest that for a small school district (less than 100 teachers) a manual program accounting system may serve its needs. In larger school districts, however, a program accounting system should be designed that will employ some type of computer or bookkeeping equipment. Both of these approaches are discussed in detail later in this chapter.

□ Another important factor in designing a program accounting system is to decide whether program costs will cut across various funds or will remain within a single fund. A fund is defined as an independent fiscal and accounting entity with a self-balancing set of accounts.[1] Normally, a school district maintains a general fund, several construction funds, a school lunch fund, and perhaps special revenue funds.

fund accounting

An example of a fund accounting problem, in remedial reading, shows that costs for this program are accounted for in the general fund, but if the district has a federal grant for remedial reading, it is also accounted for separately in a federal aid fund. The following chart illustrates the situation:

PROGRAM—REMEDIAL READING

	General Fund	Federal Aid Fund	Total Program
Salaries and Employee Benefits	$100,000	$20,000	$120,000
Supplies	20,000	3,000	23,000
Purchased Services	15,000	5,000	20,000
Total	$135,000	$28,000	$163,000

As the chart indicates, a program accounting system designed to cut across various funds will provide summaries of complete costs for a program regardless of the number of funds by which the program is supported. An accounting system that does not cut across funds may give an incomplete picture of the total effort that may be made in a program area. The above chart illustrates that if one looks at a single fund, i.e., general fund, then decisions on the remedial reading program would be made based only on the cost figure of $135,000.

□ The factor of depreciation can create considerable confusion in a school district accounting system. The concept of depreciation may not be appropriate to education, particularly public education, because there are no tax benefits to this activity. Under standard municipal and school district practice, depreciation on general fixed assets is not recorded in the accounting records.[2]

depreciation

□ Special provisions must be made for costs that cannot logically be allocated to any of the adopted program categories. For instance, a tax refund or a negotiated settlement on litigation may not be charged to a particular program area. These special costs could be accounted for as uncategorized activities. In most districts costs in nonprogram categories will be very small and will not significantly affect financial reporting and analysis.

nonprogram costs

[1] *Governmental Accounting, Auditing, and Financial Reporting,* Chicago, Municipal Finance Office Association, 1968, p. 6.
[2] Ibid, p. 10.

accounting base

☐ The method of accounting—cash or accrual—determines when and how revenues and expenditures are reported in the accounting records. Receipts under a cash accounting system are recorded when monies are received and disbursements are reported when monies are paid. Revenues under an accrual accounting system are recorded when they are earned and expenditures are recorded when they are incurred. In order to minimize disruption in the existing accounting system, the method of accounting—cash or accrual—presently in use should be continued.

encumbrance accounting

☐ Encumbrances are obligations in the form of purchase orders, contracts, or salary commitments chargeable to an appropriation and for which part of the appropriation is reserved. An encumbrance accounting system provides for the recording and liquidation of encumbrances. Those districts presently engaged in encumbrance accounting should modify their system to provide for encumbrances on a program basis. Again, this can be accomplished by expanding the account code as explained in Chapter 5. An encumbrance accounting system is not a necessary component of a PPB system. However, this technique can be used as a control device to insure that program accounts are not overexpended.

revenue accounting

☐ Certain revenues—such as admission fees for sports events—are directly attributable to specific program areas as discussed in Chapter 5. They are of assistance in determining net costs of certain program categories. Most revenues—such as property tax and state aid revenues—can not be charged directly to any one program; instead, they support all programs. Exceptions to this rule, like admission fees, ought to be accounted for in the formal accounting system. This can be done by utilizing the program code established as part of the program budget structure. This program code can be used in addition to the regular revenue source code.

fiscal control

☐ The district's adopted program budget should serve as a basis for fiscal control. The program accounting system that was designed in relation to the district's program budget provides the framework under which the control is exercised. The purpose of fiscal control in program areas is to insure that the program decisions that have been made will be implemented. Once the program accounting system has been established it should be the responsibility of the business administrator to see that program budget categories are not overexpended unless the appropriate revision of the budgeted amount has been made.

internal control

☐ The program accounting system should be based on accepted internal control procedures, that is, an arrangement of duties, records, and procedures to maintain organizational control over assets, liabilities, and expenditures. The school district's independent auditor might review the internal control procedures for the program accounting system.

☐ The type of equipment required or available to do the accounting ought to be examined. The mechanics of the program accounting system will depend upon the type of bookkeeping or computer equipment that is available.

program accounting equipment

After the factors that can affect the development of a program accounting system have been considered, a decision must be made on the actual method of accounting to be employed.

APPROACHES TO PROGRAM ACCOUNTING

The two basic approaches to accounting are manual and computerized, and both can satisfy the program accounting requirements of a PPB system. The decision on which approach to use will depend on the size of the school district, the availability of equipment, and the amount of program information for decision making required by the staff. The final decision should also obviate the necessity of maintaining two accounting systems.

a manual program accounting system

☐ A PPB system can be supported through the use of a manual accounting approach. Manual accounting envisions the posting of accounts by hand, with equipment limited to standard adding machines or calculators. In a school district of one hundred teachers or less this approach may be appropriate.

The manual program accounting system, as described in this section, can be accomplished without a duplication of accounting effort. The basic accounting practices currently in use in the district may serve as a foundation for installing a program accounting system.

It is not mandatory, particularly in a small school district, to use a computer in order to perform the necessary program accounting functions. Existing bookkeeping equipment ought to provide the necessary support for program accounting. Although a PPB system does not require a small school district to adopt a sophisticated data processing capability if it had none before, a manual program accounting system can be converted to computers or bookkeeping equipment at a later time if the need arises. The following represents some areas in which a modification of existing practices in order to integrate a program accounting system may be practical.

Accounting Cycle

A suggested accounting cycle—the process of recording, summarizing, posting, and reporting financial transactions for a manual program accounting—is displayed in the chart on page 94.

ACCOUNTING CYCLE FOR MANUAL PROGRAM ACCOUNTING SYSTEM

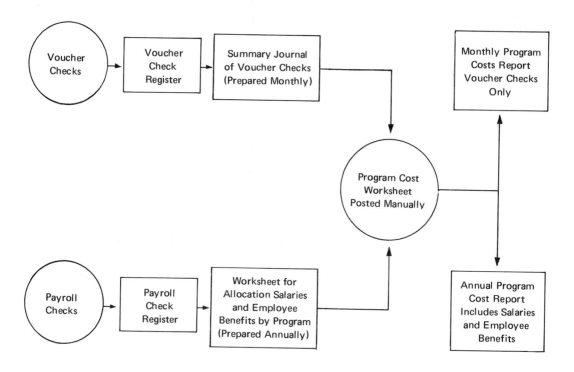

Recording Transactions

Salary costs can be charged against the various program categories; however, salaries can also be charged to the regular function-object codes and then be transferred to the program budget categories when the actual total salaries have been determined at the end of the budget year. The latter approach is preferable because it requires the least amount of additional accounting. There does not appear to be any reasonable need to maintain salary costs on a program budget basis during the budget year.

Employee benefits can be handled in the same manner by first charging them directly to function-object codes and then transferring them at the end of the school year to the appropraite program categories. Figures 37 and 38 illustrate suggested worksheets for summarizing salary costs and benefits by program.

As suggested in Chapter 5, general supply items purchased on a standard list can be allocated to programs on an estimated percent of use basis. After these materials have been purchased, the actual costs of the standard lists can be determined. By applying the percentage estimated for each program area to the actual costs of the standard supply list, costs can be distributed among the various programs. A worksheet for computing this allocation is shown in Figure 39.

Summarizing and Posting Ledgers

At the end of each month accounting data is summarized—journalized—
and posted to ledgers in accordance with the existing accounting system.
The following steps are suggested to perform program accounting
functions:

1. Review the purchase orders and payment vouchers paid during the
month and record the program codes on the check register. This can
be done by hand in the margin of the check register.
2. Prepare a summary of the voucher checks issued during the month and
show the program codes. This data is prepared by adding up the amount
of checks issued under each program code as shown on the check register.
This journal is illustrated in Figure 40.
3. Post the journal by program code to the program cost worksheet
monthly. A separate worksheet could be prepared for each program.
The worksheets and the summary of voucher checks issued for the
month should be filed in a loose-leaf notebook. A suggested program
cost worksheet is shown in Figure 41.
4. At year's end the actual salary and employee benefit costs should be
posted to the program costs worksheet. The total expenditures for
each program are then determined by adding voucher costs, salary costs,
and employee benefits at the bottom of the program costs worksheet.

Financial Reports

The manual program accounting system can be used to generate monthly
expenditure reports by program. Such reports ought to display expenditures for equipment, supplies, and contract services on a program basis. The
reports can be used by administrators for program management purposes.
A suggested format for a monthly program expenditure report is shown in
Figure 42.

An annual program expenditure report, including actual salary and
employee benefit information as well as equipment, supply, and contract
service costs, could be prepared using the same format. Data for this report
can be obtained from the program costs worksheets.

**a computerized
program accounting
system**

☐ In those school districts that have been operating their accounting
systems with the support of computer technology and equipment, the
existing system can be modified to accommodate the program accounting
system requirements. Moreover, in large school systems (more than 100
teachers) where computer capability does not now exist, consideration
should be given to leasing or contracting for some minimal computer
assistance.

While larger school districts can install a program accounting system
without computer or bookkeeping machine capability, it may be much
more efficient and effective if some type of modern data processing
equipment were provided. In order to obtain this type of support a school
district may lease, contract with a regional center, contract with a private
service bureau, or purchase its own equipment. Such equipment can be

FIGURES 40-42

PAGES 259-261

leased in part or total. It may be economical, for instance, to lease the key punch and sorter equipment and contract computer time on a "time used" basis.

Under a computerized program accounting system the coding should be arranged so that data may be entered only once for both function-object and program category purposes. This can be accomplished, as discussed in Chapter 5, through the use of codes—one for function-object and the other for program—which can be key-punched into a single card.

The areas of accounting that may require modification in order to integrate a program accounting system with the existing accounting system are given below.

Accounting Cycle

A suggested accounting cycle for a computerized program accounting system is shown in the chart on page 97.

Recording Transactions

Salaries can be recorded in a computerized accounting approach in a manner similar to that which was described in the manual accounting approach. That is, salaries may be posted to function-object categories and then transferred at the conclusion of the budget year to the appropriate program categories. However, with the use of computers salaries can be allocated to program categories on a current basis. With this system, overtime and substitute salary payments can be charged directly to the appropriate program category. Because of the capability of the equipment, a computer-oriented accounting system would allow salary allocations to be made directly to programs and simultaneously to function-object code funds.

Fringe benefits ought to be accounted for in the same manner that has been adopted for allocating salary expenditures. They may be charged on a current basis or they may be charged to the traditional function-object categories and transferred to program categories at the conclusion of the budget year.

The maintaining of actual costs for salaries and fringe benefits on a current basis by program categories is important only in those districts that are of such a size that this type of information is required in order to maintain cost control. In most school districts, however, the system of allocating these costs to function-object codes and transferring them to program codes at the conclusion of the budget year is adequate and will save considerable accounting time over the course of the year.

Financial Reports

The computer is capable of generating various reports, depending upon the financial information entered into the system. Financial reports are described in Figures 43-50. Additional reports can be programmed to provide summaries of program costs at the various levels of the program structure for a variety of priority or analytical reasons. The potential misuse of computers should be recognized.

FIGURES 43-50
PAGES 262-269

. . . Keep decisions on computers at the highest level. Make sure the climate is ruthlessly hard-nosed about the practicality of every system, every program, and every report. "What are you going to do with that report?" "What would you do if you didn't have it?" Otherwise your programmers will be writing their doctoral papers on your machines, and your managers will be drowning in ho-hum reports they've been conned into asking for and are ashamed to admit are of no value.[3]

ACCOUNTING CYCLE FOR COMPUTERIZED PROGRAM ACCOUNTING SYSTEM

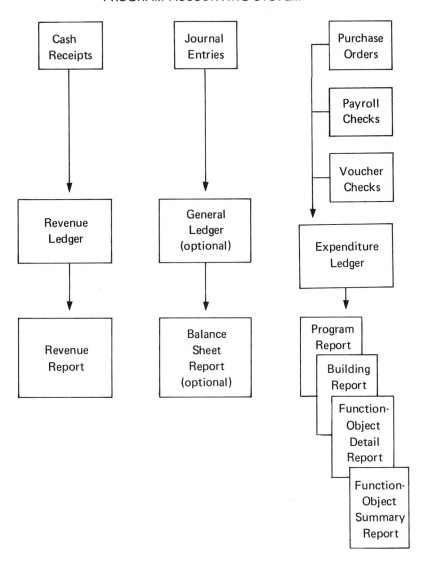

---

[3] Robert Townsend, *Up the Organization,* New York, Knopf, 1970, p. 36
©Robert Townsend.

ALTERNATIVE
STARTING POINTS FOR
INSTALLING A PROGRAM
ACCOUNTING SYSTEM

School districts installing PPBS can approach program accounting in at least three different ways. A district may analyze existing fiscal data to determine program costs. A second approach is to select one target program area for the gradual installation of a program accounting system. Finally, a district may apply its program accounting system to all programs concurrently.

**determine
costs by analyzing
function-object data**

☐ An administrator of a small district could feasibly obtain program cost data by analyzing existing line item accounts. If this approach is to work, the volume of transactions must be small and their actual program use clear. The small district could choose this alternative starting point if it wanted to achieve the benefits of a program budget without committing the resources required to design and operate a program accounting system.

In this alternative, program costs are maintained separately from the existing function-object accounting system through the use of program cost worksheets. This approach is practical in a district using a manual accounting system. The number of accounts should probably be less than fifty and the volume of transactions low.

**install a program
accounting system
gradually through
selected programs**

☐ Separate program accounts may be designed for selected program categories. If the school district has decided to install one or more programs per year, gradually leading to a full implementation of a PPB system, then the accounting system may be designed accordingly. The phasing in on a program-by-program basis allows the business office personnel to develop and operationalize a program accounting system over an extended period of time. The major disadvantage of this approach is that it may require maintaining two accounting systems during the installation period.

**design a program
accounting system
for all programs**

☐ This alternative would be to design an accounting system consistent with the adopted program structure and coding system. It will display total costs for every program category in the district's program structure. This approach provides the most immediate comprehensive data for a PPB system. The disadvantage of this starting point is that it is the most difficult because it attempts to account for all program categories simultaneously.

SUMMARY

Program accounting is the process of recording, classifying, and summarizing financial transactions in accordance with the program structure. It accounts for both the budgeted and actual revenues and expenditures by program area.

There are a number of factors that might affect the design of a program accounting system. For instance, the type of fund accounting, the legal reporting requirements, the size of the district, and the type of equipment available, among others, will all have an impact on the development of a program accounting system.

There are two basic approaches to accounting—manual and computerized—and both satisfy the program accounting requirements of a PPB system. Manual program accounting envisions the posting of accounts by hand. A computerized program accounting system will, of course, require the support of computer technology and equipment. Regardless of the approach used, the final decision should obviate the necessity of maintaining two accounting systems. However, the existing accounting cycle, methods for recording transactions, summarizing and posting ledgers, and determining financial reports might need to be modified to accommodate a program accounting system.

There are at least three alternative starting points for installing a program accounting system. Existing fiscal data may be analyzed to determine program costs, or a target program area may be selected with the phasing in of the remaining program areas. Finally, a program accounting system may be adopted to account for all program categories simultaneously.

programming: how to provide for program review, analysis of alternatives, and multi-year planning

While it may be important to preserve aspects of the present curriculum and to introduce changes gradually, we need more than haphazard attempts to modernize. We need a systematic approach to the whole problem.   Alvin Toffler *

Programming, or program analysis, is essentially a procedure allowing the decision maker to ask vital questions in a systematic manner about the benefits and cost implications of alternative approaches that have been generated to reach objectives. Briefly, program analysis is common sense by design.[1]

Analysis provides information comparing the cost and effectiveness of the several alternative programs. The questions: Why? What? Where? How? For whom? and When? can be clarified and given specificity by careful analysis.[2]

Programming represents a rational method for seeking the best solution to each particular problem. Essentially, the purpose of analysis is to show the cost of each alternative and the predicted contribution of the alternatives toward meeting a particular objective.

Program analysis is not intended, however, to replace or eliminate professional judgment or intuition—the process should only sharpen it.

---

*Alvin Toffler, *Future Shock,* New York, Random House, 1970, p. 364. © Alvin Toffler.

[1] Bela H. Banathy, *Instructional Systems,* Palo Alto, Calif., Fearon, 1968, p. 16.

[2] *Planning for Educational Development in a Planning, Programming, Budgeting System,* Washington, D.C., Committee on Educational Finance, National Education Association, 1968, p. 25.

In practically no case should it be assumed that the results of the analysis will "make" the decision. The really interesting problems are just too difficult, and there are too many intangible (e.g., political, psychological, and sociological) considerations that cannot be taken into account in the analytical process, especially in the quantitative sense.[3]

Programming as used here is a simplified form of systems analysis. Unlike systems analysis, however, it does not rely on statistical or other advanced scientific techniques of analysis. It is an approach that can reasonably be used by decision makers without an extensive background in statistics. This is not to depreciate the value of sophisticated cost-benefit or systems analysis but, rather, recognizes the limitations of most school districts to provide for this type of analysis. It should be recognized that a high level of training and expertise is necessary to function in the systems analysis area.

Systems analysis in education should probably best be left to universities, the federal government, or private foundations, because these agencies generally have greater access to the experts and they will encounter less resistance to experimental approaches in education. In addition, the majority of school districts in the United States are too small to allow for the adequate testing of alternative methods for achieving objectives. Therefore, most school districts should devote their efforts to implementing a type of analysis that is practical and useful in their situation.

PPBS generates, organizes, and displays information that can be used for program analysis purposes. The program structure discussed in Chapter 3 provides the framework for program analysis. The objectives, program budget, and program accounting system, as discussed in previous chapters, furnish the required data for both a program review of all programs and a program analysis of one specific program area.

PROGRAM REVIEW
TECHNIQUES

Programming requires the development and analysis of a series of alternatives for the accomplishment of an objective. As discussed earlier, the analysis can be based on a highly sophisticated statistical method. It does not appear, however, that it is necessary to utilize such a method in order to derive some benefits from the data that has been gathered during the PPBS process. A technique referred to as program review will allow the decision maker to make more intelligent decisions in developing programs without requiring the expertise and time necessary for an in-depth program analysis.

---

[3] G. H. Fisher, *"The World of Program Budgeting,"* The Rand Corporation, Santa Monica, Calif. A speech presented at conference on program budgeting and cost analysis, UCLA, June 2, 1966, p. 11.

To accomplish a program review, the administration and staff must describe existing programs and the program changes that they recommend in order to achieve the objectives. In other words, the staff must describe what they are doing now, the resources they need in order to continue at existing levels, and the changes, if any, they feel will improve the existing programs in order to meet an objective.

To facilitate the acquisition of information, the central administrative staff ought to develop forms that the staff can use for reporting the data. The first form which should be completed for all program areas would describe existing programs. The information required would include a brief summary of existing programs, student test material, staff, and student enrollment by section. The form should also make provision for reporting in these areas on a multi-year basis. A sample form for describing existing programs is illustrated in Figure 51.

A second form that ought to be developed by the central administration deals with proposed program changes. This form would allow all members of the staff and student body to submit recommended program changes—modifications, additions, and deletions—to the superintendent. The advantage of this approach is that it provides an opportunity for broadly based participation in making recommendations directly to the superintendent. To the extent that the superintendent considers and responds to each proposed program change, he will give meaning to this procedure. This is not to say that he must adopt every suggestion or recommendation, but rather that for whatever decision he makes he furnish a supporting rationale to the individual who initiated the proposed change.

The program change proposal may be used for all program changes whether or not they have budgetary implications. For example, a change from a required program in high school social studies to an elective program may not require any additional costs, but this change should be reflected on a program change proposal. This procedure will supply the information needed to review proposed changes in programs.

The central administration should develop a program change proposal form to facilitate the reporting of data in a comprehensive and systematic manner. This form might include a description of the issue or problem, the rationale for change, the number of students to be served, the plans for implementation, and a long-range (three-year) fiscal estimate. A sample program change form is shown in Figure 52.

ANALYSIS OF ALTERNATIVES FOR A PROGRAM AREA

While the program review technique is appropriate for all programs, one or more program areas might receive an in-depth analysis. Program analysis can be viewed as an intermediate step between program review and sophisticated systems analysis. Program analysis, like systems analysis, is concerned with the orderly analytical study to help a decision maker identify a preferred course of action from possible alternatives. It is not, however, a highly theoretical "general systems theory" approach as described by Donald Levine.[4]

Although program analysis is a simplified version of systems analysis, it will require considerable time and commitment from members of the staff. Due to these requirements, a district should probably not attempt to provide for the analysis of all programs within a single school year.

A district ought to select one program or several programs for analysis. Consideration should be given to the following criteria in determining which program should be analyzed:

= Programs that are listed as high priority—those that have been identified as the most important for the ensuing academic year. (See "Establishing Priorities," Chapter 4.)

= Programs that have high visibility—those that have received considerable criticism or attention from students, staff, or the public. (See program change proposal forms illustrated in Figure 52.)

= Programs that have high cost—those that have a high total cost or a high per pupil served cost. (See "Program Budget" as described in Chapter 5.)

The district's PPBS task team could facilitate both the determination of programs to be analyzed and the building of commitment for program analysis on the part of the staff by inviting their participation in the process. Involvement might be achieved through the use of the program change proposal concept previously described and through the selection of members of the staff to serve on a subcommittee to perform the program analysis. If the PPBS task team decides to have more than one program area analyzed, it would be well advised to establish a subcommittee for each program area.

The subcommittee should be encouraged to complete the analysis in a systematic, comprehensive manner. It should also attempt to document the analysis. Guidelines for conducting the analysis can be prepared and distributed to the various subcommittees. These guidelines ought to insure that the program analysis data is displayed in a standardized format for the uniform consideration of all factors. The data provided in the description of existing programs, as well as program change proposals, if any, may serve as a base for analysis.

Guidelines for conducting the analysis are shown in Figure 53. These guidelines, referred to as a program analysis memorandum, have been divided into three parts. The first part requires general background data—statement of problems, program objectives, description of pupils to be served, and lists of alternatives or options to be considered. After

---

[4] Donald M. Levine, *Some Problems in Planning-Programming-Budgeting for Education*, Cambridge, Mass., Harvard University Press, May 1969, p. 8.

FIGURE 53

PAGES 274-279

completing the first part, the next part is completed for each alternative or option that has been listed. The second part contains the factors required to complete the analysis. The final section of the program analysis contains the recommended alternative, the major factors that influenced this recommendation, and a suggested plan for implementing the recommended alternative.

Factors that ought to be considered in analyzing the program alternatives before making a recommendation are:

= relevance to school district's priorities
= reasonableness of the assumptions presented
= validity of the data presented
= relevance of the supportive data to the recommended alternatives
= adequateness of the plan to implement the recommended alternative
= relationship of the recommended alternative to other program decisions being considered
= analysis of other alternatives not included in the original list
= recommended alternative possesses a distinct advantage to the status quo or existing practice

It is vital to remember that any final decision will be based on a prediction of effectiveness. Decision makers must exercise judgment, common sense, professional knowledge, and even intuition in rejecting or endorsing a specific program alternative. Analysis does not produce automatic decisions nor in any way reduce the decision makers' responsibilities. Program analysis simply assists a decision maker to identify a preferred course of action from among the possible alternatives.

MULTI-YEAR PLANNING

The concept of multi-year planning is an important part of program analysis because of the necessity for predicting the long-term consequences of program decisions. Also, decision makers are not limited to a single academic year in analyzing the priorities for allocating resources. The multi-year concept assures the recognition of the educational and financial impact of program decisions over a long-term period. For instance, if a foreign language program is installed in the sixth grade, then provisions must be made for continuing that language in subsequent grades. Initial decisions should take into account a multi-year impact on the program. Will a five-year sequence be offered or will the existing four-year language program be spread among grades six through twelve? If the decision is to expand the existing foreign language program by a course in the literature of the language, will this require a more highly trained staff? The decision should also consider the resources (staff, space, equipment, time, and materials) required to support the program change not only for the ensuing year but on a long-range basis.

A three-year time frame—the budget year plus two additional years—has been suggested for multi-year planning because it represents a practical time period. Multi-year planning can be done on a five-, ten-, or even twenty-year basis. The utility of such an extended period of time, at a school district level, is questionable because of staff turnover, the rapid rate of change in educational technology, and the fluctuations of the cost of living index.

Some of the elements of a multi-year plan are as follows:

= demographic data
= predicted enrollment in program areas
= forecast of revenues by source
= forecast of expenditures based on long-range plans
= school building needs and capital outlay projections

The Westport, Connecticut, *Report of the Advisory Committee on a Long-Range School Budget* represents an example of a complete multi-year fiscal and curricular plan. (See Figure 54.)

The sequence for the development of the multi-year plan should provide for the statement of the educational plan on a long-range basis. This will permit the school business administrator to predict and assign cost to this plan. The multi-year plan should reflect the philosophical objectives that have been determined for the school district. Finally, the multi-year plan should be updated and extended for an additional year on an annual basis using the current data, thus insuring a continuous three-year program plan.

SUMMARY

Programming is the component of PPBS which focuses on the predicted benefits and cost implications of the alternative approaches that have been generated to reach objectives. Program analysis is intended to sharpen professional judgment and intuition.

Because of the limitations of most school districts in providing for systems analysis, this type of analysis should be left to other institutions or agencies. The two types of practical analysis techniques that districts may use are program reviews for all programs and program analysis for a target program area.

Program review techniques require a description of all existing programs and the program changes recommended to achieve the objectives. Program analysis for a target program area requires a statement of general background data, a list of alternatives to be considered, and the documentation of the factors that influenced the recommendation for a particular alternative.

Multi-year planning is an important element of program analysis because of the necessity for predicting the long-term consequences of program decisions. A three-year time frame has been suggested for multi-year planning purposes. Finally, the multi-year plan should be updated on an annual basis.

FIGURE 54
PAGE 280

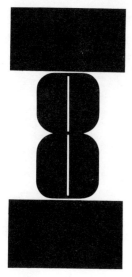

documenting:
how to prepare the
ppbs document

...we as school administrators propose to work for a joint lay and professional program of public information which will lead to an appreciation and understanding of the work and needs of the schools and to the development of ways and means of meeting those needs.   AASA Platform, 1969-1970 ∎

The various components of a PPB system have been discussed in detail. In Chapter 3, for example, procedures were suggested for designing a program structure. Chapter 4 outlined the process associated with the preparation of objectives, the establishment of priorities, and the development of related evaluation criteria. Chapters 5 and 6 furnished a process for establishing program budgeting and accounting systems. Chapter 7 presented a practical approach to program analysis—the determination of alternatives and selection of activities to reach the established objectives.

The purpose of this chapter is to present a scheme for organizing in summary form all the data related to the various components of an installed PPB system. This data serves as the information base for the preparation of a comprehensive PPBS document. The PPBS document, unlike the documents illustrated previously—such as the program analysis document, program budget document, and so forth—cannot be prepared until all the components of the system have been installed. For example, the program budget documents as discussed in Chapter 5 represent only the budget components of a PPB system, while the PPBS document provides for the integration of all of the components of the system, including a statement of the objectives, evaluation, criteria, the program budget on a multi-year basis, and program analysis data. A comparison

---

*1969-70 AASA Official Report, Washington, D.C., American Association of School Administrators, 1970, p. 149.

between three basic documents—a function-object budget document, a program budget document, and a PPBS summary document—is shown in Figure 55. If a school district has phased in the various components of a PPB system over an extended period of time, the PPBS document must be delayed until all components have become operative.

The PPBS document represents the synthesis—for possibly the first time—of the planning, programming, and budgeting activities of a school district. The most significant feature of the PPBS document is that it displays in one place the recommended educational plan with the recommended fiscal plan. Because the document reflects all of the components of a PPB system, it can serve as a powerful communications instrument. It supplies information to the staff on district priorities, objectives, program changes, and allocation of resources. It furnishes the school board with a comprehensive view of the entire school district's operations, and it provides the community with a summary of program data, objectives, and related evaluation information displayed in a relatively easy to understand manner.

The PPBS document may also serve as the plan of action for the day-to-day operation of the school system. The concept of management by objectives may be applied through the use of the information contained in a PPBS document.

THE PPBS INFORMATION SYSTEM

The information generated as a result of the installation of a PPB system will be useful for decision making only to the extent that it is well organized and can be readily retrieved. Such organization should provide the decision makers with easy access to all relevant data for any particular issue.

It is suggested that a series of notebooks be used to facilitate the organization of this information. One notebook could be prepared for each program area in the program structure. The notebooks should be numbered in sequence with the contents displayed in a consistent manner for each program. Loose-leaf notebooks are suggested for this purpose so the materials can be added or deleted to this system. The use of a notebook provides flexibility in placing related documents together. Tabs can be used on the notebooks for easy retrieval of information. It may also be desirable to color-code the various documents in the notebook. For example, all objectives might be placed on green paper, descriptions of existing programs on yellow paper, and so forth.

The following types of information are essential to utilizing the PPB system and therefore should be assembled for each program and placed in the appropriate program notebooks:

FIGURE 55
PAGE 281

1. objectives, priorities, and evaluation data
2. multi-year resource requirements based on existing programs
3. program change proposals and related fiscal information
4. program analysis studies that have been completed for selected programs

Although not a product of the PPB system, other studies and reports relating to each program should also be included in this information system.

It is important that a careful index be prepared on the information available for each program. The index should cross-reference materials in related programs. Again, the PPBS information system will only be useful if the information can be easily retrieved in a useful format for decision making.

PREPARATION
OF THE
SUMMARY DOCUMENT

The PPBS information system generates a considerable amount of data on the various programs of the school district. Due to the large volume of material, it might be desirable to condense all of this information into one document. For instance, depending upon the program structure adopted, a district may have as many as thirty-five separate notebooks containing program information. Obviously, this amount of data cannot be reproduced and disseminated to every member of the staff, school board, and community. Therefore, it is necessary to prepare a summary containing the major highlights of each program area. A PPBS summary document, then, would serve as a simple synopsis of the most relevant program data.

The PPBS summary document may be given wide distribution within the school district community. Certainly, copies should go to each principal and members of the professional staff as well as to the board of education. Support service supervisors should also receive copies so that they can understand the total education program and the relationship of their activities to that program. The summary may also serve as a communications instrument for school personnel. Finally, it can be distributed to various community leaders, community service groups, parent-teacher organizations, and other special interest groups, such as the budget advisory committee, that have expressed a desire for more information on the school district.

The PPBS document should be prepared annually upon the completion of the budget cycle, so that the fiscal resources, as approved in the operating budget for the next school year, will be integrated with the educational program plan. It is important that the document reflect all of the major program and fiscal decisions made during the budget cycle, as well as the long-range program decisions.

The suggested format for the PPBS summary document is outlined below:

1. Title page. It is suggested that a different title, such as "Educational and Fiscal Plan," be used to distinguish this document from the traditional budget document.
2. Table of contents.
3. Statement of the philosophical objectives of the school district. This statement would outline the purpose of the educational program.
4. Board of Education message. This is a vital part of the summary document because it provides the board with an opportunity to present its major objectives and priorities for the education program. This message may also serve as a statement for reporting to the press and other news media.
5. Description of PPBS and the district's program structure. The description of PPBS is desirable to assist those persons reading the document to understand the concepts involved. The district's program structure should be displayed along with the rationale for its adoption. This is important because the balance of the document will present program and financial information at various levels within the program structure.
6. Various summary tables should be presented next to furnish an overview of the entire document on a summary basis without the necessity of reviewing each program. Summary tables provide for a quick review of the major decisions and display costs and personnel allocations between the various programs. The following tables are suggested:

   = summary of major program changes
   = multi-year financial data
   = summaries of personnel, both certificated and classified by program areas
   = proposed additions or deletions in personnel by program and by type of position
   = allocation of student time by programs, grade levels, and building
   = presentation of multi-year program statistics, the number of students to be served, number of staff, number of classrooms, and so forth

7. Following the sections containing the various summary tables, some detailed information on each program should be displayed. This section will constitute the major portion of the summary of the PPBS document. Care should be taken to provide data in a consistent format for each program area so that during a review of the various programs it will not be necessary to search for information in order to make comparisons. Information on each program should include the following:

   = objectives and evaluation criteria
   = description of existing program
   = recommended program changes
   = summary of program analysis, if completed
   = presentation of multi-year fiscal plan, including offsetting revenues, if any
   = multi-year program statistics, such as number of students to be served by grade level, student time allocations, teaching staff, etc.
   = references to other reports, documents, or information available on the program

8. A detailed section on revenue presented by each fund. This section would show the source of revenues as well as prior year's comparable data and projections for future years.

9. Detailed expenditures by traditional function-object code by each fund. This section would provide comparative data as well as projections for future years. It is suggested that it be presented in this document so that comparable data on the traditional budget format would be available. This data may also serve as a basis for reporting expenditures to state and federal agencies.

10. A comprehensive index may be prepared for the entire document. This would provide for the easy location of specific information.

The PPBS summary document should be prepared by the central office administrative staff and submitted to the PPBS task team for review. The purpose of such a review would be to provide the administrative staff with information for the revision or restating of specific data in order to make it more readable and understandable prior to the final printing for public consumption.

The PPBS summary document should be prepared in such a way that it can easily be understood. To accomplish this, educational jargon should be eliminated and financial figures should be rounded to the nearest whole dollar. It could be attractively packaged with a distinctive cover and divider pages could be used to separate the various sections of the document. The reproduction process used for this summary document should result in clear, sharp, easy to read copy.

THE LIMITATIONS
OF A PPBS DOCUMENT

Once the document has been developed and presented in written form, it tends to give the impression of rigidity. Indeed, to some extent it is rigid because it represents a commitment of the staff and board for specific programs, and it therefore serves as the basis for future action. This does not mean, however, that programs cannot be changed on the basis of new information or demands. However, the PPBS document may be seen as the symbolic manifestation of the loss of autonomy, the forcing of conformity, and dehumanization. This impression will occur to the degree that the staff does not understand the rationale for a comprehensive document, and to the extent that they have not been involved in the entire PPBS process. The PPBS document is a tool for communications and its limitations will be as great as the board's and administration's failure to use it as such.

Further, because the document necessarily has to be in summary form, it will not contain a sufficient level of detail to be useful to those vitally interested in a particular program. A summarization can also oversimplify the complexity of a particular program or programs.

PROGRAM MANAGEMENT

The printed summary PPBS document does not represent the end. Its utility will, for the most part, depend upon its very use. If it is used solely by the school business administrator for budgetary control purposes, the effort devoted to the installation of a full PPB system will have been wasted. It is incumbent upon the board of education, the administrative staff, and the professional staff to be familiar with the contents of the document and to make day-to-day operational decisions based on the commitments contained in the approved PPBS document.[1]

SUMMARY

The PPBS document represents the synthesis of the planning, programming, and budgeting activities of a school district. It can serve as a powerful communication instrument because it displays, in one place, the recommended educational plan with the recommended fiscal plan.

The information generated from a PPB system will be useful for decision making only if it is well organized and readily retrieved. Thus, a simplified information system should be installed.

Because the volume of information is large, some type of summary document should be prepared for dissemination to the staff and community. This document should reflect all the major program and fiscal decisions. Consideration should also be given to including various summary tables and some detailed information for each program area. The printed summary document must be used as a guide for making day-to-day operational decisions.

CONCLUSION

An attempt has been made to present, in an understandable manner, the basic components of a Planning, Programming, Budgeting System. The various strategies and alternatives suggested for installing the system were predicated on the belief that each district should adapt, develop, and determine its PPB system in accordance with its uniqueness. In the words

---

[1] W. Hartman, H. Matthes, and A. Proeme. *Management Information Systems Handbook,* New York, McGraw-Hill, 1968.

of John Gardener, "We do not want all institutions to be alike. We want institutions to develop their individualities . . . so long as it is striving for excellence in performance."[2]

PPBS has also been presented in the belief that through the installation of the system, classroom experiences for students can be significantly improved. Although it is easy to identify the problems and risks associated with installing PPBS, the potential benefits more than justify the effort required to overcome these problems in order to operationalize the system.

The specification of desired outcomes and the funneling of resources directly toward the attainment of those desired outcomes and the concomitant integration of these two elements of a school system are the basic and most profound benefits of a PPB system. The implication for the systematic linkage of the school district's activities are enormous for both the constituents and the clients in the school community. This system suggests that schools can become institutions ". . . capable of continuous change, continuous renewal, continuous responsiveness."[3]

One of the sadder lessons of bureaucratic life is that large public institutions inevitably atrophy unless their members establish a mechanism to insure continuous change and evaluation. There is simply no way to eliminate a public institution that has withered into obsolescence. Unlike industry, which must assimilate new technology and accommodate changing markets, there is no essential reason why a public institution must change anything it does. Its members, through tenure, are secure in their jobs; its financial support is assured; its clients are usually captive; its competition does not exist.

For this reason, educators must be aware of the special dangers their institutions face. The nature of the school system forces them to rely on planned internal mechanisms to renew themselves and to respond to a changing society. As the foregoing indicates, the planning, programming, budgeting system can serve this purpose.

---

[2] John W. Gardner, *Excellence: Can We Be Equal and Excellent Too?* New York, Harper & Row, 1961, p. 83.

[3] John W. Gardner, *The Recovery of Confidence,* New York, Norton, 1970, p. 25.

part

two

procedure for the preparation of the educational program

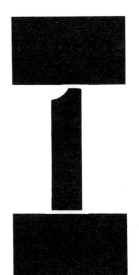

The following represents a comprehensive example for the collection and analysis of PPBS information. The procedures manual details the necessary steps, the assignment of responsibilities to the various tasks and activities, and a suggested time frame to operationalize PPBS.

1. Philosophy for Preparation of the Educational Program

It is our philosophy that each staff member should be involved in the development of the educational program for his area of interest and expertise. It is our judgment that "programming," "planning," "budgeting," and "evaluation" should be blended together.

We believe that the budget process can be used to improve instruction. It is our judgment that this process provides a discipline and vehicle to accomplish this purpose by bringing together in one comprehensive package the expression of our educational goals in fiscal and program terms.

2. What Is PPBS?

A Planning, Programming, Budgeting System (PPBS) provides the information necessary for planning educational programs that will meet the needs of the community, and for choosing among the alternative ways a school district can allocate resources to achieve their goals and objectives. . . .

A PPBS differs from current planning and budgeting systems in emphasizing the definition of district needs, goals, and objectives; and the application of systems analysis techniques.[1]

---

[1] *Conceptual Design for Planning, Programming, Budgeting System for State of California School Districts,* Peat, Marwick, Mitchell & Co., June 1969.

The purpose of this section is to present the concepts of PPBS.

The Association of School Business Administrators has developed a design for a Planning, Programming, Budgeting System for education. This design is known as an Educational Resource Management Design (ERMD).[2]

Shown below is a brief description of this design:

...the educational process is intended to result in the production of outputs for society in the form of specific growth of learnings such as increase in knowledge, skills and attitudes. It is out of this process that we are going to direct your attention to the first description of the Educational Resource Management Design that we are developing . . . (See below.)

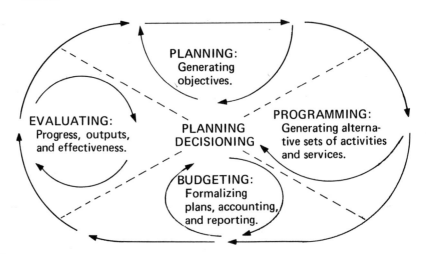

We divide the parts of the Educational Resource Management Design or PPBS in Education into four distinct parts. . . .these parts are planning, programming, budgeting, evaluation, all surrounding planning and decisioning. . . .

Now let me briefly give you our definition of planning. It is those acts devoted primarily toward qualifying the school system to meet its responsibility to society. In effect, it is decision-making concerned with guiding internal change to the end that the school as an institution adapts effectively to the dynamic society of which it is a part. Planning, then, is directed toward keeping the school doing what it is supposed to do, and we say specifically and briefly that it is generating objectives.

Now programming, on the other hand, consists of those acts which are included in developing a configuration of interrelated services and activities, with each configuration representing a design for attaining a specific objective. It is the development of different programs.

[2]*Education Resource Management Design,* developed by Research Corporation, Association of School Business Officials, Chicago, Illinois, as published in *Report of the First National Conference on PPBS in Education,* Association of School Business Officials, Chicago, Ill., 1969. This Conference was held on June 10, 1969, in Denver, Colorado.

Next, we say that budgeting *is broader, perhaps, than we normally think of it. We say it is the sum of the acts involved in final reconciliation of programs and available resources according to established priorities, plus it is preparation of the budget document, plus it is approval by the Board of Education, plus it is execution of the budgetary plans insofar as this involves management of, accounting for, and reporting use of resources.*

Finally, we define evaluating *as being those acts involved in developing subjective and objective data, descriptive, first, of progress in attaining stated objectives, and second, descriptive of the outputs which constitute final attainment wholly or in part of stated objectives.* [3]

3. Definition of PPBS Terms

3.1 Goals

A goal is a statement of broad direction, purpose, or intent based on identified needs. A goal is general and timeless, that is, it is not concerned with a specific achievement within a specified time period. [4]

3.2 Objectives

Objectives are desired accomplishments which can be measured within a given time frame. Achievement of the objective advances the system toward a corresponding goal. Accordingly, objectives must be developed that support and contribute to the achievement of the established goals. [5]

3.3 Evaluation Methods

Evaluation methods need to be developed for each objective to provide the means to determine if the objective has been achieved. Evaluation methods, both objective and subjective, provide means to determine program effectiveness and performance standards.

3.4 Program Structure

A program structure is a hierarchical arrangement of programs which represents the relationship of activities to goals and objectives. The structure contains categories of activities with common output objectives. [6]

The program structure is the basis for program accounting. It provides the framework for program description, review, and analysis.

3.5 Description of Existing Program

A program is a group or package of interdependent, closely related services or activities progressing toward or contributing to a common objective or set of allied objectives. [7]

---

[3] *Ibid.,* p. 43-46.

[4] *Conceptual Design for Planning, Programming, Budgeting System for State of California School Districts,* Peat, Marwick, Mitchell & Co., June 1969, p. 1-5.

[5] *Ibid.,* p. I-8.

[6] *Ibid.,* p. I-15.

[7] *Ibid.,* p. I-13.

The existing program description provides information, in a uniform manner, on the services and activities presently being performed during the year for each program area. It provides background data for budget review and proposed program changes.

3.6 Program Coding
Programs are coded by number to facilitate the collection of data such as costs and statistics in a variety of combinations and formats consistent with the program structure. These data are used to control program expenditures, evaluate program effectiveness in terms of stated objectives, and to analyze the cost effectiveness of alternative programs.[8]

3.7 Program Budget
The program budget in a PPBS is a plan that relates proposed expenditures for programs, within a specific time frame to goals and objectives, based upon a program structure classification. It includes the proposed revenue sources for financing programs.[9]

3.8 Multi-Year Financial and Statistical Plan
This plan presents cost estimates and statistical data by program for a multi-year period. The information presented is for activities and services performed in the school district for the current year and future years.

3.9 Program Proposal Paper
This one-page paper provides an opportunity for direct communications to the Superintendent of Schools by all staff members and students of program proposals and new ideas.

3.10 Program Change
The program change describes proposed new education programs and modifications to existing programs. Reasons for the change, projected achievements to be obtained, and multi-year cost and statistical projections are made.

3.11 System Analysis
System analysis is an approach to decision-making that emphasizes:

Definition of educational problems

Development of alternative programs

Analysis of alternative solutions

Recommendation of preferred program(s).[10]

3.12 Education Program Forms
This series of forms provides descriptive, statistical, and financial information on existing educational programs and proposed educational program changes. This is a new series of forms which integrates the various elements of a PPBS.

---

[8] *Ibid.,* p. I-15.

[9] *Ibid.,* p. I-16.

[10] *Ibid.,* p. I-29.

3.13 Budget Forms

This series of traditional forms provides the budget details by object code. These forms have been modified so that this detail is broken down by program.

4. Description of Roles in Preparation-of Educational Program

4.1 Teacher

= Contributes his professional judgment in defining educational objectives, considering alternatives, selecting a plan of action, programming that plan, and evaluating the results achieved in terms of the plan.

= Assists building principal and district curriculum coordinators in developing educational programs.

= Provides assistance in the preparation of estimated costs of various programs.

= Reacts to educational program presentations.

4.2 Building Principal

= Coordinates the educational program as it relates to his building. Advocates the best possible educational program for his building with some realization of the fiscal situation.

= Directs the development of an educational program for his building with the assistance of teachers and the district curriculum coordinators.

= Prepares, with the assistance of teachers and the district curriculum coordinators, the estimated costs of his educational program.

4.3 District Curriculum Coordinator

= Coordinates the educational program in his area. Advocates the best program on a K-12 basis that promotes articulation and student achievement. Has primary responsibility for "project planning" once educational goals are established. Project planning involves a detailed plan of action to accomplish the specified objectives. It includes a time schedule and development of evaluation methods.

= Coordinates the development of a K-12 educational program working with the building principals and teaching staff.

= Assists the building principals in preparing the estimated cost of this program.

4.4 Central Office Staff

Reviews budgets on a K-12 basis and makes recommendations to the superintendent of schools on the educational program and the allocation of resources.

4.5 Superintendent of Schools

Establishes systemwide educational goals and priorities. Allocates limited financial resources based on a systemwide viewpoint and in terms of district goals. Recommends an educational program and budget to the board of education.

4.6 Citizens' Budget Advisory Committee

A group of community residents will review the entire program. This committee will serve two purposes: (1) to make suggestions and recommendations to the superintendent and the board, and (2) to give the community a greater vote in shaping the educational program of the district.

4.7 Board of Education

Reviews and approves a program that provides for the educational needs of the students and that is fiscally responsible and educationally defensible.

4.8 Individuals Responsible

The individual(s) responsible for preparation of Education Program Forms is shown in Appendix A.

The individual(s) responsible for preparation of Budget Forms is shown in Appendix B.

The individual(s) responsible for preparing revenue estimates and reviewing standard supply lists prior to issuance is shown in Appendix C.

5. Program Proposal Paper

The Program Proposal Paper is a one-page memorandum to the superintendent of schools from members of the staff and students. Its purpose is to define a need or problem in the school district; the first step in any program analysis.

The paper may stand by itself as a description of the problem areas in order to provide an improved perspective or, preferably, can be used to set the framework to act as the first phase of an in-depth analysis of the problem.

The Program Proposal is used to assist the superintendent of schools in determining priorities for the review and analysis of existing programs and proposed program changes. The concept of the use of a Program Proposal Paper recognizes that all program areas cannot be reviewed and analyzed in depth each year.

Through his response to the Program Proposal Paper, the superintendent can indicate his priority for review of existing programs and proposed program changes. The areas designated will have more formal reviews and additional documentation prepared.

The superintendent will prepare a reaction to each Program Proposal Paper. This reaction will be sent to the person preparing the proposal and other staff members directly involved.

6. Program Structure

The program structure provides for a maximum of five program levels. These levels are indicated on Charts 1 and 2.

An example of the program structure for the basic instructional program of social studies, K-12, is shown below:

CHART 1

Program Level	Program Level Description
I	Total District
II	Instructional Programs
III	Basic Education Programs
IV	Social Studies, K-12
V	Each Grade Level, K thru 12

Grade	Level
K-5	Elementary
6-8	Middle School
9-12	High School

7. Program Coding

A twelve-digit account code is used to record all general fund expenditures. This account code includes a two-digit program code. The format for the account code is:

Fund	Program	Location	Function	Object
AO General	62 Mathematics K-12	02 Evans Park Elementary School	220 Teaching	200 Equipment

This code is written AO-62-02-220-200.

See Appendix D for definitions for fund, location, function, and object. See Appendix E for listing of program codes. See Appendix F for location codes. See Appendix G for explanation of basic object codes.

8. Presentation of Documents

Please type and submit one copy of all Education Program Forms. Supplemental data should be typed on separate sheets.

Please prepare in pen, pencil, or type one copy of each of the Budget Forms.

Materials should be well organized, referenced to basic forms, and ready for xeroxing and distribution.

Please retain a file copy for your use of all materials submitted.

9. Educational Program Forms

The use of the various Education Program Forms for preparation of the Educational Program is described in Chart 3. These forms are used to describe the educational program as it exists during the current year and projections of that program for future years.

CHART 2
Detail Program Structure—Effective July 1

Program Level					Program Code			Program Description
I	II	III	IV	V	Level III	Level IV	Level V	
*								School District
	*							Instructional Programs
		*			N/A			Basic Education

CHART 2
Detail Program Structure (continued)

Program Level					Program Code			Program Description
I	II	III	IV	V	Level III	Level IV	Level V	
			*			60		English, Language Arts, and Reading, K-12
			*			61		Science (including health), K-12
			*			62		Mathematics, K-12
			*			63		Social Studies, K-12
			*			64		Physical Education, Intramural and Interscholastic Athletics, K-12
			*			65		Business, 9-12
			*			66		Foreign Language, 7-12
			*			67		Unified Arts (Industrial Arts, Home-making, Driver Education, and Mechanical Drawing), 6-12
			*			68		Art, K-12
			*			69		Music, K-12
				*			Note	Each Grade, K-12
		*			76			Special Education
			*			Note (2)		Educable
			*			"		Emotionally Disturbed
			*			"		Learning Disability
			*			"		Physically Handicapped
			*			"		Trainable
		*			77			Vocational Education
			*			Note (2)		Air Conditioning and Refrigeration
			*			"		Auto Body and Fender
			*			"		Automotive Repair
			*			"		Building Maintenance
			*			"		Construction Trades
			*			"		Cosmetology
			*			"		Data Processing
			*			"		Distributive Education
			*			"		Drafting and Design
			*			"		Electricity
			*			"		Electronics
			*			"		Food Trades
			*			"		Grounds Maintenance
			*			"		Instrumentation
			*			"		Landscaping
			*			"		Machine Shop

CHART 2
Detail Program Structure (continued)

I	II	III	IV	V	Level III	Level IV	Level V	Program Description
			*				"	Practical Nursing
			*				"	Public Communications (Printing)
			*				"	Service Station
			*				"	Small Appliances
			*				"	Welding
	*				N/A			Continuing Education
		*				74		Adult Education
*								Instructional Support Program
	*				N/A			Learning Resources
		*				71		Libraries, K-12
	*				N/A			Pupil Personnel Services
		*				72		Guidance and Psychological Services, K-12
		*				73		Health Services, K-12
	*				N/A			Facilities
		*				83		Acquisition and Improvement of Facilities
		*				81		Operation and Maintenance of Plant
				*			Note (3)	Custodial Cleaning
			*				"	Building Maintenance
			*				"	Ground Maintenance
			*				"	General Services
	*				N/A			District Management
		*				85		School Management
		*				86		Central Office Management
				*			Note (4)	Board of Education
			*				"	Superintendent
			*				"	Instruction
			*				"	Personnel
			*				"	Finance
			*				"	Community Relations
			*				"	Planning and Research
	*				80			Transportation
	*				84			Food Service
*								Community Service Programs
	*				Note (3)			Recreational Agencies
	*				"			Community Groups

N/A = Not Applicable—Code not needed.

CHART 3

Use of Education Program Forms

Form	Form Title	Use
A	Program Goals and Objectives	To describe program level IV goals for all programs, and level V goals for English, Language Arts, and Reading (Code 60).
B	Description of Existing Program	Used for all programs at level V, or lowest program level as applicable.
C	Multi-Year Financial and Statistical Plan	Used for all programs at level V, or lowest program level as applicable.
D-1	Program Proposal Paper	Used by staff and students to communicate ideas to the superintendent of schools.
D-2	Proposed Program Change	Used for program changes.
E	System Analysis of Alternatives	Used on a very limited basis as directed.

The various Educational Program Forms are prepared by the district curriculum coordinators with the assistance of the building principal and staff.

9.1 <u>Goals</u>

Goals are prepared for program levels I through V. For this year goals will be prepared for all programs at level IV and English, Language Arts, and Reading at level V. The philosophy of education for the school district (see Appendix H) will be used as a guide in preparing goals.

The top-level goals will be quite broad and based on the identified needs of the community. The lower-level goals must be more specific and will support the higher-level goals.

Examples of typical goals are given below. Note that in these examples some goals are more specific than others and none of the goals can be quantified.

To provide quality education that will help every child acquire the habits and attitudes associated with responsible citizenship.

To provide quality education that will help every child acquire the greatest possible understanding of himself and an appreciation of his worthiness as a member of society. . . .

As some goals are more specific, related goals can be arranged in a hierarchy with the lower-level more specific goals contributing to the higher-level broader goals.

An example of a goal structure is shown in Figure 1.

Goals can stand alone or be expanded if desired. It is possible to have more than one goal at any level. . . .

The development of goals should be a coordinated process to ensure that communication exists at all levels, and that goals at any level are consistent with the goals of the total district.[11]

---

[11] *Ibid.*, p. I-6 through I-8.

Education Program Form A, *Program Goals and Objectives,* will be used to record program goals.

9.2 Objectives and Evaluation Methods

Objectives and evaluation methods will be prepared for program levels and for English, Language Arts, and Reading only at level V.

The relationship of goals and objectives at various program levels is illustrated below for Social Studies:

FIGURE 1

Typical Goal Structure

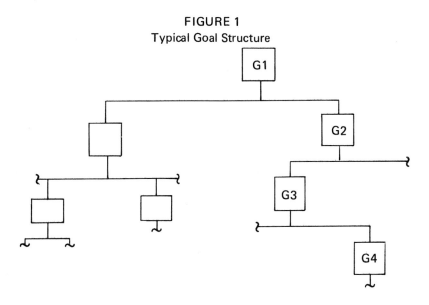

G1 — To provide all students the opportunity to develop skills enabling them to gain employment.

G2 — To provide all students the opportunity to develop skills in business, home economics, and agriculture.

G3 — To provide all students the opportunity to develop skills in typing, shorthand, bookkeeping, and office machine operation.

G4 — To provide all students the opportunity to develop skill in book-keeping.

Program Level	Program Level Description	Levels at Which Goals are Prepared	Levels at Which Objectives and Evaluation Methods are Prepared
I	Total District	X	
II	Instructional Programs	X	
III	Basic Education Programs	X	
IV	Social Studies, K-12	X	X
V	Each Grade Level, K-12	X	X

The process for developing objectives is similar to that for the development of goals and a goal structure. Objectives, like the goals they support, can be grouped and arranged in a hierarchy with lower-level more specific objectives contributing toward higher-level, broader objectives. A hierarchy of objectives may be structured. . . .

Examples of typical objectives are given below. These examples are quantifiable within a time frame and state as specifically as practical how the degree of achievement will be determined or measured.

Upon completion of the term, a sixth grade student will be able to read and pronounce with 80% accuracy a list of sixth grade words selected from the basic Stanford Achievement Test—Reading.

Upon completion of the term, 60% of eleventh grade students will score at least at the Los Angeles County average on standardized tests on reading comprehension.

Figure 2 presents a hierarchy of goals and objectives for which achievement is measured subjectively.

More than one objective may be desired for a given goal. . . .

FIGURE 2

Hierarchy of Goals and Objectives with
Subjective Measurements of Achievement

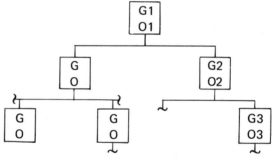

G1 O1	To provide all students the opportunity to develop an appreciation of music. 90 Percent of all graduating seniors will have either participated in band, vocal music, or completed a course in music appreciation within three years of high school.
G2 O2	To provide all students the opportunity to develop an understanding and appreciation of music history, music theories, and music listening. 90 Percent of the students completing the course in music appreciation understand the history of music and differences among program music, absolute music, opera, orations, art songs, and overtures as measured by listening and other classroom tests.
G3 O3	To provide all students the opportunity to develop an appreciation for music listening. Upon course completion, 90 percent of the students will express verbally that they appreciate listening to music.

The formulation of objectives should be a coordinated process to ensure communication and consistency at all levels.

The approved and documented objectives will provide the basis for evaluation and analysis of the performance of the program carried out by the school district. [12]

Form A, *Program Goals and Objectives,* will be used to record objectives as they relate to specific goals. Evaluation methods will be presented.

9.3 Description of Existing Program

Education Program Form B, *Description of Existing Program,* will be used to describe the existing services and activities for each program. A separate form will be prepared as indicated below:

The high school will prepare a separate form for each course.

The middle school may prepare a separate form for each program, grades 6 thru 8 or a separate form for each grade by program.

The elementary schools will prepare a separate form for each program, grades K thru 5.

9.4 Multi-Year Financial and Statistical Plan

Education Program Form C, *Multi-Year Financial and Statistical Plan,* will be used to record data for each program. A separate form will be prepared for grades K-5, 6-8, and 9-12 for each program.

9.5 Program Proposal Paper

Education Program Form D-1 will be used by members of the staff and students. See Section 5 for detailed description of the purpose and use of this form.

9.6 Proposed Program Change

Education Program Form D-2, *Proposed Program Change,* will be prepared for all proposed program modification and for new programs.

Form D-2 is designed to provide basic information to consider the program change. However, it does not provide a system analysis of alternative solutions.

9.7 System Analysis of Alternatives

Education Program Form E, *System Analysis of Alternatives,* provides a systematic way of reviewing alternative solutions to a problem. Very limited use will be made of this approach because of limited staff resources.

Problems on which system analysis will be applied will be identified by the superintendent of schools.

System analysis will be used on selected problem areas. Areas selected for analysis will be related to the district's priorities and the resources required to make the analysis in relation to the possible "pay off."

It is recognized that the district has limited resources for this type of analysis. Therefore, activities to be reviewed must necessarily be limited in number and carefully selected.

---

[12] *Ibid.,* p. I-9 through I-12.

10. Budget Forms

The Budget Forms show the estimated cost of the *existing* educational program for the next school year. Estimated cost for proposed program additions and modifications *are not included in these forms.*

Estimated costs for proposed program changes are shown on *Proposed Program Change,* Education Program Form D-2. This procedure is being used so that program change costs can be readily identified for review purposes.

Samples of the various budget forms are shown in Appendix I.

10.1 Personnel
Budget Form 1 can be used to summarize your budget requests. Budget Forms 2 thru 5 are used to record various personnel budget items. Budget Forms 14 and 15, showing personnel detail, are only used by the business office.

10.2 Equipment
Budget Forms 6 and 7 show equipment requests.

10.3 Supplies and Materials
Budget Forms 8 thru 10 are used to request supplies and materials.

10.4 Standard Supply Lists
The inventory columns on the standard supply lists should be completed based on an actual inventory of supplies on hand. The date of the inventory should be shown on the list.

Each building principal should prepare one copy of each standard list. District curriculum coordinators will review these lists. An allocation of the estimated cost of the standard supply list by program will be jointly prepared by the building principal and district curriculum coordinator. This allocation will be shown on the standard list in the space provided.

CHART 4
Educational Planning and Budgeting Cycle

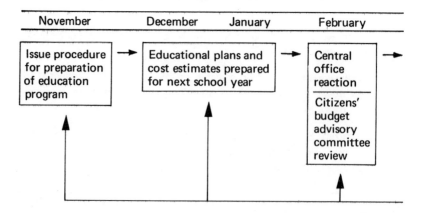

10.5 Other Expenses
Budget Forms 12 and 13 are used to detail other expense budget requests.

10.6 Improvements to Facilities
The superintendent of buildings and grounds has the basic responsibility for preparing the operation and maintenance of plant budget. He will consult with each building principal prior to preparing his recommendations.

Building principals, in cooperation with the teaching staff and district curriculum coordinators, are requested to prepare and submit to the superintendent of buildings and grounds suggested building improvements.

10.7 Revenue Estimates
Persons responsible for preparing revenue estimates are requested to submit the following information in a memorandum:

- account code
- account title
- actual revenue
- budgeted revenue

- budgeted revenue
- basis of estimate
- reasons for major change, if any, from last year's budget.

11. PPBS Implementation Plan

It is felt that a fully integrated and operating PPBS will take five years to implement. Appendix L shows a suggested implementation schedule.

12. Educational Planning and Budgeting Cycle

The educational planning and budgeting cycle for the next school year starts in November and ends the following October. This cycle attempts to integrate educational planning with the fiscal resources required to carry out the plans. Chart 4 shows this cycle.

CHART 4
Educational Planning and Budgeting Cycle
(continued)

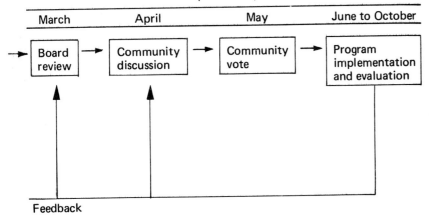

Feedback

12.1 Due Dates

Action	Due Date
Review procedure for preparation of educational program	November
Issue procedure	December 1
Briefing sessions on procedure	December 1-4
Due date for program proposal papers	January 5
Education program and budget forms due	February 2
Superintendent's reaction	February

12.2 Budget Calendar

Date	Week Day	Action
1. December 1	Monday	Issue procedure for preparation of Educational Program.
2. February 2	Monday	Education Program Forms and Budget Forms due.
3. February 2-25		Superintendent's review of budget and conferences with selected staff.
4. February 27	Friday	Superintendent approves his recommended budget for duplication.
5. February 27	Friday	Citizens' Budget Advisory Committee presents Report.
6. March 13	Friday	Superintendent presents his recommended budget to Board of Education.
7. March 26	Thursday	Last day to publish Notice of Annual Budget Vote and Public Hearing (25 days before public hearing date as required by law).
8. April 3	Friday	Last day for Board of Education to approve budget in order to allow time for printing and mailing.
9. April 10	Wednesday	Mail Budget Summary (at least 13 days prior to vote in accordance with Board policy).
10. April 21	Tuesday	Public Budget Hearing (not more than 30, nor less than 10 days before budget vote as required by law).
11. April 29	Wednesday	Last date for submitting to Board of Education a financial resolution revising the published budget (6 days prior to budget vote as required by law).
12. May 6	Wednesday	Budget vote and election of Board Members (first Wednesday after first Tuesday in May as required by law).

APPENDIX A
RESPONSIBILITY FOR PREPARATION
OF EDUCATION PROGRAM FORMS

Code No.	Description	District Curriculum Coordinator	General Fund Function Code(s)
60	English, Language Arts, and Reading, K-12		212, 220
61	Science (including Health), K-12		220
62	Mathematics, K-12		220
63	Social Studies, K-12		220
64	Physical Education, Intramural and Inter-scholastic Athletics, K-12		212, 220, 281
65	Business, 9-12		220
66	Foreign Language, 7-12		220
67	Unified Arts (Industrial Arts, Homemaking, Driver Education, and Mechanical Drawing), 6-12		220
68	Art, K-12		212, 220
69	Music, K-12		212, 220
71	Libraries, K-12		213
72	Guidance and Psychological Services, K-12		291, 292
73	Health Services, K-12		294
74	Adult Education		320
76	Special Education		220
77	Vocational Education		220
80	Transportation		510
81	Operation and Maintenance of Plant		600
83	Acquisition and Improvement of Facilities		800
84	Food Service		Separate Fund
85	School Management		211
86	Central Office Management		010's, 100'

APPENDIX B
RESPONSIBILITY FOR PREPARATION
OF BUDGET FORMS

Function Code No.	Functional Description	Responsibility
A 010	Board of Education	
A 020	District Clerk	
A 030	District Treasurer	
A 040	Tax Collector	
A 050	Auditor Services	
A 060	Legal Services	
A 070	District Meeting	
A 080	Census	
A 110	Superintendent of Schools	
A 120	Assistant Superintendent-Instruction	
A 130	Assistant Superintendent-Business	
A 150	Personnel	
A 160	School Community Relations	
A 211*	Building Principals	
A 212	Special Teachers	
A 213	Library Services, K-12	
A 220*	Teaching	
A 220-525	Board of Cooperative Educational Services (BOCES)	
A 281	Interscholastic Athletics	
A 291*	Guidance	
A 292	Psychological Services, K-12	
A 294	Health Services, K-12	
A 320	Adult Education	
A 321	Summer School	
A 430	Use of Building by Community	
A 510	Transportation	
A 600*	Operation and Maintenance of Plant	
A 720	Data Processing	
A 730	Employees' Benefits	
A 750	BOCES Facilities and Consultants	
A 800	Debt Service	
A 900	Interfund Transfers	
C 790	School Lunch Fund	

*Function codes budgeted for by building. All other functions are budgeted district-wide.

APPENDIX C
RESPONSIBILITY FOR PREPARATION OF REVENUE
ESTIMATES AND REVIEW OF STANDARD SUPPLY LISTS

General Fund Revenue Account No.	Description	Responsibility
AO-00-1220	Adult Education Tuition	
AO-00-1230	Summer School Tuition	
AO-00-1435	Admissions (Interscholastic Athletics)	
AO-00-1469	Sales of Adult Education Textbooks	
AO-00-1471	Loss Books	
None	Federal Aid	
None	School Lunch Fund	

Standard Supply Lists

Responsibility for review of standard supply lists prior to their issuance is assigned to the persons indicated below:

Standard List No.	Description	Person Responsible for Review of List Prior to Issuance
1	General Supplies	
2	Paper Supplies and Spirit Masters	
3	Art Supplies	
4	Clay	
5	Art Supplies (all Craft Tool and Supply Co.)	

APPENDIX D
DEFINITION OF FUND, LOCATION,
FUNCTION, AND OBJECT CODES

Fund (2 digits). A sum of money or other resources segregated for the purpose of carrying on specific activities or attaining certain objectives in accordance with special regulations, restrictions, or limitations and constituting an independent fiscal and accounting entity.

Location (2 digits). This shows the building location. See Appendix F for list of these codes.

Function (3 digits). The term function has reference to the primary classification and description of expense as to purpose. It identifies groups of services to achieve certain purposes or ends, i.e., "Board of Education," "Central Administration," etc. See Appendix B for a listing.

Object (3 digits). This term has reference to the secondary classification of description of expense. It identifies expense by the article purchased or service obtained in order to carry out the function. This object classification identifies expenses as those for personal services, equipment, supplies and materials, and other expenses. See Appendix G for an explanation of various objects of expenditure.

APPENDIX E
PROGRAM CODES

Program Code	Program Description	Program Level
00	Non-Program	—
60	English, Language Arts, and Reading, K-12	IV
61	Science (including Health), K-12	IV
62	Mathematics, K-12	IV
63	Social Studies, K-12	IV
64	Physical Education, Intramural and Interscholastic Athletics, K-12	IV
65	Business, 9-12	IV
66	Foreign Language, 7-12	IV
67	Unified Arts (Industrial Arts, Homemaking, Driver Education, and Mechanical Drawing), 6-12	IV
68	Art, K-12	IV
69	Music, K-12	IV
71	Libraries, K-12	IV
72	Guidance and Psychological Services, K-12	IV
73	Health Services, K-12	IV
74	Adult Education	IV
76	Special Education	III
77	Vocational Education	III
80	Transportation—Home to School and BOCES	III
81	Operation and Maintenance of Plant	IV
83	Acquisition and Improvement of Facilities	IV
84	Food Service	III
85	School Management	IV
86	Central Office Management	IV

APPENDIX F
LOCATION CODES

Description	Code
Districtwide	00
Administration Building	01
Elementary Schools, grades K-5	
Evans Park	02
Franklin	03
Lincoln Avenue	04
Nauraushaun	05
Middle School, grades 6-8	30
High School, grades 9-12	08*
Warehouse	40

*High School Code 08 will be used for interscholastic athletics—AO-64-08-281-XXX.

APPENDIX G
EXPLANATION OF BASIC OBJECT CODES

Code

---

100 Staff Salaries (Personnel Services)

Record under this object compensation including overtime paid full or part-time employees of the school district.

Remuneration paid individuals hired as consultants or to do a specific task under an agreement which does not create an employer-employee relationship is not considered personal services; such remuneration is entered as object 400 Other Expenses.

200 Equipment—Unit Price of $25 or over

Expenditures for initial, replacement, or additional pieces of furniture or equipment are entered under this object.

Criteria for Equipment Items

An equipment item is movable or fixed unit of furniture or furnishings, an instrument, a machine, an apparatus, or a set of articles which meets all of the following conditions:

1. It retains its original shape and appearance with use.
2. It is nonexpendable, that is, if the article is damaged or some of its parts are lost or worn out, it is usually more feasible to repair it rather than replace it with an entirely new unit.
3. It represents an investment of money which makes it feasible and advisable to capitalize the item.
4. It does not lose its identity through incorporation into a different or more complex unit or substance.

300 Supplies and Materials

Enter under this classification the costs of supplies except textbooks for which a special object is provided. Supplies are defined as items of an expendable nature that are consumed, worn out, or deteriorated in use; or items that lose their identity through fabrication or incorporation into a different or more complex unit or structure. Includes printing and *purchase* of film strips, workbooks, records, tapes, library books, sheet music, professional books, maps, globes, and charts.

Criteria for Supply Items

A supply item is any article or material which meets one or more of the following conditions:

1. It is consumed in use.
2. It loses its original shape or appearance with use.
3. It is expendable, that is, if the article is damaged or some of its parts are lost or worn out, it is usually more feasible to replace it with an entirely new unit rather than repair it.

4. It is an inexpensive item, having characteristics of equipment, whose small unit cost makes it inadvisable to capitalize the item.
5. It loses its identity through incorporation into a different or more complex unit or substance.

398 Textbooks—Grades K-6
Used for purchase of textbooks for pupil use.

399 Textbooks—Grades 7-12

400 Other Expenses
Expenses of the school district not provided for under other objects of expense will be shown under this classification. Such items include travel expenses, mileage, postage, rental of film strips, maintenance of equipment, book binding, professional services, and other contracted services.

APPENDIX H
DISTRICT PHILOSOPHY OF EDUCATION

Inherent in a democratic society is the recognition of the importance of the individual and of the responsibility of preparing him for an effective role in its growth, management, and preservation. The school is an institution committed to the creation of an environment in which individual capacities can be guided and developed to their fullest extent, in which the individual can be helped to find and understand himself and his role in society, and in which the culture and values of society can be maintained and improved.

This Public School System aspires to carry out this philosophy through working toward attainment of the following aims and objectives:

1. Fundamental Processes of Intellectual Growth
a. To develop a command of fundamental skills and knowledge to meet the challenge of a dynamic, competitive society.
b. To develop the ability to think critically, constructively, and creatively.
c. To nourish the innate spirit of man to seek, discover, and adapt himself to new horizons of knowledge which have become part of our way of life.

2. Self-realization
a. To develop desirable attitudes toward the ethical, moral, and cultural values in our society.
b. To provide for experiences which will develop proper attitudes and the self-discipline necessary to meet everyday situations realistically.
c. To foster appreciation of literature and the arts.
d. To develop sound physical and mental health.
e. To provide for growth in understanding and utilization of one's individual capabilities.

3. Human Relationships
To develop an understanding and appreciation of intergroup relationships and to encourage acceptance of responsibilities within these groups (i.e., family, neighborhood, community, state, nation, world).

4. Citizenship

a. To develop an understanding and knowledge of governmental processes.
b. To encourage desirable practices which will reflect the ideals and principles of our democratic way of life.
c. To develop a knowledge of the cultural, economic, and political backgrounds of the peoples and nations of the world and an understanding of their interrelationship and interdependence.

5. Economic Efficiency

a. To develop an understanding of the relationship of the command of fundamental skills and knowledge to one's further education and career as an adult.
b. To develop an understanding of the need to maintain a necessary degree of economic independence within the framework of socially acceptable practices.

APPENDIX I
SUGGESTED PPBS IMPLEMENTATION SCHEDULE

PPBS Element	1st Year	2nd Year	3rd Year	Future Years
1. Goals	Described goals for all programs without regard to program level or related objectives. Social Studies goals for level IV and V (grades 3, 6, and 11 only) prepared under PPBS project.	Develop Program IV goals for all programs. Develop level V goals for English, Language Arts, and Reading Program (code 60).	Develop program level V goals for one additional instructional area and one instructional support area.	Continue development of goals at all program levels and areas.
2. Objectives and Evaluation Methods	Objectives were developed without regard to specific goals or program levels. Objectives were general in nature. Objectives for social studies at level V (grades 3, 6, and 11) prepared under PPBS project.	Develop level IV and V objectives for English, Language Arts, and Reading (Code 60).	Develop program level IV and V objectives for one additional instructional area and one instructional support area.	Continue development of objectives at all program IV and V levels.
3. Program Structure	Initial program structure was developed.	Revision of program structure.	Continue same structure.	Consider going to program level VI on some instructional areas.
4. Existing Program	General descriptions were prepared in various formats and amounts of detail.	Request on uniform formats for all programs at each program level.	Revise and update.	
5. Program Coding	Developed initial coding system. Started new BOCES accounting system. Breakouts provided through level IV. Level V breakouts for instructional programs are K-5, 6-8, 9-12, and not by grade.	Basic system to continue.	Consider modification of computer programming to go to program level V.	Consider impact of regional data processing center on account coding.
6. Program Budget	Program presentation to Board and Citizens' Budget Advisory Committee.	Program presentation to be made to public.	Refine and more fully develop public and Board presentations.	
7. Multi-Year Financial and Statistical Plan.	Three years' projects prepared, on limited data.	Prepare three-year projections of more fiscal and statistical data.	Continue on same basis as last year.	Prepare five-year projections.
8. System Analysis	Done on a limited and informal basis for new programs.	Initiate formal system analysis of a few selected target problems.	Expand system review to selected areas.	Same as last year.

illustrative example of a program budget document

The display document provides an example of a comprehensive PPB system. It has been condensed for readability, understanding, and general distribution to the staff and to the community. Following the budget are representative forms that have been helpful in one local school district's implementation of PPBS.

PROPOSED
PROGRAM AND
FISCAL PLAN

Board of Education	Administration
Mr. Henry C. Leidel, Jr. President	Dr. Robert F. Alioto Superintendent
Mr. Roberts W. Smithem Vice-President	Dr. Stanley A. Schainker Assistant Superintendent- Personnel
Mr. Andrew D. McCahill	Dr. David M. Jones Assistant Superintendent- Instruction
Mr. Francis J. Nilan, Jr.	
Dr. Lee N. Starker	Mr. J. A. Jungherr Assistant Superintendent- Business
	Mr. E. A. Vollbrecht Administrative Assistant

SUPERINTENDENT'S EDUCATION MESSAGE

The Proposed 1970-1971 Educational Program and Fiscal Plan

March 25, 1970

Dear Board Members:

On May 6, 1970, the Pearl River voters will for the first time in the history of the Pearl River School District be given the opportunity to vote on the budget in which fiscal requests have been displayed on a program basis. For information purposes, we have provided for the integration of the educational program with the fiscal plan. The traditional function-object budget data is also provided for those individuals who wish to make comparisons with previous years' budgets. We anticipate that in future years as we become more sophisticated in the program budgeting process there will be further refinements of the format contained in this report.

You will find, in addition to the statistical data, a brief overview of the goals of our programs, a description of existing programs, and a description of the major program changes which we are recommending for your adoption.

Based on our analysis of existing test data, teacher and administrative evaluations, and discussions with members of the community, we have established as our top priorities the areas of reading and health education with particular emphasis on narcotics education. You will find, therefore, that the allocation of resources, both in terms of staff and material, will reflect in a significant increase in expenditures in these two areas and a concomitant decrease in other areas which have been deemed to be desirable but not absolutely necessary.

The proposed 1970-1971 budget totals $5,825,081 compared to the 1969-1970 revised budget of $5,444,027. The total dollar increase over the revised 1969-1970 budget is $381,954. It should be noted that $100,000 of the revised 1969-1970 budget was due to the settlement of the high school litigation and is therefore a non-recurring expense. The proposed 1970-1971 budget reflects a true increase, therefore, of $481,054 of which $415,000 must be considered as mandated increases as follows: BOCES, $131,000; insurance costs, $10,000; retirement, social security, and other fringe benefits costs, $88,000; Middle School health program, $15,000; debt service (for the bond issue passed by the voters on November 12, 1969), $77,000; and increases in salaries based on existing salary schedules, $94,000. This increase has been held to a minimum through the modification of existing programs, the redistribution of staff and fiscal resources, and the elimination of some staff as a result of the closing of Central Avenue school. Monies have been allocated to maintain the Central Avenue school for one year's continued use on a limited basis for community and school recreation purposes. It is anticipated that the Board of Education will dispose of this property sometime during the 1970-1971 school year. It may be necessary, however, to use this building for several months in the event that the elementary classroom additions have not been completed.

The tax rate increase required to support the proposed budget will be approximately 11%. This increase takes into account additional State aid monies which are dependent upon final passage by the State Legislature.

The dilemma of contract negotiations continues to cause the budget to be tentative in nature. The budget does not include monies beyond the experience increments in the existing salary schedules for the staff. When negotiations with staff bargaining units have been completed, further adjustments will have to be made in the budget.

The educational program and fiscal plan as outlined is the direct result of contributions made by students, the entire staff, and members of the Budget Advisory Committee. Members of the staff were given the opportunity to submit recommended program changes and many of these were adopted. In addition, curriculum coordinators made presentations to various staff committees in order to solicit their professional judgment on the proposed programs. Several high school students took advantage of the offer to make suggestions regarding programs for the 1970-1971 school year. The Budget Advisory Committee carefully reviewed and analyzed the initial program and budget proposals from the staff and submitted its recommendations for consideration.

Recommendations from the various groups involved in the budget process, as well as supporting detail, are available upon request for your review and consideration.

Recognizing the fiscal, human, and program limitations contained in this proposal, we are confident that we will be able to continue our goal to eliminate the articulated deficiencies in the Pearl River School District as well as to build on the strengths that have been developed over the past several years.

Respectfully submitted,

Robert F. Alioto
Superintendent of Schools

PROGRAM BUDGET SUMMARY TABLE 1
SUMMARY OF EXPENDITURE BUDGET BY PROGRAM LEVEL II

Programs	1969-1970 Revised Budget	1970-1971 Recommended Budget	Change
Instructional programs	$3,072,763	$3,285,692	$+212,929
Instructional support programs	2,367,115	2,436,130	+69,015
Sub total			
Community service program	4,149	7,041	+2,892
Total	$5,444,027	$5,728,863	$+284,836

This table is based on Table 4 and Table 5, without allocation of district management.

PROGRAM BUDGET SUMMARY TABLE 2
SUMMARY OF REVENUE BUDGET

Source of Revenue	1969-1970 Revised Budget	1970-1971 Recommended Budget	Change
Real property taxes	$2,868,593	$3,145,183	$+276,590
State aid	2,180,370	2,522,000	+341,630
Prior year's surplus	317,394	–	−317,394
Other local revenues	77,670	61,680	−15,990
Total	$5,444,027	$5,728,863	$+284,836

PROGRAM BUDGET SUMMARY TABLE 3
SUMMARY OF BUDGET BY PROGRAM LEVEL III WITH
ALLOCATION OF DISTRICT MANAGEMENT TO
INSTRUCTIONAL PROGRAMS AND
INSTRUCTIONAL SUPPORT PROGRAMS

	1970-1971 Recommended Budget
Instructional Programs	
Basic education	$3,677,596
Special education	84,987
Vocational education	77,166
Continuing education	12,108
Total	$3,851,857
Instructional Support Programs	
Learning resources	$ 169,282
Pupil personnel services	338,069
Facilities	1,140,861
District management	103,594
Transportation	192,968
Food service	—
Nonprogram	20,000
Total	$1,964,774
Community Services Program	
Recreation agencies	$ 3,704
Community groups	4,746
Total	$ 8,450
Grand Total	$5,825,081

Note: Allocation of District Management to other programs was made as follows: District Management—15% of program costs; Operation and Maintenance of Plant—3% of program costs; Transportation—2% of program costs; Community Service—$1,408; Other Programs—balance of district management not allocated above. Proportion was made based on relationship of each program's cost to cost of programs receiving allocation. Allocations were not made to debt service or nonprogram (refund of prior year's revenues).

PROGRAM BUDGET SUMMARY TABLE 4
SUMMARY OF BUDGET BY PROGRAM LEVEL III

	1969-1970 Revised Budget	1970-1971 Recommended Budget	Change
Instructional Programs			
Basic education	$2,962,892	$3,152,844	$+189,952
Special education	52,628	73,371	+20,743
Vocational education	43,130	49,064	+5,934
Continuing education	14,113	10,413	−3,700
Total	$3,072,763	$3,285,692	$+212,929
Instructional Support Programs			
Learning resources	$ 135,032	$ 145,295	$ +10,263
Pupil personnel services	255,909	292,350	+36,441
Facilities	992,478	1,129,695	+137,217
District management	695,002	672,495	−22,507
Transportation	161,394	176,295	+14,901
Food service	−	−	−
Nonprogram	127,300	20,000	−107,300
Total	$2,367,115	$2,436,130	$ +69,015
Community Services Programs			
Recreation agencies	$ 1,185	$ 3,000	$ +1,815
Community groups	2,964	4,041	+1,077
Total	4,149	7,041	+2,892
Grand Total	$5,444,027	$5,728,863	$+284,836

PROGRAM BUDGET SUMMARY TABLE 5
SUMMARY OF BUDGET BY PROGRAM LEVEL IV

Code	Program Title	1969-1970 Revised Budget	1970-1971 Recom- mended Budget	Change
Instructional Programs				
	Basic education			
60	English, language arts, K-12	$ 811,547	$ 942,116	$130,569
61	Science (including health), K-12	393,246	447,945	54,699
62	Mathematics, K-12	445,507	455,593	10,086
63	Social studies, K-12	384,932	391,437	6,505
64	Physical education, K-12	317,203	303,415	−13,788

TABLE 5 (continued)

Code	Program Title	1969-1970 Revised Budget	1970-1971 Recommended Budget	Change
65	Business, 9-12	56,229	69,749	13,520
66	Foreign languages, 7-12	141,182	154,797	13,615
67	Unified arts, 6-12	135,074	126,292	−8,782
68	Art, K-12	100,658	102,243	1,585
69	Music, K-12	135,715	144,067	8,352
00	Nonprogram	41,599	15,190	−26,409
	Total basic education	$2,962,892	$3,152,844	$189,952
76	Special education	52,628	73,371	20,743
77	Vocational education	43,130	49,064	5,934
74	Continuing education-adult education	14,113	10,413	−3,700
	Total Instructional Programs	$3,072,763	$3,285,692	$212,929
	Instructional Support Programs			
	Learning resources			
71	Libraries, K-12	$ 135,032	$ 145,295	$ 10,263
	Pupil personnel services			
72	Guidance and psychological services, K-12	158,540	194,753	36,213
73	Health services, K-12	97,369	97,597	228
	Total pupil personnel services	$ 255,909	$ 292,350	$ 36,441
	Facilities			
83	Acquisition and improvement of facilities	$ 439,333	$ 516,608	$ 77,275
81	Operation and maintenance of plant	553,145	613,087	59,942
	Total facilities	$ 992,478	$1,129,695	$137,217
	District management			
85	School management	$ 351,756	$ 361,374	$ 9,618
86	Central office management	343,246	311,121	−32,125
	Total district management	$ 695,002	$ 672,495	$−22,507
80	Transportation	161,394	176,295	14,901
84	Food service	—	—	—
00	Nonprogram	127,300	20,000	−107,300
	Total Instructional Support Programs	$2,367,115	$2,436,130	$ 69,015
	Community Service Programs	4,149	7,041	2,892
	Grand Total	$5,444,027	$5,728,863	$284,836

PROGRAM BUDGET SUMMARY TABLE 6
SUMMARY BY PROGRAM LEVEL IV SHOWING BUDGETED
EXPENDITURES PER STUDENT SERVED BY
GRADE SPAN (In whole dollars)

Code	Program Title	Elementary K-5	Middle School 6-8	High School 9-12	District-wide
Instructional Programs					
	Basic education				
60	English, language arts, K-12	$305	$280	$172	$ 1
61	Science (including health), K-12	66	145	214	2
62	Mathematics, K-12	112	138	154	1
63	Social studies, K-12	98	78	133	1
64	Physical education, K-12	31	82	163	—
65	Business, 9-12	—	—	174	—
66	Foreign languages, 7-12	—	100	154	—
67	Unified arts, 6-12	—	51	169	—
68	Art, K-12	35	41	126	—
69	Music, K-12	43	68	56	—
00	Nonprogram	—	2	7	1
76	Special education	—	—	—	49
77	Vocational education	—	—	90	—
74	Adult education	—	—	—	14
Instructional Support Programs					
71	Libraries, K-12	48	37	30	—
	Pupil personnel services				
72	Guidance and psychological, K-12	13	63	81	4
73	Health services, K-12	19	15	17	8
	Facilities				
83	Acquisition of facilities	—	—	—	140
81	Operation and maintenance of plant	77	115	128	63
	District management				
85	School management	94	101	95	2
86	Central office management	—	—	—	84
80	Transportation	—	—	—	109
84	Food service	—	—	—	—
00	Nonprogram	—	—	—	5
Community Service Programs		Not Applicable			

PERSONNEL SUMMARY TABLE 7
SUMMARY OF CERTIFICATED AND NONCERTIFICATED STAFF
(In full-time-equivalent personnel)

	1969-1970 Actual	1970-1971 Recom- mended	Change
Certificated staff			
Central office administrators	5.0	4.4	−0.6
Building administrators	9.0	8.6	−0.4
Teachers	203.1	210.2	+7.1
Total	217.1	223.2	+6.1
Noncertificated staff			
Clerical	31.8	30.8	−1.0
Custodial, maintenance, and transportation	28.6	27.1	−1.5
Teacher aides and monitors	9.5	14.2	+4.7
Total	69.9	72.1	+2.2
Grand total	287.0	295.3	+8.3

Note:
1. Does not include food service personnel. These salaries are budgeted in a separate school lunch fund.
2. Does not include census takers (seasonal employees) and part-time dentists.

PERSONNEL SUMMARY TABLE 7A
SUMMARY OF CERTIFICATED STAFF BY LEVEL
(In full-time-equivalent personnel)

Level	1969-1970 Actual	1970-1971 Recom- mended	Change
Elementary	81.1	79.8	−1.3
Middle school	56.5	60.1	+3.6
High school	73.9	78.3	+4.4
Districtwide	5.6	5.0	−0.6
Total	217.1	223.2	+6.1

PERSONNEL SUMMARY TABLE 7B
CERTIFICATED STAFF BY LEVEL AND PROGRAM
(In full-time-equivalent personnel)

I. Elementary Certificated Staff

Program Code	Program	1969-1970 Actual	1970-1971 Recommended	Change
60	English	30.1	30.8	+0.7
61	Science	6.2	6.2	—
62	Math	11.7	11.1	−0.6
63	Social studies	10.7	10.1	−0.6
64	Physical education	3.8	3.8	—
65	Business	—	—	—
66	Foreign language	—	—	—
67	Unified arts	—	—	—
68	Art	3.2	3.2	—
69	Music	4.2	4.0	−0.2
71	Library	3.6	3.6	—
72	Guidance and psychology	0.6	1.0	+0.4
73	Health services	2.0	2.0	—
85	School management	5.0	4.0	−1.0
	Total elementary	81.1	79.8	−1.3

II. Middle School Certificated Staff

Program Code	Program	1969-1970 Actual	1970-1971 Recommended	Change
60	English	11.7	16.4	+4.7
61	Science	7.5	8.7	+1.2
62	Math	7.3	7.5	+0.2
63	Social studies	6.5	5.7	−0.8
64	Physical education	5.7	5.1	−0.6
65	Business	0	0	0
66	Foreign language	2.9	2.3	−0.6
67	Unified arts	2.7	2.0	−0.7
68	Art	2.3	2.1	−0.2
69	Music	3.7	3.0	−0.7
71	Library	1.2	1.2	—
72	Guidance and psychology	2.2	2.5	+0.3
73	Health services	0.8	1.0	+0.2
85	School management	2.0	2.6	+0.6
	Total middle school	56.5	60.1	+3.6

PERSONNEL SUMMARY TABLE 7B (continued)

III. High School Certificated Staff

Program Code	Program	1969-1970 Actual	1970-1971 Recommended	Change
60	English	11.0	11.7	+0.7
61	Science	10.1	11.4	+1.3
62	Math	8.3	8.6	+0.3
63	Social studies	9.7	10.6	+0.9
64	Physical education	7.5	6.5	−1.0
65	Business	3.6	4.0	+0.4
66	Foreign language	7.0	7.3	+0.3
67	Unified arts	5.0	5.0	—
68	Art	1.3	1.3	—
69	Music	0.7	1.6	+0.9
71	Library	1.2	1.2	—
72	Guidance and psychology	4.2	4.5	+0.3
73	Health	1.0	1.0	—
85	School management	3.3	3.6	+0.3
	Total high school	73.9	78.3	+4.4

IV. Districtwide

Program Code	Program	1969-1970 Actual	1970-1971 Recommended	Change
78	Health	0.6	00.6	—
86	Central office management management	5.0	4.4	−0.6
	Total districtwide	5.6	5.0	−0.6

PERSONNEL SUMMARY TABLE 8
SUMMARY OF CERTIFICATED AND NONCERTIFICATED
STAFF CHANGES (In full-time-equivalent personnel)

Certificated Staff

	Changes	Net Change
Elementary		
Classroom teachers, grade 1-5	−2.0	
Principal, Central Avenue	−1.0	
Music coordinator—reallocation of time to high school	−0.2	
Subtotal	−3.2	
Reading specialists	+1.5	
Psychologist	+0.4	
Subtotal	+1.9	
Total elementary		−1.3
Middle school		
Classroom teachers (reading specialist, net after reallocations)	+1.7	
Health teacher (mandated by State of New York)	+1.0	
Psychologist	+0.3	
Assistant to principal (reallocation from central office)	+0.6	
Total middle school		+3.6
High school		
Physical education teacher	−1.0	
Classroom teacher	+4.8	
Psychologist	+0.3	
Dean	+0.3	
Subtotal	+5.4	
Total high school		+4.4
Districtwide		
Administrative assistant, reallocation to the middle school		−0.6
Grand Total		+6.1

Noncertificated Staff

	Changes
Clerical	
Central Avenue secretary	−1.0
Custodial, maintenance, and transportation	
Central Avenue head custodian	−1.0
Central Avenue custodian	−0.5
Total	−1.5

PERSONNEL SUMMARY TABLE 8 (continued)

Teacher aides and monitors

Franklin Avenue—walking monitor	−0.2
Elementary—teacher aides for reading program	+3.7
Middle school—teacher aides for reading program	+0.4
Middle school—monitors for cafeteria	+0.4
High school—monitors for cafeteria	+0.4
Total	+4.7
Total noncertificated staff	+2.2
Total Staff	+8.3

PERSONNEL SUMMARY TABLE 9
SUMMARY OF CERTIFICATED STAFF BY PROGRAM
(In full-time-equivalent personnel)

Code	Program Title	1969-1970 Actual	1970-1971 Recommended Budget	Change
	Instructional Programs			
	Basic education			
60	English, language arts, K-12	52.8	58.9	+6.1
61	Science (including health), K-12	23.8	26.3	+2.5
62	Mathematics, K-12	27.3	27.2	−0.1
63	Social studies, K-12	26.9	26.4	−0.5
64	Physical education, K-12	17.0	15.4	−1.6
65	Business, 9-12	3.6	4.0	+0.4
66	Foreign language, 7-12	9.9	9.6	−0.3
67	Unified arts, 6-12	7.7	7.0	−0.7
68	Art, K-12	6.8	6.6	−0.2
69	Music, K-12	8.6	8.6	—
00	Nonprogram	—	—	—
	Total basic education	184.4	190.0	+5.6
	Instructional Support Programs			
	Learning resources			
71	Libraries	6.0	6.0	—
	Pupil personnel services			
72	Guidance and psychological, K-12	7.0	8.0	+1.0
73	Health services	4.4	4.6	+0.2
	Total pupil personnel services	11.4	12.6	+1.2
	District management			
85	School management	10.3	10.2	−0.1
86	Central office management	5.0	4.4	−0.6
	Total district management	15.3	14.6	−0.7
	Total Instructional Support Programs	32.7	33.2	+0.5
	Grand Total	217.1	223.2	+6.1

FINANCIAL AND STATISTICAL SUMMARY TABLE 10
SUMMARY OF REVENUES BY SOURCE AND
EXPENDITURES BY FUNCTION

	1969-1970 Revised Budget	1970-1971 Recom-mended Budget	Change
Revenues by Source			
Real property tax	$2,868,593	$3,145,183	$+276,590
State aid	2,180,370	2,522,000	+341,630
Prior year's surplus	317,394	—	−317,394
Other local revenue	77,670	61,680	−15,990
Total	$5,444,027	$5,728,863	$+284,836
Expenditures by Function			
Board of education	$ 36,880	$ 23,275	$ −13,605
Central administration	202,906	196,180	−6,726
Instruction, regular day school	3,151,016	3,333,310	+182,294
Instruction, special schools	25,044	22,275	−2,769
Community service	3,500	6,000	+2,500
Transportation	171,134	182,015	+10,881
Operation and mainte-nance of plant	474,366	511,995	+37,629
Undistributed	939,548	937,205	−2,343
Debt service	439,633	516,608	76,975
Interfund transfers	—	—	—
Total	$5,444,027	$5,728,863	$+284,836

FINANCIAL AND STATISTICAL SUMMARY TABLE 11
SUMMARY OF BUDGET BY OBJECT OF EXPENDITURE

Object of Expenditure	1969-1970 Revised Budget	1970-1971 Recommended Budget	Change
Personal service and employee benefits	$3,946,404	$4,144,315	$ 197,911
Equipment	52,709	43,255	−9,454
Supplies, materials, and textbooks	218,796	218,105	−691
Contracted services	527,030	547,890	20,860
Services from BOCES	109,381*	202,725	93,344
Data processing, insurance, and debt service	489,707	572,573	82,866
High school litigation settlement	100,000	—	−100,000
Total	$5,444,027	$5,728,863	$ 284,836

*Estimated BOCES contract prior to adjustment is $106,037. See Table 19.

FINANCIAL AND STATISTICAL SUMMARY TABLE 12
PERCENTAGE DISTRIBUTION OF BUDGET BY
OBJECT OF EXPENDITURE

Object of Expenditure	1969-1970 Revised Budget	1970-1971 Recommended Budget	Change
Personal service and employee benefits	72.5	72.3	−0.2
Equipment	1.0	.9	−0.1
Supplies and materials	4.0	3.8	−0.2
Contracted services	9.7	9.6	−0.1
Services from BOCES	2.0	3.5	+1.5
Data processing, insurance, and debt service	9.0	9.9	+0.9
High school litigation settlement	1.8	—	−1.8
Total	100%	100%	—

FINANCIAL AND STATISTICAL SUMMARY TABLE 13
ASSESSED VALUATIONS

School Year	Equalization Tax Ratio	Year	Assessed Valuation	Equalized Valuation	Tax Rate per $1000 of Assessed Valuation Actual	Equalized	Change
1961-1962	28%	1961	16,313,751	58,263,396	68.00	19.03	+0.14
1962-1963	26%	1962	17,142,754	65,933,669	77.10	19.96	+0.93
1963-1964	24%	1963	18,598,500	77,493,750	80.00	19.20	−0.76
1964-1965	24%	1964	19,072,917	79,470,487	85.15	20.42	+1.22
1965-1966	23%	1965	19,580,647	85,133,248	93.37	21.39	+0.97
1966-1967	23%	1966	19,970,637	86,828,857	93.51	21.50	+0.11
1967-1968	23%	1967	20,476,997	89,030,422	113.70	26.15	+4.65
1968-1969**	38%*	1968	34,729,126A	91,392,437	78.53	29.84	+3.69
1969-1970	38%	1969	36,133,020	95,086,895	79.33	30.15	+0.31
1970-1971 (est.)	38%	1970	36,833,020	96,929,000	85.39	32.45	+2.30

*The 1968 assessment roll is used for the state aid calculation of monies to be received in 1969-1970.

**Town of Orangetown was completely reassessed as of May 1, 1968. Therefore, tax rate figures for 1968-1969 are not comparable with prior years.

Note A: This is assessed valuation on which tax rate was applied. Subsequent to the levy several errors were found. The adjusted assessed valuation for 1968-1969 is $34,475,026. True value of $88,397,503 and true tax rate of $30 .85/$1000, assessed valuation.

FINANCIAL AND STATISTICAL SUMMARY TABLE 14
TAX RATE PER $1000 ASSESSED VALUATION

School Year	School District Amount	Increase	Public Library Amount	Increase	Total Amount	Increase
1961-1962	68.00	6.20	1.00	0	69.00	6.20
1962-1963	77.10	9.10	1.00	0	78.10	9.10
1963-1964	80.00	2.90	2.00	1.00	82.00	3.90
1964-1965	85.15	5.15	2.05	0.05	87.20	5.20
1965-1966	93.37	8.22	2.67	0.62	96.04	8.84
1966-1967	93.51	0.14	4.74	2.07	98.25	2.21
1967-1968	113.70	20.19	6.30	1.56	120.00	21.75
1968-1969*	78.53	−35.17*	4.32	−1.98*	82.85	−37.15*
1969-1970	79.33	0.80	4.58	0.26	83.91	1.06
1970-1971 (est.)	85.39	6.06	4.97	0.39	90.36	6.45

*Town of Orangetown was completely reassessed as of May 1, 1968. Therefore, tax rate figures for 1968-1969 are not comparable with prior years.

FINANCIAL AND STATISTICAL SUMMARY TABLE 15
MISCELLANEOUS STATISTICS

	1964-1965 Actual	1965-1966 Actual	1966-1967 Actual	1967-1968 Actual	1968-1969 Actual	1969-1970 Budget	1970-1971 Budget
1. Enrollment (January 1st)	3,223	3,372	3,429	3.512	3,568	3,664A	3,688
2. Average daily attendance (ST-4) beginning in 1968-1969 (AT-6)	3,019	3,147	3,221	3,313	3,261	3,387	3,390
3. Weighted average daily attendance (Entry 3 SA 129)	3,210	3,349	3,467	3,602	3,637	3,750	3,800
4. Number of buildings used (district-owned)	6	6	7	8	8	8A	7A
5. District assessed valuation per pupil (based on resident weighted average daily attendance) (Entry 3, SA 124)	$20,293	22,967	22,544	25,169	24,746	24,425A	24,641A
6. State average assessed valuation per pupil (in dollars)	$28,300	29,300	29,800	31,200	31,400	31,500A	32,300A
7. Amount district assessed valuation per pupil is less than state assessed valuation per pupil (in dollars)	$ 8,007	6,333	7,256	6,031	6,654	7,075A	7,659A
8. State aid ratio (in percent)	57.2%	55.8%	58.2%	58.9%	59.9%	60.5A	?
9. Net current expenditures per pupil (total expenditures less debt service, capital outlay, and transportation-based on average daily attendance (in dollars)	$ 838	894	1,001	1,075	1,310	1,411*	1,496
10. Total cost per pupil-based on average daily attendance (in dollars) excludes encumbrances	$ 931	1,023	1,177	1,284	1,506	1,607*	1,718
11. Total expenditures (in millions of dollars)	$2.8	3.2	3.8	4.2	4.9	5.4*	5.8
12. Total tax levy (in millions of dollars)	$1.6	1.8	1.9	2.3	2.7	2.9*	3.2
13. Percent tax levy is of total revenue budget	58.0%	54.0%	50.0%	55.0%	54.0%	56.0%	55.0%
14. State aid (in millions of dollars)	$1.1	1.4	1.7	1.8	2.2	2.2*	2.5
15. Percent state aid is of total revenue budget	40.0%	41.0%	45.0%	43.0%	44.0%	43.0%*	43.0%

*Based on revised budget.

Note A: Indicates an actual figure.

FINANCIAL AND STATISTICAL SUMMARY TABLE 16
ENROLLMENT BY GRADES

Grade		Sept. 1967	Sept. 1968	Sept. 1969	Sept. 1970 (Est.)	No. of Change	% of Change
K		303	289	328	312	−16	
1		260	218	221	243	+22	
2		246	258	222	225	+3	
3		279	250	265	221	−44	
4		275	280	257	270	+13	
5		280	285	288	260	−28	
	Total	1643	1580	1581	1531	−50	−3
6		288	304	288	293	+5	
7		264	294	316	295	−21	
8		271	263	293	322	+29	
	Total	823	861	897	910	+13	+1
9		266	344	336	362	+26	
10		305	247	327	315	−12	
11		248	289	237	320	+83	
12		223	240	289	250	−39	
	Total	1042	1120	1189	1247	+58	+5
	Grand Total	3508	3561	3667	3688	+21	+1

FINANCIAL AND STATISTICAL SUMMARY TABLE 17
ENROLLMENT BY SCHOOLS

		Sept. 1967	Sept. 1968	Sept. 1969	Sept. 1970	Change
Elementary						
Central Avenue		264	306	261	0*	−261
Evans Park		351	347	327	463	+136
Franklin		456	372	449	366	−83
Lincoln		285	271	273	420	+147
Nauraushaun		287	284	271	282	+11
	Total	1643	1580	1581	1531	−50
Middle School		823	861	897	910	+13
High School		1042	1120	1189	1247	+58
	Grand Total	3508	3561	3667	3688	+21

*The new additions at Evans Park and Lincoln Avenue will be used for the first time in 1970-1971. Central Avenue will not be used in 1970-1971. New elementary districts will become effective September 1, 1970 to reflect the above changes.

FINANCIAL AND STATISTICAL SUMMARY TABLE 18
ENROLLMENT FOR BOARD OF COOPERATIVE
EDUCATIONAL SERVICES

	1967-1968 Actual	1968-1969 Actual*	1969-1970 Actual**	1970-1971 Estimate	Change
Special Education					
Brain-injured and emotionally disturbed	16	11	15	20	+5
Educables	12	15	13	13	0
Hard-of-hearing	1	2	4	4	0
Physically handicapped	2	3	2	2	0
Trainables	4	7	7	10	+3
Total special education	35	38	41	49	+8
Vocational and Technical Education	72	75	75	90	+15
Grand Total	107	113	116	139	+23

*As of March 28, 1969
**As of March 3, 1970

FINANCIAL AND STATISTICAL SUMMARY TABLE 19
BOARD OF COOPERATIVE EDUCATIONAL
SERVICES (BOCES) CONTRACT
(All figures are shown net of state aid received by BOCES)

Function-Object Code	1968-1969[A] Actual	1969-1970[B] Actual	1970-1971[C] Actual	Change
A-220-525 Teaching				
Special education	$ 41,271	26,451	69,371	+42,920
Occupational education	30,406	33,985	49,064	+15,079
Itinerant teacher services	1,622	5,482	9,601	+4,119
Testing, counseling, and test scoring	2,641	3,803	6,429	+2,626
Total	$ 75,940	69,721	134,465	+64,744
A-510-525 Transportation				
Special education	0	0	22,968	+22,968
Occupational education	2,639	6,118	1,742	−4,376
Total	$ 2,639	6,118	24,710	+18,592
A-720-525 Data Processing	$ 12,814	9,592	19,842	+10,250
A-750-526 Administrative Costs				
Administration	4,068	3,162	6,638	+3,476
Rentals and leases	7,737	17,444	17,070	−374
Total Administrative Cost	$ 11,805	20,606	23,708	+3,102
Grand Total	$103,198	106,037	202,725	+96,688

Notes:
A. Based on adjusted BOCES contract dated June 3, 1969.
B. Based on estimated contract dated September 22, 1969. This contract will be adjusted to its final amount in June 1970. This amount is $3,344 less than budget amount of $109,381 shown in Table 11.
C. Based on BOCES budget dated April 2, 1970.

PROGRAM GOALS AND DESCRIPTIONS, PROGRAM CHANGES,
PERSONNEL SUMMARY, AND PROGRAM BUDGET

Description of Information Presented for Each Program

This section is a summarization of each program. The following
information is presented:

A. Goals, grades K-12
B. Description of existing program
C. Program changes
D. 1970-1971 personnel summary
E. 1970-1971 program budget.

Goals, grades K-12, presents a summary of districtwide goals for grades
K-12 (or other grade spans as appropriate) for each subject area.

Description of existing program shows the program description as it exists
for the school year 1969-1970. Where it is applicable this section is given
by grade span, elementary, middle school, and high school.

Program changes outline the major changes in each educational program
proposed for the school year 1970-1971. A rationale for the change is also
given.

Each program is concluded with a personnel summary and a program
budget. These tables summarize the certificated and noncertificated
personnel involved in the program and the budget for the program for
elementary, middle school, high school, and districtwide categories.

Program Title: English, Language Arts,   Program Code: 60
and Reading, K-12

GOALS, GRADES K-12

1. To develop the students' ability to learn and to utilize basic reading
   skills.
2. To develop students' understanding of the relationship between
   written thoughts and human behavior.
3. To develop intellectual curiosity.
4. To develop increasingly mature standards of personal enjoyment and
   aesthetic taste.
5. To develop students' ability to express themselves in a creative
   manner.
6. To develop positive student attitudes regarding all aspects of
   communication.
7. To develop students' ability to empathize with others and to
   understand their own feelings.

DESCRIPTION OF EXISTING PROGRAM

Elementary

Kindergarten classes have a general Language Arts program, and a reading-readiness program is introduced. A Reading-Readiness Test is given in May to facilitate grouping in the first grade.

The *Read Series* of the American Book Company was introduced this year as the basal reader for grade 1.

In grade 2 the program continues in the Read Series, with its accompanying skill books and two basal readers are available for supplementary work.

In grade 3 the sequential program of the Read Series continues, and more supplementary material for individualized reading is introduced.

In grade 4 the reading program is based on the premise that a child becomes a facile reader by reading not only under instruction but independently. In addition to the basal reader and its skill book, two other readers are introduced for supplementary reading.

In grade 5 the Read Series' *Kings and Things* is a collection of many types of literature which serve as a springboard to more extensive reading for all pupils. All classes are supplied with *SRA Reading Kits,* Macmillan's *Spectrum,* and other materials for supplementary reading and skill building.

In grades 3-5 there is a remedial reading program for students who are two or more years behind in achievement. Students are oriented to the school library.

Middle School

In grade 6 the program strives to:
A. Develop an understanding of the structure of simple sentences through an understanding of language patterns.
B. Teach correct usage of sentences through an understanding of language patterns.
In grade 7 there is a continued study of syntax to further the use of correct writing and speaking patterns. There is development of the ability to write a well-constructed paragraph using the principles of unity and coherence. Study of the short story and novel takes place by developing an understanding of setting, characterization, plot, and theme.

The 8th grade continues the focus on the 7th grade and adds:
A. Composition using three paragraphs.
B. Study of various types of writing.
C. Study of various forms of literature.
In developmental reading, all 6th grade students have forty minutes of reading instruction each day as part of the related studies program.

Seventh and 8th grade students who are not involved in the foreign language program also have forty minutes per day scheduled for reading.

In the remedial reading program for grades 6, 7, and 8, we strive to improve the students' reading through the emphasis of basic concepts in phonics, vocabulary development, and comprehension.

High School

In grade 9 the formal study of grammar terminates. After diagnostic testing the curriculum is adjusted within classes to intensify work on the weak areas. A structured course in writing is given to all pupils.

In grade 10 there are two areas of focus: one in journalism and the other in speech.

In grade 11 the area of concentration is American literature.

In grade 12 a strong effort is made to have students who share similar post-graduate goals scheduled in the same classes. Composition techniques that best fit the goal of each particular group are used. All seniors have one semester of composition and one semester of literature during this year.

PROGRAM CHANGES

Over the past year reading has evolved to the point where it has become the number one priority for the school district. Basal readers have been provided for all elementary classrooms and a 30-hour teacher workshop has been devoted to the problems of teaching reading. On the national scale, reading has been selected as the number one priority due to the fact that a youngster's success in most phases of formal education is dependent upon his acquisition of basic reading skills. In Pearl River we have prepared for the next step in the sequential development of our K-12 reading program.

Elementary

At the elementary level, additional basal reading books will be purchased to complete the sets that have been purchased to date. The major change in the program will be the addition of 1.5 elementary reading specialists together with 3.7 additional teacher aides. This personnel change will mean that next year 3 full-time reading specialists will be working in the elementary school with their emphasis at the primary grade levels. It is intended that two of the reading specialists will serve as resource people for classroom teachers and one will work as a remedial teacher. The teacher aides, while functioning basically in the area of reading, will also assist teachers where disproportionate class size exists.

The language arts program at the elementary level will continue to operate within the framework established during the past year.

Middle School

The middle school program will be expanded to include a developmental reading program in grades 6 and 7. To help accomplish this an additional full-time reading specialist will be added to the staff. Furthermore, reallocation of existing staff will be made in order to provide for a reading staff of seven full-time specialists which will be supplemented by the efforts of teachers in other academic areas to stress basic teaching skills. Under this arrangement a total of 11.3 teachers will devote their full attention to reading instruction. Each student will receive a minimum of 160 minutes per week of formal reading instruction. In grade 8 there will be one reading specialist to work with those students who have demonstrated basic reading skill deficiencies.* The additional staff and instructional time for the reading program will be provided by placing the industrial arts, homemaking, music, and art programs in grade 7 and 8 on an elective basis and by redefining qualifying standards for foreign language at the 7th and 8th grade levels.

The existing language arts program will continue. The developmental reading program will be in addition to the instruction now being given in the area of language arts. The implementation of a developmental reading program will also provide an opportunity for new grouping patterns at the middle school. It is anticipated that by regrouping the students to concentrate on various types of academic problem areas, the teaching and administrative staff will have an opportunity to eliminate the source of many of the existing student discipline problems.

High School

Ninth grade English sections will be scheduled on a back-to-back basis in groups of three. Since students will be grouped within the sections according to their academic strengths and weaknesses, greater flexibility for movement of youngsters within the sections will occur as the result of this back-to-back scheduling.

At the tenth and eleventh grade levels, C group students will be grouped into general English sections according to common academic deficiencies rather than according to grade levels.

In the twelfth grade, the expansion of the existing elective program, including independent study and English seminars will occur. Electives will include half-year courses in the areas of: mass media, speech, drama, humanities, and contemporary literature. The new High School English program will require no substantial increases in the area of staff. An increase of .7 of a teacher, however, will be required to accommodate the anticipated enrollment increases.

---

*The reading texts selected for this program will be an extension of the reading series now being used at the elementary level.

1970-1971 PERSONNEL SUMMARY
(In full-time equivalent personnel)

Position Title	1969-1970 Actual	1970-1971 Recommended Budget	Change
Summary of Staff			
Certificated staff	52.8	58.9	+6.1
Noncertificated staff	1.8	5.9	+4.1
Total	54.6	64.8	+10.2
Certificated Staff			
Elementary			
Curriculum coordinator	0.2	0.2	—
Classroom teachers, K	2.7	2.7	—
Classroom teachers, 1-5	24.8	24.0	−0.8
Reading teachers	1.5	3.0	+1.5
Speech therapist	0.9	0.9	—
Total elementary	30.1	30.8	+0.7
Middle school			
Curriculum coordinator	0.3	0.3	—
Classroom teachers	6.9	4.7	−2.2
Reading specialists	4.4	11.3	+6.9
Speech therapist	0.1	0.1	—
Total middle school	11.7	16.4	+4.7
High school			
Curriculum coordinator	0.5	0.5	—
Classroom teachers	10.5	11.2	+0.7
Total high school	11.0	11.7	+0.7
Noncertificated Staff			
Elementary			
Teacher aides	—	3.7	+3.7
Middle school			
Teacher aides	1.2	1.6	+0.4
High school			
Teacher aides	0.6	0.6	—

| 1970-1971 PROGRAM BUDGET | | | | |
	Elementary	Middle School	High School	District-wide	Total
Certificated Staff					
Regular salaries	$334,709	$188,337	$160,008	$2,250	$685,304
Substitutes and overtime	8,929	5,056	4,840	—	18,825
Employee benefits	88,551	47,775	41,500	565	178,391
Total	$432,189	$241,168	$206,348	$2,815	$882,520
Noncertificated Staff					
Regular salaries	$ 18,000	$ 7,703	$ 2,958	—	$ 28,661
Substitutes and overtime	—	—	—	$ 250	250
Employee benefits	3,124	1,337	514	43	5,018
Total	$ 21,124	$ 9,040	$ 3,472	$ 293	$ 33,929
Other Expenses					
Equipment	$ 448	$ 105	$ 275	—	$ 828
Supplies	8,867	2,800	1,641	—	13,308
Textbooks	4,174	1,377	1,723	—	7,274
Contract services	200	500	1,487	$2,070	4,257
Total	$ 13,689	$ 4,782	$ 5,126	$2,070	$ 25,667
Grand Total	$467,002	$254,990	$214,946	$5,178	$942,116
Number of Students Served	1,531	910	1,247	3,688	3,688
Budget Per Student Served (whole dollars)	$ 305	$ 280	$ 172	$ 1	$ 255

Program Title: Science (including Health),   Program Code: 61
Grades K-12

GOALS, GRADES K-12

Science:

1. To develop understandings of scientific facts, principles, and concepts as they relate to the students' immediate and future needs.
2. To develop skills related to the experimental method of problem solving.
3. To develop the attitudes of respect for open-mindedness, intellectual curiosity and honesty, suspended judgment, and sustained effort.
4. To prepare all of our students, upon high school graduation, to function successfully in a science-oriented world.

Health:

1. The Health and Family Life Curricula will be carefully planned to offer sequential information appropriate to the age and grade level of the students.
2. Family Life Education will provide the knowledge, understanding, and appreciations that are the foundations of wholesome attitudes and mature behavior.
3. To inform students of the effects of alcohol, tobacco, and narcotic drugs.

DESCRIPTION OF EXISTING PROGRAM

Elementary

Each classroom has a classroom laboratory kit. The six major concepts are:

A. conservation of energy
B. conservation of matter
C. interdependence of living things
D. a living thing is the product of its heredity and environment
E. living things are in constant change
F. the universe is in constant change

Middle School

In grades 6-8 students are exposed to content in the following areas:

A. Chemistry
B. Physics
C. Astronomy
D. Biology
E. Anatomy

High School

Science:

In grade 9C students are exposed to content in the following areas:

A. Geology and Oceanography
B. Meteorology and Astronomy and Space Travel

This course is designed for students with severe reading limitations and restricted learning ability.

The curriculum for 9A and 9B stresses the topics of geology, meteorology, and astronomy.

Biology N.R. deals with a scientific study of the world of living things. topics include:

A. Human anatomy
B. Physiology
C. Genetics
D. Disease
E. The plant and animal kingdom
F. Conservation

Chemistry N.R. deals with the properties of elements and compounds, principles of chemical reactions, and the applications of chemistry to medicine, industry, and nutrition.

Chemistry A and B is concerned with the major principles of chemistry. The nature of qualitative and quantitative chemical reaction is studied.

Physics N.R. deals with topics of mechanics, heat, electricity, light and sound, electronics, and nuclear energy.

In Physics B, the concept of energy unifies the classical topics of physics.

Advanced Biology is open to highly talented science students. The course deals in depth with various biology areas.

Health:

In grade 7 the following topics are covered:

A. Maturation
B. Personal health and hygiene
C. Sociological health (tobacco, alcohol, and drugs)

In grade 12 a ½ unit course is required of all seniors where the following topics are covered:

A. Physical and personal health
B. Sociological health (tobacco, alcohol, and drugs)
C. Family life education
D. Mental health

PROGRAM CHANGES

The health dimension of the science program will be the number two priority for the 1970-1971 school year. This is due not only to the state mandate but to our increasing awareness of the importance of modern health instruction for helping to solve the problems related to the areas of drug abuse, smoking, alcoholism, and family life education. An in-service training course may be provided for classroom teachers in the area of health education. We are also considering the possibility of providing a grant for an elementary teacher to pursue a summer study program in order to acquire the knowledge necessary to assist the classroom teachers during the academic year to improve their teaching skills in this important area.

Elementary

The improvement of the science program has been hampered somewhat due to the lack of adequate facilities and science backgrounds of teachers at the elementary level. Since in-service training programs have to date been devoted to the priority areas of mathematics and reading, there has been no concerted effort to provide teachers with an opportunity to improve their instructional skills related to science. There has been a significant change, however, in the type of materials and instructional guidelines provided for our elementary school staff. Although we do not claim that this approach represents the ideal program, we do believe that the use of these materials has provided students throughout the district with an opportunity to become exposed to scientific concepts which would have otherwise been denied to them.

Middle School

The introductory physical science course (I.P.S.) will be expanded at the 8th grade level. This is a nationally sponsored physical science course that has been used on a limited basis in this district for the past two years. An attempt will be made to schedule the sections of science at the middle school for a minimum of 200 minutes per week.

The state-mandated health course will be implemented at the 6th grade level for the 1970-1971 school year pending approval of the State Education Department. Each 6th grade student will be required to take one-half unit of health instruction. An additional 1.2 teachers will be needed to teach this health program and the expanded 8th grade science program.

High School

The high school science program will be modified to provide two academic tracks, a Regents track and a Non-Regents track. The advanced student will continue to have the opportunity to take an accelerated program. The course entitled Advanced Biology will continue to be offered to our seniors who have demonstrated a high degree of interest and achievement in the area of science. However, an independent study program stressing laboratory-oriented experiences will be offered as part of the Advanced Biology course.

The health course will be modified from a required course at the 12th grade level to an elective course at that level with an emphasis on family living. At the 10th grade level, a one-half unit of health instruction will be required for every student in lieu of one semester of physical education. An additional 1.3 teachers will be required to teach the new health course and to accommodate increasing student enrollments.

1970-1971 PERSONNEL SUMMARY (In full-time-equivalent personnel)			
Position Title	1969-1970 Actual	1970-1971 Recommended Budget	Change
Summary of Staff			
Certificated staff	23.8	26.3	+2.5
Noncertificated staff	0.4	0.4	—
Total	24.2	26.7	+2.5
Certificated Staff			
Elementary			
Curriculum coordinator	0.3	0.3	—
Classroom teachers, K	0.5	0.5	—
Classroom teachers, 1-5	5.4	5.4	—
Total elementary	6.2	6.2	—
Middle school			
Curriculum coordinator	0.3	0.3	—
Classroom teachers	7.0	8.4	+1.4
Nurse-teacher	0.2	—	−0.2
Total middle school	7.5	8.7	+1.2
High school			
Curriculum coordinator	0.4	0.4	—
Classroom teachers	9.7	11.0	+1.3
Total high school	10.1	11.4	+1.3
Noncertificated			
High school			
Teacher aides	0.4	0.4	—

1970-1971 PROGRAM BUDGET				
	Elementary	Middle School	High School	District-wide	Total
Certificated Staff					
Regular salaries	$ 71,642	$ 94,381	$147,700	$3,250	$316,973
Substitutes and overtime	1,815	3,025	4,840	–	9,680
Employee benefits	18,139	25,847	41,069	816	85,871
Total	$ 91,596	$123,253	$193,609	$4,066	$412,524
Noncertificated Staff					
Regular salaries	–	–	$ 1,714	–	$ 1,714
Substitutes and overtime	–	–	–	–	–
Employee benefits	–	–	298	–	294
Total	–	–	$ 2,012	–	$ 2,012
Other Expenses					
Equipment	$ 1,219	$ 2,130	$ 2,500	–	$ 5,849
Supplies	5,200	3,950	7,550	–	16,700
Textbooks	1,292	1,868	2,890	–	6,050
Contract services	1,040	750	950	$2,070	4,810
Total	$8,751	$8,698	$13,070	$2,070	$33,409
Grand Total	$100,347	$131,951	$209,511	$6,136	$447,945
Number Of Students Served	1,531	910	978	3,419	3,419
Budget Per Student Served (whole dollars)	$ 66	$ 145	$ 214	$ 2	$ 131

Program Title: Mathematics, K-12   Program Code: 62

GOALS, GRADES K-12

1. To give students an appreciation of the place of mathematics in the history of civilization and realization of its importance in our scientific age.
2. To prepare students to cope with quantitative problems that arise in their personal lives as well as in connection with their vocations.
3. To develop the ability to think or reason soundly in problem solving.
4. To develop the ability to understand and work in abstracts.
5. To develop the students' ability to understand the basic concepts of logic.

DESCRIPTION OF EXISTING PROGRAM

Elementary

The following topics are covered:

A. Mathematical structure
B. Use of sets
C. Number-numeral distinction
D. Development of equations and inequalities
E. Metric and non-metric geometry
F. Introduction of fractional numbers
G. Patterns including an intuitive introduction to functions
H. Development of computational skills
I. Introduction to topics in number theory, such as primes.

Middle School

In grade 6 remedial steps are introduced to improve each youngster's arithmetic skills and content background.

In grade 7 students are specifically prepared to use arithmetic in the world around them. Students are assisted in solidifying their thinking about particular mathematical concepts.

In grade 8 students are provided with additional mathematical concepts and an attempt is made to improve their attitudes regarding further study of mathematics.

Mathematics 9 is a generalization of the fundamental processes of arithmetic in grade 8.

High School

Pre-Algebra is a course intended for those students who desire to continue their study of mathematics, but need more preparation before enrolling in Elementary Algebra.

Mathematics 9 is a generalization of the fundamental processes of arithmetic grade 9.

Mathematics 9 N.R. is designed to acquaint the students with symbolic notation, equations, inequalities, functions, statistics, graphs, and numerical trigonometry.

Mathematics 10 stresses the nature of deductive and inductive proofs, the meaning of logical sequence, and the requirements of necessary and sufficient conditions for proof.

Mathematics 10 N.R. integrates plane geometry with arithmetic, algebra and numerical trigonometry.

Mathematics 10A is the same as Mathematics 10 with Solid Geometry as enrichment.

Mathematics 11 is a course which represents a combination of intermediate algebra, plane trigonometry, and co-ordinate geometry.

Mathematics 11X is the same as Mathematics 11 except offered over one and one half years.

Mathematics 11Y is the third semester of Mathematics 11X.

Mathematics 11 N.R. provides a review of Elementary Algebra and covers functional relationships, graphic representation, linear and quadratic equations, exponents and logarithms, trigonometric functions, series, variations and binomial expansion.

Mathematics 12X is a course which is designed to satisfy not only the basic requirements of advanced algebra and solid geometry, but also topics of modern mathematics.

Calculus is offered for the student who has followed the accelerated mathematics program beginning in the middle school.

Consumer Mathematics is a terminal mathematics course designed to give mathematical skills that are needed to function effectively in the everyday world.

PROGRAM CHANGES

The mathematics program has been the top priority throughout the school district for the past two years. The scope and sequence of the mathematics program have been carefully developed and the materials selected, including textbooks, are directly related to the program as it has been developed. Two 30-hour in-service workshops for classroom teachers dealing with articulated deficiencies of Pearl River students have been held. Test data, administrative evaluation, and teacher assessment support the conclusion that student performance in computational skills has improved significantly over the past two years. Therefore, we feel that the program is moving in the right direction and we see no modification other than the change of course nomenclature at the high school level at this time. Refinements may be made during the year based upon continuing evaluation reports and data.

The cooperative teaching arrangements at the middle school will require an increase of .2 of a teacher in this program. At the high school, an additional .3 of a teacher will be needed to accommodate anticipated increase in student enrollment.

| | | 1970-1971 | |
| 1970-1971 PERSONNEL SUMMARY (In full-time-equivalent personnel) | | | |
Position Title	1969-1970 Actual	1970-1971 Recommended Budget	Change
Summary of Staff			
Certificated staff	27.3	27.2	−0.1
Noncertificated staff	0.6	0.6	—
Total	27.9	27.8	−0.1
Certificated Staff			
Elementary			
Curriculum coordinator	0.3	0.3	—
Classroom teachers, K	0.5	0.5	—
Classroom teachers, 1-5	10.9	10.3	−0.6
Total elementary	11.7	11.1	−0.6
Middle school			
Curriculum coordinator	0.3	0.3	—
Classroom teachers	7.0	7.2	+0.2
Total middle school	7.3	7.5	+0.2
High School			
Curriculum coordinator	0.4	0.4	—
Classroom teachers	7.9	8.2	+0.3
Total high school	8.3	8.6	+0.3
Noncertificated			
High school			
Teacher aides	0.6	0.6	—

1970-1971 PROGRAM BUDGET				
	Elemen-tary	Middle School	High School	District-wide	Total
Certificated Staff					
Regular salaries	$119,482	$ 90,413	$110,775	$2,250	$322,920
Substitutes and overtime	3,630	3,025	3,025	—	9,680
Employee benefits	32,246	24,823	29,940	565	87,574
Total	$155,358	$118,261	$143,740	$2,815	$420,174
Noncertificated Staff					
Regular salaries	—	—	$ 2,934	—	$ 2,934
Substitutes and overtime	—	—	—	250	250
Employee benefits	—	—	509	43	552
Total	—	—	$3,443	$ 293	$3,736
Other Expenses					
Equipment	$ 1,320	$ 1,983	$ 1,280	—	$ 4,583
Supplies	11,900	3,000	1,650	—	16,550
Textbooks	2,118	1,957	3,635	—	7,710
Contract services	270	500	500	1,570	2,840
Total	$15,608	$7,440	$7,065	$1,570	$31,683
Grand Total	$170,966	$125,701	$154,248	$4,678	$455,593
Number of Students Served	1,531	910	1,000	3,441	3,441
Budget Per Student Served (whole dollars)	$ 112	$ 138	$ 154	$ 1	$ 132

Program Title: Social Studies, K-12   Program Code: 63

GOALS, GRADES K-12

1. To develop students' ability to identify the resources and forces of nature which affect how men live.
2. To develop students' ability to identify the high degree of world interdependence that exists today.
3. To develop students' ability to understand and apply geographic concepts.
4. To develop students' ability to understand the dignity and worth of the individual.
5. To develop students' ability to recognize that individuals and groups are responsible for achieving democratic social action.
6. To allow students to develop moral and spiritual values.
7. To develop students' ability to apply social studies concepts to their everyday life.

DESCRIPTION OF EXISTING PROGRAM

Elementary

The social studies program begins with local environment in kindergarten and builds out to major culture regions for grade 5.

Middle School

In grade 6 Eastern and European culture regions are studied. In grade 7 New York State is studied and in grade 8 United States history is the topic.

High School

Grade 9 is devoted to a study of Asian and African culture studies.

Grade 10 is devoted to a study of world history to 1900.

Grade 11 deals with American history to 1900 and grade 12 is a problems of democracy study.

PROGRAM CHANGES

Middle School

The social studies program at the middle school will basically remain the same as it is in 1969-1970. Personnel in this area, however, will be reduced and re-allocated into the developmental reading program.

High School

The social studies program has been under extensive review for the past year and the primary emphasis of this effort has been directed towards improving the program at the senior high school level.

At the 12th-grade level, a program of electives has been proposed that focuses on significant concepts in the various social studies disciplines.

Electives will include:

A. The Human Condition—modern social problems, affluence, poverty, crime, pollution, etc.
B. Human Rights—racial, ethnic, religious, and socioeconomic class conflicts among the peoples of the world.
C. The Human Society—understanding ourselves, culture, society, and social behavior.
D. International Relations—African studies, Latin American studies, Asian studies.
E. Ideas That Changed the World—Capitalism, Communism, Socialism, Fascism, religion, the revolutionary spirit in history.
F. Social Studies Seminar—an independent study program.

The 11th-grade students who have successfully completed social studies 10A will be invited to select an elective in addition to their required American studies program. Students will be grouped into two basic tracks, Regents and Non-Regents.

An independent study program will be provided for the accelerated students in grades 9 and 10 in addition to the required courses. An additional .9 of a teacher will be required to accommodate anticipated increases in student enrollment.

1970-1971 PERSONNEL SUMMARY
(In full-time-equivalent personnel)

Position Title	1969-1970 Actual	1970-1971 Recom- mended Budget	Change
Summary of Staff			
Certificated staff	26.9	26.4	−0.5
Noncertificated staff	—	—	—
Total	26.9	26.4	−0.5
Certificated Staff			
Elementary			
Curriculum coordinator	0.3	0.3	—
Classroom teachers, K	0.5	0.5	—
Classroom teachers, 1-5	9.9	9.3	−0.6
Total elementary	10.7	10.1	−0.6
Middle school			
Curriculum coordinator	0.3	0.3	—
Classroom teachers	6.2	5.4	−0.8
Total middle school	6.5	5.7	−0.8
High school			
Curriculum coordinator	0.4	0.4	—
Classroom teachers	9.8	10.2	+0.9
Total high school	9.7	10.6	+0.9

1970-1971 PROGRAM BUDGET					
	Elemen-tary	Middle School	High School	District-wide	Total
Certificated Staff					
Regular salaries	$109,131	$ 50,056	$123,084	$2,250	$284,521
Substitutes and overtime	3,025	1,815	3,630	—	8,470
Employee benefits	28,506	14,836	32,252	565	76,159
Total	$140,662	$ 66,707	$158,966	$2,815	$369,150
Noncertificated Staff					
Regular salaries	—	—	—	—	—
Substitutes and overtime	—	—	—	—	—
Employee benefits	—	—	—	—	—
Total	—	—	—	—	—
Other Expenses					
Equipment	$ 839	$ 200	$ 608	—	$ 1,647
Supplies	4,000	2,500	3,000	—	9,500
Textbooks	4,600	1,200	3,100	—	8,900
Contract services	—	310	360	$1,570	2,240
Total	$ 9,439	$ 4,210	$ 7,068	$1,570	$ 22,287
Grand Total	$150,101	$ 70,917	$166,034	$4,385	$391,437
Number of Students Served	1,531	910	1,247	3,688	3,688
Budget Per Student Served (whole dollars)	$ 98	$ 78	$ 133	$ 1	$ 106

Program Title: Physical Education,   Program Code: 64
  Intramural and Interscholastic Athletics, K-12

GOALS, GRADES K-12

Physical Education:

1. To develop student physical fitness.
2. To foster social and emotional development of students.
3. To initiate and expose students to the worthy use of leisure time through the development of special skills related to lifetime sports.

Interscholastic athletics:

The goal of the interscholastic athletic program is to plan for a sport or activity for every student and to have every student participate in a sport or activity of his own choosing with maximum efficiency and safety.

DESCRIPTION OF EXISTING PROGRAM

Physical education:

Elementary

In grades 1-2 we have instruction two days per week and in grades 3-5 we have three days per week of instruction.

We continue to not meet the New York State recommendation of a daily physical education program.

Middle School

Instruction takes place in teaching the fundamentals of team sports, and there is the introduction to individual and carryover lifetime activities. There is also an intramural program.

Physical education classes continue to meet below the state recommendation.

High School

In grade 9 team sports are stressed. Refinements of team sports are stressed in grades 10 and 11. A coeducational program has been introduced in grade 12 for ½ year, the other ½ year is devoted to health education.

Interscholastic athletics:

A total of 27 teams compete interscholastically including girls' twirling and cheerleading.

PROGRAM CHANGES

The physical education program has been sharply upgraded over the past several years. It is anticipated that with the completion of the building program, adequate facilities will be provided for the improved instruction and safety of all students.

Middle School and High School

Due to the State mandate for the inclusion of a health program, there will be some modification of time and staff allocations for the middle school and high school. There will be a reduction of one teacher at the high school and one-half teacher at the middle school.

There will be a moderate expansion of the intramural program at the middle school. This expansion is based on individual lifetime recreational activities. In the area of interscholastic athletics the expansion of our existing intramural gymnastics program to an interscholastic sport is proposed. Pending further review, the 12th-grade physical education program will be placed on an elective basis.

The remainder of the programs will continue within the existing framework.

1970-1971 PERSONNEL SUMMARY
(In full-time-equivalent personnel)

Position Title	1969-1970 Actual	1970-1971 Recommended Budget	Change
Summary of Staff			
Certificated staff	17.0	15.4	−1.6
Noncertificated staff	—	—	—
Total	17.0	15.4	−1.6
Certificated Staff			
Elementary			
Curriculum coordinator	0.2	0.2	—
Classroom teachers, K	0.6	0.6	—
Physical education teachers, 1-5	3.0	3.0	—
Total elementary	3.8	3.8	—
Middle school			
Curriculum coordinator	0.3	0.3	—
Physical education teachers	5.4	4.8	−0.6
Total middle school	5.7	5.1	−0.6
High school			
Curriculum coordinator	0.5	0.5	—
Physical education teachers	7.0	6.0	−1.0
Total high school	7.5	6.5	−1.0

1970-1971 PROGRAM BUDGET				
	Elemen- tary	Middle School	High School	District- wide	Total
Certificated Staff					
Regular salaries	$ 36,928	$ 56,156	$ 86,158	—	$179,242
Substitutes and overtime	956	1,291	25,310	—	27,557
Employee benefits	9,608	13,317	27,975	—	50,900
Total	$ 47,492	$ 70,764	$139,443	—	$257,699
Noncertificated Staff					
Regular salaries	—	—	—	—	—
Substitutes and overtime	—	$ 605	$ 2,519	—	$ 3,124
Employee benefits	—	105	437	—	542
Total	—	$ 710	$ 2,956	—	3,666
Other Expenses					
Equipment	$ 1,000	$ 500	$ 1,250	—	$ 2,750
Supplies	1,000	2,600	13,500	—	17,100
Textbooks	—	—	—	—	—
Contract services	—	945	21,255	—	22,200
Total	$ 2,000	$ 4,045	$ 36,005	—	$ 42,050
Grand Total	$ 49,492	$ 75,519	$178,404	—	$303,415
Number of Students Served	1,531	910	1,089	—	3,530
Budget Per Student Served (whole dollars)	$ 31	$ 82	$ 163	—	$ 86

1970-1971 REVENUE BUDGET DETAIL

Code	Description	1968-1970 Actual Revenue	1969-1970 Original Budget	1969-1970 Revised Budget	1970-1971 Recom. Budget
	Local Sources				
A01110	Real property taxes	$2,726,116	$2,814,093	$2,868,593	$3,145,183
A01210	Day school tuition	2,596	—	—	—
A01220	Adult education tuition	10,130	11,020	11,020	9,800
A01230	Summer school tuition	—	900	900	700
A01340	Health service provided for other districts	1,340	1,500	1,500	600
A01420	Real property rental	11,826	15,790	15,790	3,800
A01435	Admissions	2,873	6,300	6,300	4,650
A01450	Interest and profits on deposits and investments	39,094	35,000	35,000	35,000
A01452	Earnings from trust funds	1,127	1,200	1,200	1,200
A01460	Sale of property	9,200	—	—	—
A01464	Sale of instructional materials and supplies	217	200	200	200
A01469	Sale of adult education textbooks	232	400	400	300
A01470	Insurance recoveries	2,379	1,000	1,000	1,000
A01471	Other compensation for loss (books)	861	1,000	1,000	800
A01486	Commissions (telephone)	181	160	160	180
A01489	Refunds of year's expenditures	2,361	1,000	1,000	500
A01490	Misc. revenues from local sources	1,859	900	900	900
A01491	Appropriation of prior years' surplus	—	142,000	317,394	—
A01492	Examination fees	—	300	300	1,050

		1970-1971 REVENUE BUDGET DETAIL (continued)			
Code	Description	1968-1969 Actual Revenue	1969-1970 Original Budget	1969-1970 Revised Budget	1970-1971 Recom. Budget
A01950	Earnings on temporary investments transferred from capital funds	–	1,000	1,000	1,000
	Total local sources	$2,812,392	$3,033,763	$3,263,657	$3,206,863
	Revenues from State Sources*				
A03110	Gross state aid-basic formula	$2,067,952	$2,067,335	$2,067,335	$2,390,000
A03120	Textbook law	22,708	21,000	21,000	21,000
A03491	In-service project aid (Lois)	1,235	1,375	1,375	1,000
A03492	High tax rate aid	90,660	90,660	90,660	110,000
	Total state sources	$2,182,555	$2,180,370	$2,180,370	$2,522,000
	Revenues from Federal Sources*				
A04110	Federal aid for vocational education	$ 715	–	–	–
A04121	Federal aid—NDEA Title III	9,803	–	–	–
	Total federal sources	$ 10,518	–	–	–
	Total Revenues	$5,005,465	$5,214,133	$5,444,027	$5,728,863

*Funds received under ESEA Title I shows in a separate Federal Aid Fund.

EXPLANATION OF 1970-1971 GENERAL FUND REVENUE BUDGET

Account Code and Title	Explanation	1970-1971 Budget
1. AO-1110 Real Property Tax	This budget is based on an estimated net assessed valuation increase of $700,000 from $36,133,020 to $36,833,020. This represents a 2% increase.	$3,241,401

The first year of the "aged" exemption was 1967. Exemptions for this purpose were:

Year	Assessed Valuation	School Tax Loss
1967	$ 80,700	$ 9,176
1968	161,700	12,698
1969	183,450	14,553
1970		

Church and clergy exemptions are as follows:

Year	Assessed Valuation	School Tax Loss
1967	$34,800	$3,957
1968	56,750	4,457
1969	56,750	4,502
1970		

The tax rate has been estimated at $88.00 per thousand of assessed valuation—an increase of $8.67 per thousand or 11 percent. As you know, the tax rate is not established until July when the final assessed valuations are known.

Account Code and Title	Explanation	1970-1971 Budget
2. AO-1220 Adult Education Tuition	Our Adult Education registration figures are as follows:	9,800

Description	Actual 1968-1969	Actual 1969-1970	Estimated 1970-1971
Resident	512	637	625
Nonresident	227	234	225
Total	739	871	850

Account Code and Title	Explanation	1970-1971 Budget
3. AO-1230 Summer School Tuition	This account shows the $3 fee to be collected from each student. This $3 fee is the maximum under the law that we can charge.	700

Shown below are enrollment and ADA figures for the past several years.

Description	Actual Summer 1968 Enrollment	ADA	Actual Summer 1969 Enrollment	ADA	Estimate Summer 1970 Enrollment
Academic	263	164	231	?	233

Account Code and Title	Explanation	1970-1971 Budget
4. AO-1340 Health Services Provided for Other Districts	This provides for reimbursement of health services provided by the school district for nonresident students who attend St. Margaret's. Reimbursement is made by the school districts where the student resides (Nanuet and Ramapo II).	600

Also included is reimbursement for BOCES for health services provided to special education classes that are housed in our school district (1 classroom at the high school).

Account Code and Title	Explanation	1970-1971 Budget
5. AO-1420 Real Property Rental	Our real property rental is estimated as follows:	3,800

A. Rental of 1 classroom to BOCES as follows:

Type of Classes	No. of Class-rooms	Rent Per Class-room	School	Total
Educable	1	2,300	H. Sch.	$2,300

B. From BOCES for instructional services provided   1,000

EXPLANATION OF REVENUE BUDGET (continued)

Account Code and Title	Explanation	1970-1971 Budget
	C. Rental of buildings for community services, including reimbursement for custodial services (for organizations outside of district) 500	
	Total Real Property Rental $3,800	
6. AO-1435 Admissions	This account shows the revenue estimates for the various home varsity athletic events including football, basketball, and wrestling.	4,650
7. AO-1450 Interest and Profits on Deposits and Investments		35,000
8. AO-1452 Earnings from Trust Funds	Interest earnings on trust and agency savings accounts are recorded in this account.	1,200
9. AO-1464 Sale of Instructional Materials and Supplies		200
10. AO-1469 Sale of Adult Education Textbooks	This amount represents the revenue from the sale of textbooks as part of the Adult Education program. A corresponding expense item for the purchase of these textbooks is budgeted under the Adult Education expense budget.	300
11. AO-1470 Insurance Recoveries		1,000
12. AO-1471 Other Compensation for Loss (Books)	This revenue comes primarily from the high school and middle school for reimbursement by students for lost textbooks and library books.	800
13. AO-1486 Commissions (telephone)	This represents commissions from the New York Telephone Company on various semi-public pay telephones installed in the schools.	180
14. AO-1489 Refund of Prior Year's Expenditure	Under the State Accounting System any refund of prior year's expenditures, such as dividends received from our Workmen's Compensation Policy, are shown as revenue.	500
15. AO-1490 Miscellaneous Revenues from Local Sources	This provides for miscellaneous revenues not otherwise accounted for. Included in this item is estimated revenue from the Xerox machine located in the middle school office.	900
16. AO-1491 Appropriation of Prior Year's Surplus	Estimated surplus is based on our fund balance at July 1, 1969, and the difference between revenues and expenditures for 1969-1970.	0
17. AO-1492 Examination Fees	This is a new revenue item resulting from a charge to students taking the Preliminary Scholastic Aptitude Test and the National Merit Examinations. These tests are given at the high school.	1,050

EXPLANATION OF REVENUE BUDGET (continued)

Account Code and Title	Explanation	1970-1971 Budget
18. AO-1950 Earnings on Temporary Investments Transferred from Capital Funds	This account records the transfer from construction funds of interest earned on the investment of idle cash balances.	1,000
19. AO-3110 Gross State Aid—Basic Formula	State aid for 1970-1971 has not been determined as yet by the legislature. The figure shown for our budget is an estimate. This figure will need to be adjusted to the actual amount once the state aid formula has been established by the New York State Legislature.	2,390,000

1969-1970 state aid is shown below:

Basic Formula	1969-1970 Actual
Operating Aid	$1,672,508
Growth Aid	41,813
Building Expense Aid	238,031
Transportation Expense Aid	116,374
Size Correction Aid	68,970
Total	$2,137,696*

*Actually received $2,047,541 due to cuts made by the 1969 New York State Legislature.

Account Code and Title	Explanation	1970-1971 Budget
20. AO-3490 Textbook Law	New York State Textbook Law (Chapter 320, Laws of 1965) became effective September 1, 1966. This law provides that school boards have the duty to purchase and loan textbooks upon individual requests to all children residing in the district enrolled in grades 7-12 of public and non-public schools. This law was further amended by Chapter 795, Laws of 1966, to provide reimbursements not to exceed $15 per pupil for the 1966-1967, 1967-1968, and 1968-1969 school years. This amendment further provided that reimbursement for the 1969-1970 school year and each year thereafter would be $10 per pupil.	21,000

We have estimated an expenditure of $5,000 under Account AO-220-397 for the purchase of textbooks (up to a $10 per student maximum) for nonpublic school children. This account shows revenue for public and nonpublic school textbooks.

Account Code and Title	Explanation	1970-1971 Budget
21. AO-3491 State Aid for Locally Initiated In-service Projects (LOIS)	This revenue item provides for 50% reimbursement from the State of New York for Teacher In-service Training Programs.	1,000

Estimated Cost	State Share @ 50%	District Share
2,000	1,000	1,000

Account Code and Title	Explanation	1970-1971 Budget
22. AO-3492 High Tax Rate Aid	This state aid was received for the first time in 1968-1969. It is designed to provide additional aid for school districts with high tax rates.	110,000

The 1970-1971 aid has been estimated on the same basis as 1969-1970. The 1970 legislature is considering changes to this aid program, the impact of which has not as yet been determined.

	Total General Fund Revenues	$5,728,863

COMPARATIVE BUDGETS DETAIL OF BUDGET
BY FUNCTION AND OBJECT CODE (All figures in dollars)

Code	Description	1968-1969 Actual	1969-1970 Revised Budget	1970-1971 Recommended Budget	Change
	BOARD OF EDUCATION				
	Board of Education				
A0-010-300	Supplies and materials	324	200	325	125
A0-010-400	Other expenses	1,771	1,806	2,000	194
	District Clerk				
A0-020-150	Personal services	2,500	2,500	2,500	—
	District Treasurer				
A0-030-150	Personal services	1,500	1,500	1,500	—
A0-030-300	Supplies and materials	—	124	100	−24
	Tax Collector				
A0-040-400	Other expenses	1,063	1,200	—	−1,200
	Auditing Services				
A0-050-400	Other expenses	—	4,500	1,800	−2,700
	Legal Services				
A0-060-400	Other expenses	15,664	18,500	7,500	−11,000
	District Meeting				
A0-070-300	Supplies and materials	1,654	1,000	1,500	500
A0-070-400	Other expenses	3,840	3,500	3,500	—
	Census				
A0-080-152	Census takers	2,174	2,000	2,500	500
A0-080-300	Supplies and materials	39	50	50	—
	Total Board of Education	30,529	36,880	23,275	−13,605
	CENTRAL ADMINISTRATION				
	Central Administration				
A0-110-101	Personal services— certificated	47,500	47,500	47,500	—
A0-110-150	Personal services— clerical	12,735	6,590	6,780	190
A0-110-200	Equipment	180	200	200	—
A0-110-300	Supplies and materials	1,863	2,023	2,200	177
A0-110-400	Other expenses	3,209	3,078	3,150	72
	Total	65,487	59,391	59,830	439
	Curriculum Development and Supervision				
A0-120-101	Personal services— certificated	22,000	22,000	22,000	—

COMPARATIVE BUDGETS DETAIL OF BUDGET
BY FUNCTION AND OBJECT CODE (continued)

Code	Description	1968-1969 Actual	1969-1970 Revised Budget	1970-1971 Recommended Budget	Change
CENTRAL ADMINISTRATION (continued)					
Curriculum Development and Supervision (continued)					
A0-120-150	Personal services—clerical	6,500	7,725	7,915	190
A0-120-200	Equipment	359	200	200	—
A0-120-300	Supplies and materials	1,065	1,396	1,500	104
A0-120-400	Other expenses	1,423	1,500	1,575	75
	Total	31,347	32,821	33,190	369
Business Administration					
A0-130-101	Personal services—certificated	33,404	34,950	23,500	−11,450
A0-130-150	Personal services—clerical	41,474	42,230	41,775	−455
A0-130-152	Clerical substitutes and overtime	*	2,060	3,000	940
A0-130-200	Equipment	1,469	1,000	2,000	1,000
A0-130-300	Supplies and materials	2,658	3,219	3,210	−9
A0-130-400	Other expenses	6,425	5,317	3,675	−1,642
	Total	85,430	88,776	77,160	−11,616
Personnel Administration					
A0-150-152	Clerical substitutes and overtime	345	2,575	3,000	425
A0-150-400	Other expenses	7,397	14,237	17,000	2,763
	Total	7,742	16,812	20,000	3,188
School Community Relations					
A0-160-300	Supplies	12	—	—	—
A0-160-400	Other expenses	2,078	5,106	6,000	894
	Total	2,090	5,106	6,000	894
	Total Central Administration	192,096	202,906	196,180	−6,726
INSTRUCTION					
Building Principals					
A0-211-101	Personal services—certificated	154,905	168,480	160,808	−7,672
A0-211-150	Personal services—clerical	60,956	57,845	55,325	−2,520
A0-211-152	Clerical substitutes and overtime	**	2,060	2,000	−60

*Included in A0-130-150.
**Included in A0-211-150.

COMPARATIVE BUDGETS DETAIL OF BUDGET
BY FUNCTION AND OBJECT CODE (continued)

Code	Description	1968-1969 Actual	1969-1970 Revised Budget	1970-1971 Recom- mended Budget	Change
	INSTRUCTION (continued)				
	Building Principals (continued)				
A0-211-200	Equipment	—	1,100	1,000	−100
A0-211-300	Supplies and materials	2,350	2,569	3,000	431
A0-211-400	Other expenses	2,392	4,950	6,500	1,550
	Total	220,603	237,004	228,633	−8,371
	Supporting Teachers (Art, Music, Physical Education, Reading, Speech)				
A0-212-101	Personal services— certificated	173,453	205,947	230,761	24,814
A0-212-149	Substitute teachers	1,948	2,700	2,700	—
A0-212-150	Personal services— clerical	11,126	26,509	26,295	−214
A0-212-152	Clerical substi- tutes and overtime	**	1,000	3,000	2,000
A0-212-200	Equipment	127	—	—	—
A0-212-300	Supplies and materials	1,045	1,569	2,000	431
A0-212-400	Other expenses	4,822	11,143	11,000	−143
	Total	192,521	248,868	275,756	26,888
	School Library Services				
A0-213-101	Personal services— certificated	71,375	78,173	79,175	1,002
A0-213-149	Substitute teachers	297	250	250	—
A0-213-150	Personal services— clerical	11,562	18,419	16,885	−1,534
A0-213-200	Equipment	142	1,650	780	−870
A0-213-300	Supplies and materials	26,265	11,847	23,200	11,353
A0-213-400	Other expenses	867	1,170	1,620	450
	Total	110,508	111,509	121,910	10,401
	Teaching				
A0-220-110	Salaries, cert.: ½ day K	58,749	62,237	58,103	−4,134
A0-220-111	Salaries, cert.: K-6	663,086	673,056	656,801	−16,255
A0-220-112	Salaries, cert.: 7-12	1,050,916	1,172,806	1,256,869	84,063
A0-220-113	Salaries, cert.: sabbatical	—	—	—	—

**Included in A0-212-150.

COMPARATIVE BUDGETS DETAIL OF BUDGET
BY FUNCTION AND OBJECT CODE (continued)

Code	Description	1968-1969 Actual	1969-1970 Revised Budget	1970-1971 Recom- mended Budget	Change
	INSTRUCTION (continued)				
	Teaching (continued)				
A0-220-114	Salaries, cert.: summer curricu- lum development	3,265	5,000	5,000	—
A0-220-120	Salaries, cert.: home teaching	7,769	5,000	5,000	—
A0-220-125	Salaries, cert.: co-curricular club and activity assign.	22,663	15,450	16,500	1,050
A0-220-149	Salaries, substitutes	39,348	43,810	44,000	190
A0-220-150	Personal services— clerical	34,294	47,626	68,435	20,809
A0-220-200	Equipment	24,059	40,591	28,850	−11,741
A0-220-300	Supplies and materials	78,316	94,559	92,225	−2,334
A0-220-397	Textbooks 7-12 (Nonpublic schools)	3,938	5,012	5,000	−12
A0-220-398	Textbooks K-6	10,362	30,865	14,475	−16,390
A0-220-399	Textbooks 7-12	18,734	18,076	22,380	4,304
A0-220-400	Other expenses	14,112	17,581	25,700	8,119
A0-220-401	State supported teacher training program	114	2,750	2,000	−750
A0-220-501	Tuition K-6 to other districts (special education)	118	—	4,000	4,000
A0-220-525	BOCES services	75,940	71,638	134,465	62,827
	Total	2,105,783	2,306,057	2,439,803	133,746
	Interscholastic Athletics				
A0-281-125	Salaries: certi- ficated coaching assignments	21,157	20,260	22,890	2,630
A0-281-200	Equipment	2,721	1,599	500	−1,099
A0-281-300	Supplies and materials	12,287	8,618	10,500	1,882
A0-281-400	Other expenses	5,513	9,042	8,340	−702
	Total	41,678	39,519	42,230	2,711
	Guidance				
A0-291-101	Personal services— certificated	89,984	91,275	94,233	2,958
A0-291-150	Personal services— clerical	13,281	15,106	16,190	1,084

COMPARATIVE BUDGETS DETAIL OF BUDGET
BY FUNCTION AND OBJECT CODE (continued)

Code	Description	1968-1969 Actual	1969-1970 Revised Budget	1970-1971 Recommended Budget	Change
	INSTRUCTION (continued)				
	Guidance (continued)				
A0-291-200	Equipment	728	340	—	−340
A0-291-300	Supplies and materials	1,909	2,588	3,525	937
A0-291-400	Other expenses	960	750	2,000	1,250
	Total	105,862	110,059	115,948	5,889
	Psychological Services				
A0-292-101	Personal services— certificated	15,191	16,201	27,730	11,529
A0-292-300	Supplies and materials	222	243	500	257
A0-292-400	Other expenses	186	250	330	80
	Total	15,599	16,694	28,560	11,866
	Health Services				
A0-294-101	Personal services— certificated	59,883	50,990	49,905	−1,085
A0-294-149	Substitute teachers	595	900	900	—
A0-294-150	Personal services: clerical physicians and dentists	21,662	23,116	23,250	134
A0-294-200	Equipment	331	900	965	65
A0-294-300	Supplies and materials	632	900	950	50
A0-294-400	Other expenses	3,312	4,500	4,500	—
	Total	86,415	81,306	80,470	−836
	Adult Education				
A0-320-101	Personal services— certificated	5,807	9,400	6,500	−2,900
A0-320-152	Clerical substitutes and overtime	358	350	600	250
A0-320-300	Supplies and materials	742	550	665	115
A0-320-399	Textbooks	189	424	300	−124
A0-320-400	Other expenses	—	720	610	−110
	Total	7,096	11,444	8,675	−2,769
	Summer School				
A0-321-101	Personal services— cert.	3,055	12,200	12,200	—
A0-321-152	Cler. subs. and overtime	*	500	500	—
A0-321-300	Supplies and materials	380	800	800	—

*Included in A0-321-101.

COMPARATIVE BUDGETS DETAIL OF BUDGET
BY FUNCTION AND OBJECT CODE (continued)

Code	Description	1968-1969 Actual	1969-1970 Revised Budget	1970-1971 Recommended Budget	Change
	INSTRUCTION (continued)				
	Summer School (continued)				
A0-321-398	Textbooks	—	100	100	—
	Total	3,435	13,600	13,600	—
	Total Instruction	2,889,500	3,176,060	3,355,585	179,525
	COMMUNITY SERVICES				
	Civic Activities (use of buildings)				
A0-430-152	Personal services—custodial overtime	2,855	3,500	6,000	2,500
A0-430-400	Other expenses	17	—	—	—
	Total Community Services	2,872	3,500	6,000	2,500
	TRANSPORTATION				
A0-510-150	Personal services—transportation	7,866	7,570	7,465	−105
A0-510-152	Personal services—substitutes and overtime	—	2,000	1,000	−1,000
A0-510-210	Purchase of bus	—	—	5,000	5,000
A0-510-300	Supplies and materials	541	600	600	—
A0-510-400	Other expenses	425	450	450	—
A0-510-451	Private carrier	125,859	144,000	130,000	−14,000
A0-510-452	Public service corporation	5,092	5,000	5,600	600
A0-510-453	Private carrier—physical education program	13,077	5,845	7,190	1,345
A0-510-525	BOCES services	2,639	5,669	24,710	19,041
	Total Transportation	155,499	171,134	182,015	10,881
	OPERATION AND MAINTENANCE OF PLANT				
A0-600-150	Personal services—custodial and maintenance	184,672	200,638	197,385	−3,253
A0-600-152	Personal services—substitutes and overtime	*	8,000	13,000	5,000
A0-600-200	Equipment	8,453	5,129	3,760	−1,369
A0-600-300	Supplies and materials	26,446	31,464	29,000	−2,464
A0-600-400	Other expenses	2,868	4,132	4,550	418

*Included in A0-600-150.

COMPARATIVE BUDGETS DETAIL OF BUDGET
BY FUNCTION AND OBJECT CODE (continued)

Code	Description	1968-1969 Actual	1969-1970 Revised Budget	1970-1971 Recommended Budget	Change
	OPERATION AND MAINTENANCE OF PLANT (continued)				
A0-600-421	Fuel oil	18,280	21,000	20,000	−1,000
A0-600-422	Gas	7,421	11,400	9,000	−2,400
A0-600-425	Electricity	50,723	51,125	52,000	875
A0-600-426	Water	4,504	5,700	6,000	300
A0-600-427	Telephone and telegraph	24,226	26,815	25,300	−515
A0-600-430	Rental (warehouse)	3,975	4,500	4,500	−
A0-600-460	Contract services (included contract custodial cleaning)	98,210	105,463	147,500	42,037
	Total Operation and Maintenance of Plant	429,778	474,366	511,995	37,629
	EMPLOYEE BENEFITS AND OTHER EXPENSES				
	Data Process Unit				
A0-720-400	Contract data processing services	6,811	4,074	−	−4,074
A0-720-525	BOCES services	12,814	8,268	19,842	11,574
	Total	19,625	12,342	19,842	7,500
	Employees' Benefits				
A0-730-611	Teachers' retirement	384,262	498,000	537,000	39,000
A0-730-613	Employees' retirement	45,369	50,000	55,000	5,000
A0-730-615	Social security	113,472	101,000	115,000	14,000
A0-730-616	Health insurance	46,093	60,000	77,500	17,500
A0-730-617	Travel insurance	364	400	390	−10
A0-730-618	Dental insurance—teachers	−	5,500	13,000	7,500
A0-730-619	Dental insurance—others	−	1,500	3,800	2,300
	Total	589,560	716,400	801,690	85,290
	Insurance				
A0-740-413	Compensation insurance	8,335	10,000	13,000	3,000
A0-740-414	Other Insurance	74,458	46,000	55,965	9,965
	Total	82,793	56,000	68,965	12,965

COMPARATIVE BUDGETS DETAIL OF BUDGET
BY FUNCTION AND OBJECT CODE (continued)

Code	Description	1968-1969 Actual	1969-1970 Revised Budget	1970-1971 Recommended Budget	Change
	EMPLOYEE BENEFITS AND OTHER EXPENSES (continued)				
	Other				
A0-750-526	BOCES debt service and rentals for special education facilities	11,805	23,806	23,708	−98
A0-750-621	Refund of prior year's revenue	—	27,000	20,000	−7,000
A0-750-623	Judgments and claims	—	100,000	—	−100,000
A0-750-625	Professional consultants	656	4,000	3,000	−1,000
	Total	12,461	154,806	46,708	−108,098
	Total Employee Benefits And Other Expenses	704,439	939,548	−108,098	−2,343
	Debt Service				
A0-800-711	Principal on bonds	223,000	223,000	233,000	10,000
A0-800-714	Principal on bond anticipation notes	—	—	30,000	30,000
A0-800-721	Interest on bonds	224,258	216,333	208,408	−7,925
A0-800-724	Interest bond anticipation notes for construction	—	—	41,700	41,700
A0-800-727	Interest on tax anticipation notes	2,238	300	3,500	3,200
	Total Debt Service	449,496	439,633	516,608	76,975
	INTER-FUND TRANSFERS				
A0-900-810	To capital funds	56,775	—	—	—
A0-900-860	To federal funds	1,282	—	—	—
	Total Inter-Fund Transfers	58,057	—	—	—
	GRAND TOTAL	4,912,266	5,444,027	5,728,863	284,836

SCHOOL LUNCH FUND BUDGET

Code	Description	1969-1970 Revised Budget	1970-1971 Recom- mended Budget	Change
	Revenues			
C-1476	Sales type A lunches	$ 73,535	$ 73,362	$ −173
C-1477	Other food sales	48,375	60,854	+12,479
C-1483	Government com- modities	8,000	12,000	+4,000
C-3410	State aid contribution	27,426	24,446	−2,980
	Total Revenues	$157,336	$170,662	$+13,326
	Expenditures			
C-790-150	Personal services	$ 61,730	$ 70,462	$ +8,732
C-790-200	Equipment	273	−	−273
C-790-300	Supplies and materials	4,590	4,100	−490
C-790-400	Other expenses	400	200	−200
C-790-520	Food and milk	82,693	84,000	+1,307
C-790-613	Employee retirement	4,400	5,100	+700
C-790-615	Social security	1,600	3,500	+1,900
C-790-616	Health insurance	1,650	3,300	+1,650
	Total Expenditures	$157,336	$170,662	$+13,236

BOARD OF EDUCATION
RESOLUTION ADOPTING BUDGET

Be it resolved, by the Board of Education, that the General Fund 1970-1971 Budget, as shown on the attached pages be and hereby is adopted for the 1970-1971 School Year.

Be it further resolved, that in accordance with Section 205L of the Regulations of the Commissioner of Education of New York State, that transfers between and within functional unit appropriations for ordinary contingent expenses may be made by the Superintendent of Schools.

SUMMARY OF BUDGET					Form 1
	Fund	Program	School/Dept.	Function	Object
CODE	A O				
DESCRIPTION	GENERAL				

Object Code	Account Title		Proposed Budget		
			Consultant Recommendation	Principal Recommendation	Superintendent Recommendation
101	Certificated Salaries				
110	Certificated Salaries, 1/2 day Kindergarten				
111	Certificated Salaries, Grades 1 - 6				
112	Certificated Salaries, Grades 7 - 12				
120	Certificated Salaries, Home Teaching				
125	Certificated Salaries, Overtime				
149	Certificated Salaries, Substitutes				
150	Non-Certificated Salaries				
152	Non-Certificated Salaries, substitutes and overtime				
200	Equipment				
300	Supplies and Materials				
398	Textbooks, Grades K - 6				
399	Textbooks, Grades 7 - 12				
400	Other Expenses				
	TOTAL				

Business Office will complete Salary items.   Prepared by   Date

NUMBER OF RECOMMENDED NEW STAFF POSITIONS (ON BASIS FULL-TIME EQUIVALENT)					Form 2
	Fund	Program	School/Dept.	Function	Object
CODE	A O				
DESCRIPTION	GENERAL				
Position Title			Consultant Recommendation	Principal Recommendation	Superintendent Recommendation
TOTAL					
Prepare for each Account Code. Attach complete justification			Prepared by		Date

	Fund	Program	School/Dept.	Function	Object
DAYS OF SUBSTITUTE TEACHERS OTHER THAN SICKNESS					Form 3
CODE	AO				149
DESCRIPTION	GENERAL				Substitute Teachers
PURPOSE (JUSTIFICATION)			Consultant Recommendation	Principal Recommendation	Superintendent Recommendation
TOTAL					
Show Number of Days Requested			Prepared by		Date

HOURS OF TEACHER OVERTIME					Form 4	
	Fund	Program	School/Dept.	Function	Object	
CODE	AO				125	
DESCRIPTION	GENERAL				Teacher Overtime	
Reason for Overtime (Justification)			Consultants		Principal		Superintendent	
			Gen.	Major	Gen.	Major	Gen.	Major
TOTAL								
		Prepared by		Date				

HOURS OF NON-CERTIFICATED SUBSTITUTES AND OVERTIME					Form 5
	Fund	Program	School/Dept.	Function	Object
CODE	AO				152
DESCRIPTION	GENERAL				Substitutes and Overtime
Reason (Justification)			Consultant Recommendation	Principal Recommendation	Superintendent Recommendation
Clerical					
Custodial					
Maintenance					
TOTAL HOURS					
Include substitutes for sickness and vacations			Prepared by		Date

SUMMARY OF EQUIPMENT					Form 6
	Fund	Program	School/Dept.	Function	Object
CODE	A 0				200
DESCRIPTION	GENERAL				Equipment

Description	Quantity	Consultant Recommendation	Principal Recommendation	Superintendent Recommendation
1.				
2.				
3.				
4.				
5.				
6.				
7.				
8.				
9.				
10.				
11.				
12.				
13.				
14.				
15.				
TOTAL				

Show items of $25 unit price or more. Complete a separate form for each year.	Prepared by	Date

	EQUIPMENT DETAILS FOR ITEMS OVER $250				Form 7
	Fund	Program	School/Dept.	Function	Object
CODE	AO				200
DESCRIPTION	GENERAL				Equipment

1. Description of item requested (include suggested vendor)

2. Number of Similar Units on hand.	11. Budget Item	Quantity	Unit Cost	Total This Year	Total Next Year
3. Intended use of requested item Weeks per year	Equipment				
No. hours used: Day Week Mo.	Installation				
4. ☐ Explain need for this item Scheduled Replacement	Freight				
☐ Present Equipment Obsolete	Building Modification				
☐ Replace Worn-out Equipment	Maintenance				
☐ Cut Personnel Time Hours per day_____	Operation (Utilities,etc)				
☐ Expanded Service	Total				
☐ New Operation	Less:Trade-in (if any)				
☐ Increase Safety	Net Total				

5. Equipment that will be replaced by the above:
    Item   Make   Age   Prior Year's Maintenance Cost

6. ☐ Replacement   ☐ Addition   Disposition of Equipment to be replaced:

7. Explain need for this item on back of form. Describe its use and work load. If this is a scheduled replacement, specifiy the schedule. Describe relationship to District's objectives.	8. Will this request require an increase in personnel at any time? ☐ yes ☐ No	9. Item requested previously (year)	10. ☐ Priority: Essential ☐ Desirable ☐ Non-Essential

Prepare only for items of a unit value or total value of over $250 requested for 1971-72   Prepared by   Date

SUMMARY OF SUPPLIES AND MATERIALS					Form 8
	Fund	Program	School/Dept.	Function	Object
CODE	A 0				300
DESCRIPTION	GENERAL				Supplies and Materials
Description			Consultant Recommendation	Principal Recommendation	Superintendent Recommendation
1. General Supplies - Standard List No. 1					
2. Paper & Spirit Master - Standard List No. 2					
3. Art Supplies - Standard List No. 3					
4. Other Standard Supplies (List No.____)					
5. Workbooks (Detail on Budget Form 9)					
6. Paper Supplies (Other than Standard List No. 1 and 2)					
7. Printed Supplies, including forms and stationery. (Please give us detailed list)					
8. Sheet Music					
9. Standardized Tests					
10. Records and Tapes					
11. Maps, globes and charts					
12. Professional Books and Periodicals					
13. Films and film strips that are purchased (rented film strips are coded "400")					
14. Library Books and Periodicals					
15. Others (specify)					
TOTAL					
Use Form 11 for detail of supplies. Complete a separate form for each year.			Prepared by		Detail

DETAIL OF WORKBOOKS				Form 9	
	Fund	Program	School/Dept.	Function	Object
CODE	A O			200	300
DESCRIPTION	GENERAL			Teaching	Supplies and Materials
Subject Area and Grade	Quantity	Unit Price	Consultant Recommendation	Principal Recommendation	Superintendent Recommendation
TOTAL					
Use a separate sheet for each program area.			Prepared by		Date

DETAIL OF SUPPLIES AND MATERIALS					Form 10
	Fund	Program	School/Dept.	Function	Object
CODE	AO				300
DESCRIPTION	GENERAL				Supplies and Materials

Description (Include Quantity and Unit Price)	Consultant Recommendation	Principal Recommendation	Superintendent Recommendation
Show suggested vendors name and address, if possible.	Prepared by		Date

DETAIL OF TEXTBOOKS					Form 11
	Fund	Program	School/Dept.	Function	Object
CODE	A O			220	398(K-6) 399(7-12)
DESCRIPTION	GENERAL			Teaching	Textbooks

Subject Area and Grade	Quantity	Unit Price	Consultant Recommendation	Principal Recommendation	Superintendent Recommendation
TOTAL					

Use a separate sheet for each program area. Indicate new adoptions. Textbook titles are not necessary at this time. Complete a separate form for each year.	Prepared by	Date

SUMMARY OF OTHER EXPENSES					Form 12
	Fund	Program	School/Dept.	Function	Object
CODE	AO				400
DESCRIPTION	GENERAL				Other Expenses
Description (Explain and justify on Form 13)			Consultant Recommendation	Principal Recommendation	Superintendent Recommendation
1. Mileage-in District @ .10/mile					
2. Mileage-out of District @ .10/mile					
3. Conferences (Show on separate sheet conference name, place, position attending, no. of days, transportation, living other expenses)					
4. Maintenance of Equipment (show on separate sheet description of equipment, no. of pieces, contractor, period of contract and unit cost)					
5. Book Binding					
6. Outside Speakers					
7. Postage					
8. Filmstrip rental (show no., purpose, etc.)					
9. District Membership (detail on separate sheet)					
10. Professional Services					
11. Consultants					
12. Other Contractural Services (Detail and Explain)					
TOTAL					
			Prepared by		Date

DETAIL OF OTHER EXPENSES					Form 13
	Fund	Program	School/Dept.	Function	Object
CODE	A 0				400
DESCRIPTION	GENERAL				Other Expenses
Detail			Consultant Recommendation	Principal Recommendation	Superintendent Recommendation
			Prepared by		Date

DETAIL OF CERTIFICATED STAFF SALARIES BY OBJECT

Date				Form 14

FTE (Full-time Equivalent)
Teacher = 10 months = 1.0
Administration = 11 months = 1.0

This form is only used by the Business Office

	Fund	Program	School/Dept.	Function	Object
Code	AO				
Description	General				

Col.	Step	Position Title	Grade	Bldg.	Name	11 mo. ✓	Base Salary	Differential	Budget	FTE This Year	FTE Next Year

DETAIL OF NON-CERTIFICATED STAFF SALARIES BY OBJECT

Date   Form 15

Fund	A O
Code	
Description	General

FTE (Full-time Equivalent)
Clerical = 1910 hours/year = 1.0
Custodial= 2080 hours/year = 1.0

This form is only used by the Business Office

Pay Grade	Loca-tion	Position Title	Shift	Name	Hr/Wk	Wk/Yr	Total Hours	Anniv. Date	Present Rate	Budget	FTE This Year	FTE Next Year
			Program	School/Dept.	Function		Object					
		OVERTIME										
		SUBSTITUTES										
		GRAND TOTAL										

part
THREE

illustrative ppbs forms and sample documents

The following figures represent samples of various forms and other materials that have been developed by school districts in order to facilitate the implementation of a PPB system. Sample budgets from small suburban to large urban districts are provided. The budget forms contained in this section may serve with some adaptation to assist in the implementation of PPBS.

FIGURE 1.   ILLUSTRATIVE SUMMARY EVENT SCHEDULE

Event No.	Event	Time Frame
1	Orientation Meeting	February 6-7
2	Training Seminars Training seminars will be conducted during this period.	March 7, March 31-April 1
3	Preparation of District Planning and Implementation Schedule A detailed event schedule with related time frames will be prepared during this phase. The event schedule will show assignment of personnel responsible for various activities.	February and March
4	Preparation of Communications Plan Communications plan will include activities directed at the various publics concerned with the schools, including board of education, staff, and community.	May-July
5	Preparation of District Training Program District training plan will be prepared.	July-August
6	Develop Program Structure Program structure is the basis for analysis and review of programs, as well as program accounting. It is important, therefore, that this structure be designed by the district to reflect its needs and priorities.	March-August

FIGURE 1.   ILLUSTRATIVE SUMMARY EVENT SCHEDULE (cont'd)

Event No.	Event	Time Frame
7	Develop Program Accounting Program Accounting system will include a program coding system related to the program structure. Systems and procedures to support program accounting will be developed as well as the possible use of computers.	July-September
8	Prepare Program Budget Program budgeting will show the allocation of budget in accordance with the program structure.	July-June
9	Prepare Objectives[1] Select the priority target programs for the purpose of the pilot project. One or more programs may be selected by the district for the purpose of the project. Separate objectives for the target programs will then be developed.	October-August
10	Develop Evaluation Plan[1] During this phase, each district will determine the output, time frame, and evaluation method to be used in relation to the objectives developed for target program areas.	February-August
11	Prepare Multi-Year Financial Plan[1] For the target program(s), multi-year financial and statistical data will be presented for a three-year period.	June-November
12	Apply Program Analysis[1] During this phase, alternative ways to achieve program objectives within the target program(s) will be considered.	October-January
13	Prepare PPBES Document This document will include objectives with related evaluation criteria as well as multi-year statistical and financial projections, review of alternatives considered to achieve program objectives and related costs.	January-June

[1] Applicable to target program(s) selected by district.

FIGURE 2.   ILLUSTRATIVE DETAIL EVENT SCHEDULE

Event: No. 6   Event: Develop Program Structure
Suggested Time Frame: March-August

Detail Event No.	Event	Person Responsible	Date to Start	Date to Finish
6.1	Determine district philosophy in developing program structure.			
6.2	Study alternative program structures.			
6.3	Prepare alternative program structure for staff review.			
6.4	Determine if programs will cut across organization lines to provide "trade-off" for purpose of analysis.			
6.5	Determine the lowest level for each program, considering ability to control, measure outputs, and allocate resources to that level.			
6.6	Determine at what administrative level decisions affecting the program can be made.			
6.7	Determine amount of administrative control desired over various programs.			
6.8	Determine if programs will cut across fund used for accounting purposes (General Fund, etc.).			
6.9	Determine what activities will be under each program.			
6.10	Design program structure.			
6.11	Review of program structure by task force team.			
6.12	Recommendation of program structure to board of education.			
6.13	Adoption of program structure by board of education.			

FIGURE 3.   ILLUSTRATIVE CALENDAR EVENT SCHEDULE

EVENT	PHASE I					PHASE II												PHASE III											
	FEB	MAR	APR	MAY	JUNE	JULY	AUG	SEPT	OCT	NOV	DEC	JAN	FEB	MAR	APR	MAY	JUNE	JULY	AUG	SEPT	OCT	NOV	DEC	JAN	FEB	MAR	APR	MAY	JUNE
1. Orientation Meeting	×								×												×								
2. Training Seminars		×	×																										
3. District Planning & Implementation Schedule	×	×	×																										
4. District Communications Plan				×	×																								
5. District Training Program						×	×																						
6. Program Structure		×	×	×	×																								
7. Program Accounting System						×	×																						
8. Program Budget						×	×	×	×	×	×	×	×	×	×	×	×	×	×										
9. District Goals & Objectives						×	×	×	×	×	×	×	×	×	×	×	×	×	×										
10. Evaluation Plan													×	×	×	×	×												
11. Multi-Year Financial Plan																×	×	×	×	×	×	×							
12. System Analysis																				×	×	×	×	×					
13. PPBES Document																								×	×	×	×	×	×

FIGURE 4.   ILLUSTRATIVE TRAINING PROGRAM SCHEDULE

Target Group	Activities	Estimated Hours* For Each Activity
Board of Education	Orientation to PPBS	2
	Total Hours Board of Education	2
Task Team	Orientation to PPBS	2
	Task Team Role	1
	Developing Implementation Plan	2
	Event Schedules	1
	Designing Program Structures	2
	Developing Objectives	2
	Establishing Priorities	1
	Evaluating Achievement	3
	Program Budget	1
	Program Accounting	1
	Program Analysis	3
	PPBS Summary Document	1
	Total Hours Task Team	20
Principals and Curriculum Supervisors	Orientation to PPBS	2
	Program Structure	2
	Developing Objectives and Evaluating Achievement	6
	Program Budget Accounting	1
	Program Analysis	6
	Total Hours Principals and Curriculum Supervisors	17
Teaching Staff	Orientation to PPBS including Task Team Role and Implementation Plan	2
	Developing Objectives and Evaluating Achievement	6
	Total Hours Teaching Staff	8
Support Service Supervisors (Food Service Manager, Superintendent of Buildings & Grounds, Transportation Supervisor, Business Office Supervisor, etc.)	Orientation to PPBS	2
	Developing Objectives and Evaluation Performance for Support Services	2
	Program Analysis for Support Services	2
	Total Hours Support Service Supervisors	6
Non-Teaching Staff	Orientation to PPBS	1
	Total Hours Non-Teaching Staff	1
Clerical Staff	Orientation to PPBS	1
	Training for Preparation of PPBS Material	4
	Total Hours Clerical Staff	5
Groups Doing Specific Program Analysis	Program Analysis	2
	Alternative Models for Analysis	2
	Workshop on Program Analysis	4
	Total Hours Program Analysis Groups	8

*The number of hours estimated for each target group provides for their orientation to the activities listed above.

Note: Some of the sessions for various target groups could be combined. For example, the orientation to PPBS (two-hour session) could be given to the teaching staff, principals, and curriculum supervisors concurrently.

FIGURE 5.   ILLUSTRATIVE PROGRAM

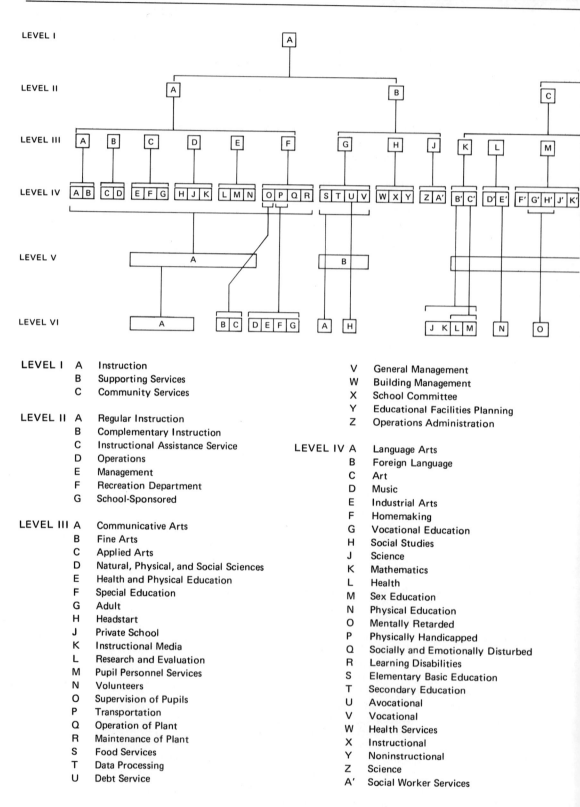

LEVEL I   A   Instruction
           B   Supporting Services
           C   Community Services

LEVEL II   A   Regular Instruction
           B   Complementary Instruction
           C   Instructional Assistance Service
           D   Operations
           E   Management
           F   Recreation Department
           G   School-Sponsored

LEVEL III A   Communicative Arts
           B   Fine Arts
           C   Applied Arts
           D   Natural, Physical, and Social Sciences
           E   Health and Physical Education
           F   Special Education
           G   Adult
           H   Headstart
           J   Private School
           K   Instructional Media
           L   Research and Evaluation
           M   Pupil Personnel Services
           N   Volunteers
           O   Supervision of Pupils
           P   Transportation
           Q   Operation of Plant
           R   Maintenance of Plant
           S   Food Services
           T   Data Processing
           U   Debt Service

           V   General Management
           W   Building Management
           X   School Committee
           Y   Educational Facilities Planning
           Z   Operations Administration

LEVEL IV   A   Language Arts
           B   Foreign Language
           C   Art
           D   Music
           E   Industrial Arts
           F   Homemaking
           G   Vocational Education
           H   Social Studies
           J   Science
           K   Mathematics
           L   Health
           M   Sex Education
           N   Physical Education
           O   Mentally Retarded
           P   Physically Handicapped
           Q   Socially and Emotionally Disturbed
           R   Learning Disabilities
           S   Elementary Basic Education
           T   Secondary Education
           U   Avocational
           V   Vocational
           W   Health Services
           X   Instructional
           Y   Noninstructional
           Z   Science
           A'   Social Worker Services

STRUCTURE WITH SIX LEVELS

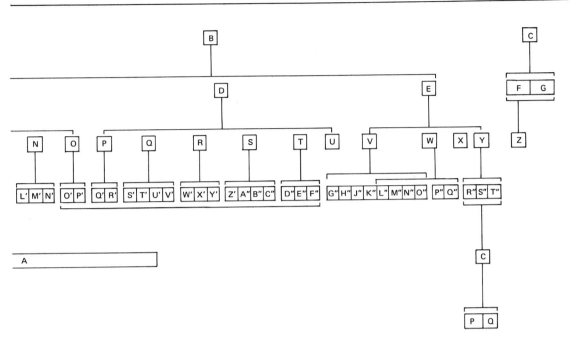

B'	Resource Center (Staff)
C'	Library (Pupils)
D'	Noninstructional Projects
E'	Instructional Programs
F'	Attendance
G'	Psychological
H'	Guidance
J'	Social Services
K'	Health
L'	Administration
M'	Operation
N'	Orientation
O'	Professional
P'	Nonprofessional
Q'	Regular
R'	Special
S'	Buildings
T'	Grounds
U'	Warehouse
V'	Management
W'	Buildings
X'	Grounds
Y'	Management
Z'	Breakfast Program
A"	Lunch Program
B"	Milk Program
C"	Management
D"	School Management Systems
E"	Student Information Systems
F"	Vocational and Instructional Systems
G"	Business Management
H"	Negotiations

J"	Noninstructional Program Development
K"	Noninstructional Program Evaluation
L"	Educational Program Development
M"	Educational Program Evaluation
N"	Community Information Program
O"	Staff Relations and Evaluation
P"	Student Relations
Q"	School Management and Operations
R"	Hall School Addition
S"	Portland West Community Elementary School
T"	Vocational

LEVEL V	A	Grade Span
	B	Grade (Systemwide or Undistributed)
	C	Grade Span (Systemwide)

LEVEL VI	A	Course
	B	Educable
	C	Trainable
	D	Speech Therapy
	E	Hospital
	F	Homebound
	G	Cerebral Palsy Center
	H	Driver Education
	J	Graphic Arts
	K	In-Service
	L	Publications
	M	Audiovisual
	N	Specific Program by Group, Class, Individual, or Project
	O	Testing
	P	Architect Selection
	Q	Project Development

FIGURE 6.   PROGRAM STRUCTURE—BY TARGET GROUP

Program Level	
I	District
II	Regular program (may be differentiated by ability levels)
II	Programs differentiated by environmental or cultural backgrounds of students
III	Culturally disadvantaged
III	Non-English speaking
IV	Individual tutoring
II	Programs for students with intellectual, physical, or emotional exceptionalities
III	Educable mentally retarded
III	Severe mentally retarded
III	Mentally gifted
III	Physically handicapped
III	Emotionally disturbed
III	Other learning disorders or educational handicaps
II	Programs differentiated according to student career options and capacities
III	Programs for training in different occupations
III	Programs to prepare for different areas of higher education
III	General programs
II	Programs for adults and others not in the normal school population
II	Programs not categorized by type of student

Source: Adopted from Table 2, A Possible Categorization of Programs by Type of Student, in S.A. Haggart et al., *Program Budgeting for School Planning: Concepts and Applications,* Englewood Cliffs, N.J.: Educational Technology Publications, 1971.

FIGURE 7.   PROGRAM STRUCTURE—BY GRADE LEVEL

1.   Preschool programs
2.   Kindergarten
3.   Elementary education—lower grades
           Grade 1
           Grade 2
           Grade 3
4.   Elementary education—upper grades
           Grade 4
           Grade 5
           Grade 6
5.   Junior high school education
           Grade 7
           Grade 8
           Grade 9
6.   High school education
           Grade 10
           Grade 11
           Grade 12
0.   Programs not categorized by level of instruction

Source: Adopted from Table 3, A Possible Categorization of Programs by Level of Instruction, in S.A. Haggart et al., *Program Budgeting for School Planning: Concepts and Applications,* Englewood Cliffs, N.J.: Educational Technology Publications, 1971.

FIGURE 8.   PROGRAM STRUCTURE—BY GRADE SPAN

1. Elementary
    - 1.01 English Language Arts
    - 1.02 Mathematics
    - 1.03 Social Studies
    - 1.04 Science
    - 1.05 Art
    - 1.06 Practical Arts
    - 1.07 Music
    - 1.08 Physical Education
    - 1.09 Foreign Languages
    - 1.10 Personal Hygiene and Sex Education
    - 1.11 Summer and Evening
    - 1.12 Vocational Courses
    - 1.13 Media
    - 1.14 Health Services
    - 1.15 Guidance and Counseling
    - 1.16 Student Activities
    - 1.17 Administration
    - 1.18 Maintenance and Operation of Plant
    - 1.19 Planning and Engineering
    - 1.20 Community Services

2. Junior High
    - 2.01 English Language Arts
    - 2.02 Mathematics
    - 2.03 Social Studies
    - 2.04 Science
    - 2.05 Art
    - 2.06 Practical Arts
    - 2.07 Music
    - 2.08 Physical Education
    - 2.09 Foreign Languages
    - 2.10 Personal Hygiene and Sex Education
    - 2.11 Summer and Evening
    - 2.12 Vocational Courses
    - 2.13 Media
    - 2.14 Health Services

FIGURE 8.   PROGRAM STRUCTURE—BY GRADE SPAN (cont'd)

      2.15 Guidance and Counseling
      2.16 Student Activities
      2.17 Administration
      2.18 Maintenance and Operation of Plant
      2.19 Planning and Engineering
      2.20 Community Services

3.   Senior High
      3.01 English Language Arts
      3.02 Mathematics
      3.03 Social Studies
      3.04 Science
      3.05 Art
      3.06 Practical Arts
      3.07 Music
      3.08 Physical Education
      3.09 Foreign Languages
      3.10 Personal Hygiene and Sex Education
      3.11 Summer and Evening
      3.12 Vocational Courses
      3.13 Media
      3.14 Health Services
      3.15 Guidance and Counseling
      3.16 Student Activities
      3.17 Administration
      3.18 Maintenance and Operation of Plant
      3.19 Planning and Engineering
      3.20 Community Services

4.   Vocational and Business Schools

5.   Adult Education

6.   Special Education for the Disabled and for Special Problems

7.   Central Administration

Source: *Organizing an Urban School System for Diversity,* Boston Public School District, prepared by Donald M. Levine as shown in mimeographed handout, October 1970.

FIGURE 9.   PROGRAM STRUCTURE—
BY BUILDING

Program Level	Program Description
I	District
II	Elementary
III	Adams
III	Jefferson
III	Lincoln
III	Hoover
III	Washington
II	Middle School
III	Windham
III	North Star
II	High School
III	North
III	West
III	East
II	Administration
II	Warehouse

FIGURE 10.   PROGRAM STRUCTURE—
BY EDUCATIONAL OBJECTIVE

Instructional Programs Aimed at Providing a Basic Education to all Students

1.   Learning fundamental intellectual skills
    1.1   Language and communication skills
    1.2   Quantitative and reasoning skills
    1.3   Study skills

2.   Learning about the world
    2.1   Learning about the U.S. and other societies
    2.2   Learning about the physical world and living things
    2.3   Learning about literature and the arts
    2.4   Learning knowledge and skills for everyday application

3.   Development of the individual physically, socially, and emotionally
    3.1   Physical development
    3.2   Development of means of self-expression
    3.3   Development of interpersonal relationships

Instructional Programs Aimed at Preparing Students for Specific Futures

4.   Learning knowledge and skills in preparation for future employment or occupational training
    (classified by occupation)

5.   Learning academic subjects to prepare for higher education
    (classified by academic field)

Direct Support of Instructional Programs

6.   Assessment, guidance, and counseling

7.   Program development and evaluation

8.   Instructional resource and media services

Ancillary and Support Programs

9.   Auxiliary services to students
    9.1   Health services
    9.2   Transportation
    9.3   Food services

10.   Community service programs

11.   Operation and maintenance of physical plant and equipment

12.   Provision of physical plant and equipment

13.   Administration and general support

Source: Table 1, Categorization of Activities into Programs According to Their Relationship to Educational Objectives, in S.A. Haggart et al., *Program Budgeting for School Planning: Concepts and Applications,* Englewood Cliffs, N.J.: Educational Technology Publications, 1971.

FIGURE 11.   PROGRAM STRUCTURE—COMBINATION OF

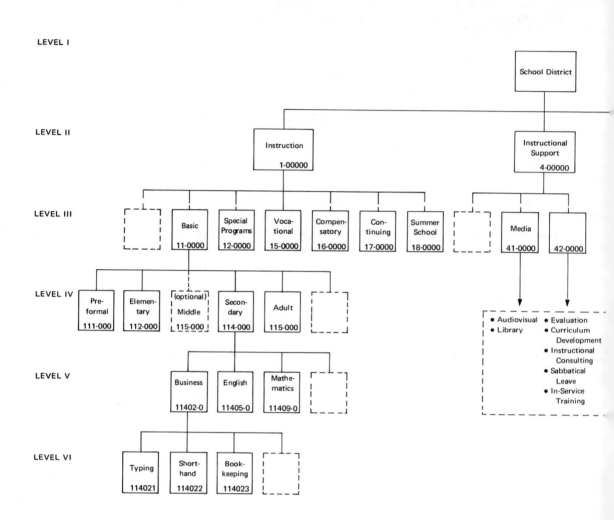

SUBJECT AREA AND GRADE SPAN

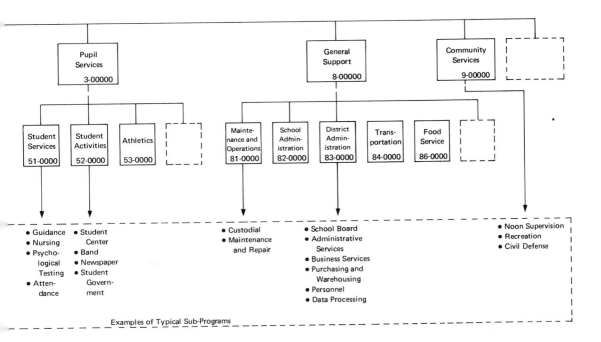

Source: Figure 5, Program Structure Guideline, *Conceptual Design for a Planning, Programming, Budgeting System for California School Districts*, Advisory Commission on School District Budgeting and Accounting, Sacramento, Calif., 1969, pp. 12 and 13.

FIGURE 12. EXAMPLES OF PHILOSOPHICAL OBJECTIVES

1. Students should acquire the intellectual skills basic to continuing self-development and further study.
2. Students should develop a capacity for critical thought and analysis.
3. Students should accept responsibility early for their own educational progress so they become adults for whom learning is a natural part of life.
4. Students should learn to practice the principles and qualities of thought needed for democratic citizenship and responsible participation in a multi-racial, multi-cultural society.
5. Students should develop the perspectives, competence, and skills needed for living in a world of close international interdependence.
6. Students should be helped to develop a full measure of self-awareness and emotional stability.
7. Students should be given opportunities for self-realization through the development of their artistic abilities and interests.
8. Students' development should include attention to, and responsibility for, the needs of physical fitness.
9. The central focus of the Westport school should be on the special needs and abilities of the individual student.
10. Our schools should seek to enhance the relevance and purpose of education.
11. Our school system should sustain an extensive program to develop and maintain a high quality of teaching performance.
12. Our school system should develop an effective program of innovation and evaluation, designed to search out and test improved means of achieving maximum educational impact.
13. Our schools should become year-round educational centers for the whole community.
14. Our school system should develop more fully its role in a regional educational community.

Source: *Report of the Advisory Committee on School Goals to the Board of Education, Westport, Conn.,* Ian H. Wilson, Chairman, June 1969, p. 3.

FIGURE 13.   ILLUSTRATIVE INSTRUCTIONAL PROGRAM
OBJECTIVES

Level I Program: Math

Example

Objective: To provide experiences that develop skills, attitudes, and understanding necessary for success with practical and theoretical mathematics.

Criteria: Upon completion of high school education:

100% of students will have 6th grade competency
90% of students will have 7th grade competency
80% of students will have 8th grade competency
70% of students will have 9th grade competency
60% of students will have 10th grade competency

as measured by standarized achievement tests in mathematics and based on national grade-equivalent norms.

Level II Program: General Math

Example

Objective: To build skills in fundamental operations of arithmetic on rational numbers.

Criteria: Upon completion of the course 90% of the students will make scores of 60% or higher on a departmental test which adequately tests for comprehension of the fundamental operations in arithmetic.

Level III Program: Third Grade Math

Example

Objective: To strive for mastery of the multiplication tables through the nines by the end of the school year.

Criteria: By the end of the third grade 90% of the students will make a score of 60% or better on a teacher-made test which adequately tests for mastery of the multiplication tables through the nines.

FIGURE 14. SUPPORT SERVICE OBJECTIVES
—FOOD SERVICE

Goal: School officials must provide adequate food service to alleviate hunger and to meet the nutrition needs of all students in the district.

Specific Objectives

Activities

1. Food service must be available in every school within the five-year period. Currently, the district has 25 schools and approximately 30,000 students without food service. Five schools should be selected to have centralized kitchen facilities installed; each of the five schools will serve hot meals to five additional schools.

1. The school district shall proceed with financial arrangements to provide the funds for construction of five central kitchen operations.

    a. Correlate the timing of a bond issue with the reports on the needs from the health authorities.

    b. Investigate the possibility of securing federal funds.

    c. Contact the state authorities for possible assistance.

2. Menus shall be planned which will provide nutritionally adequate, nonprofit food service programs for all students.

2. All food service programs shall serve Type A meals to all students. Vitamin A shall be served daily and Vitamin C rich food at least three times each week. Institute a program of nutrition education. All schools shall have appropriate, planned programs of nutrition education as part of the curriculum at all grade levels instituted within the five-year period.

    The program must be "popularized" to the students.

FIGURE 14. SUPPORT SERVICE OBJECTIVES
—FOOD SERVICE (continued)

Specific Objectives	Activities
	a. Improve pupil acceptance (this might be done through multiple choice Type A lunches).
	b. Arouse concern among the parents. This may be accomplished through visits of public health nurses to the homes and study groups.
	c. "Spot announcements" in the news media to attract attention to the value of the menu and also to the necessity of eating nutritionally adequate meals.
3. Additional food programs shall be instituted to meet the needs of the students as the needs are identified through documented evidences of the county health department.	3. Needs must be identified by: a. Documentation through use of such services as the county health department, dental societies, and medical groups. b. Needs must be made known to the public. c. Reports coordinating information which has been developed by the applicable agencies shall be published.

Source: Irene Y. Ponti, *A Guide for Financing School Food and Nutrition Services,* Chicago, Ill., American School Food Service Association and the Research Corporation of the Association of School Business Officials, 1970, pp. 47-48.

FIGURE 15.   DEVELOPMENT OF OBJECTIVES

Program Level	Program Structure	Type of Objective	Year of PPBS Installation	
			1st	2nd
I	District	Philosophical	Prepare objective	Review and update
II	Instruction	Philosophical	Prepare objective	Review and update
III	Regular Instruction	Philosophical	Prepare objective	Review and update
IV	Subject Area, Grades K-12	Instructional Program	Prepare English Language Arts only	Prepare all programs
V	Course	Instructional Program	—	Prepare English Language Arts

OVER A FIVE-YEAR TIME SPAN

Year of PPBS Installation		
3rd	4th	5th
Review and update	Review and update	Review and update
Review and update	Review and update	Review and update
Review and update	Review and update	Review and update
Review and update	Review and update	Review and update
Review English, Language Arts, do Mathematics and Science	Review previous programs, do Social Studies and Physical Education	Review previous programs, do balance of pro- grams

FIGURE 16.   IOX OBJECTIVE

Objective 1   Biology
Major Category: Biological Themes   Grade 10-12
Sub-Category: The Nature of Scientific Inquiry

Objective: Given any observable phenomenon, either static or
                dynamic, the student will first collect data on the
                phenomenon and then categorize this data as either
                quantitative or qualitative observations.

Criteria: The *quantitative* observations must be based on some sort
                of measurement. They must not include any judgments of
                cause-and-effect that are not measured.

                The *qualitative* observations can be based on sense
                impressions and may include judgments that are not
                measures. Statements of color and touch sensations are
                relative to the individual and may be permitted in
                qualitative observations but not in quantitative.

Sample Item: Observe a candle burning. Write down as many things as
                you can about the burning candle. Then put all the
                quantitative observations under the heading of "quantita-
                tive" and the qualitative observations under the heading
                of "qualitative."

Sample Answer:

Quantitative	Qualitative
1. The candle is 6" high.	1. The flame of the candle is hot to the touch.
2. The flame of the candle is 1" high when left to burn undis-turbed.	2. The flame of the candle is mostly yellow.
3. After 3 minutes, 3 oz. of wax dripped down the side of the candle and formed a puddle at the base.	3. The melted wax is soft to the touch.
4. The candle weighs 10 oz.	4. Waving the hand rapidly over the candle makes the flame move.
5. After 5 minutes of burning, the candle weighs 9.5 oz.	5. The wick turns black where the flame has been.

Source: *Instructional Objectives Exchange, Biology, 10-12*, Study of Evaluation,
UCLA Graduate School of Education, 1970, p. 1.

FIGURE 17.   AMERICAN BOOK COMPANY OBJECTIVES

Checkup Test 1   And So You Go!

A.1. Given five known words with three of the words rhyming, the pupil will be able to recognize and draw a line under the words that rhyme (me, she, we)—all being personal pronouns.

A.2. Given three groups of words with four words in each group. In two of the groups all of the words rhyme while in the third group, the words do not rhyme. The two rhyming groups are composed of personal pronouns. The pupil will be able to identify and draw a circle around the group in which the words do not rhyme (and, pat, man, I), and the pupil will be able to underline two words in this group that he can read.

B.1. Given the spoken words, "he, she, and me," and three words, one of which rhymes with the spoken words. The pupil will be able to identify and circle the word that rhymes with the spoken words he, she, and me (be).

B.2. Given four known words (he, me, she, and we) all of which rhyme and are personal pronouns. The pupil will be able to identify and circle the personal pronoun that he could use to talk about himself. Given four new words with one rhyming with the four known words, the pupil will be able to recognize and circle the word in the new-word group that rhymes with all of the words in the known-word group he, me, she, and we (be).

Comprehension

C.1. Given two sentences, punctuated with a question mark and exclamation point respectively, and the spoken instructions to circle the sentence that asks a question. The pupil will be able to identify and correctly circle the sentence that uses a question mark to indicate that it is a question (Me?).

C.2. Given two sentences, punctuated with a question mark and an exclamation point respectively, the pupil will be able to identify and put a line under the sentence that asks a question (He and she?). The pupil will also be able to circle the part of the sentence that tells him it is a question (?).

C.3, Given the spoken referents boy, girl, and children and three words,
 4, with two or more being personal pronouns, the pupil will be able to
 5. draw a circle around the pronoun (he) for the referent boy; the pupil will be able to circle the pronoun (she) for the referent girl; the pupil will be able to circle the pronoun (we) referring to all the children in his class.

C.6, Given three spoken referents father, mother, and family, and three
 7, words two or more being personal pronouns, the pupil will be able to
 8. circle the pronoun (we) for the referent family; the pupil will be able to circle the pronoun (she) for the referent mother; the pupil will be able to circle the pronoun (he) for the referent father.

Source: *Preliminary Compilation of Behavioral Objectives, The Read System,* New York, N.Y., Litton Educational Publishing, Inc., 1970, p. 1.

FIGURE 18. EVOLUTION OF OBJECTIVES

Project Title: *Diagnostic Reading Clinic*

1966 Objectives: The Diagnostic Reading Clinic will be organized to attain the following objectives:
1. To provide services related to diagnosing reading problems.
2. To provide prognostic information that can be translated into instructional practices.
3. To provide in-service training for elementary school teachers.
4. To provide remedial reading for selected pupils.

1967 Objectives: The aims of this program include the following:
1. To improve reading skills of children with serious reading disabilities in an effort to bring them to an appropriate functioning for their grade level.
2. To provide services related to the diagnosis of reading difficulties.
3. To increase the competency of the classroom teachers in using diagnostic and remedial information.

1968 Objectives: The aims of the Diagnostic Reading Clinic include the following:
1. To improve the reading skills of children with serious reading disabilities in an effort to bring them up to an appropriate level for their reading expectancy, which shall be determined by the Bond-Tinker formula.

   Two criteria will be considered indicative of appropriate functioning:
   a. Independent performance by the pupil with materials in use in his regular classroom at least half of the time, and
   b. Achievement on standardized test and inventories within at least a half-year of his reading-expectancy level.
2. To coordinate services of related disciplines in the diagnosis and correction of reading difficulties.
3. To facilitate parental involvement and support in remediation of pupil reading disabilities.
4. To increase competency of classroom teachers of pupils referred in the use of diagnostic and remedial information through consultation with clinic staff and follow-up service for pupils in their classrooms.

Source: Joseph L. Davis and Martin W. Essex, *Educational Evaluation,* Columbus, Ohio: State Superintendent of Public Instruction, 1969, p. 54.

FIGURE 19.   PROGRAM OBJECTIVES

☐ Philosophical Objective	Program Area	Level	Code
☐ Instructional Program Objective	Program Description		
☐ Support Service Program Objective			
Objective	Evidence that will indicate that the objective was achieved	Time Frame	
Prepared By	Date	Reviewed By	Date

FIGURE 20.   TESTS RELATED

EDUCATIONAL OBJECTIVE TEST NAME		MEASUREMENT VALIDITY		EXAMINEE APPROPRIATENESS						
				Compre-hension		Format			
		Content and Construct	Concurrent and Predictive	Content	Instruc-tions	Visual Principles	Quality of Illustrations	Time and Pacing	Recording Responses
Rating Range		0-10	0-5	0-4	0-4	0-2	0-2	0-2	0-2
Performance									
9. CREATIVITY									
Torrance Tests of Creative Thinking Total	(GC)	7	3	3	3	1	2	1	2
A. Creative Flexibility									
Torrance Tests of Creative Thinking Figural Flexibility	(GC)	7	3	4	3	1	2	1	2
Torrance Tests of Creative Thinking Verbal Flexibility	(GC)	7	3	4	3	1	2	1	2
B. Creative Fluency									
Illinois Test of Psycholinguistic Abilities Verbal Expression	(UIP)	6	0	3	3	2	2	1	2
Reading Aptitude Tests Language	(HMC)	5	0	3	4	1	1	0	2
Torrance Tests of Creative Thinking Figural Elaboration	(GC)	7	3	4	3	1	2	1	2
Torrance Tests of Creative Thinking Figural Fluency	(GC)	7	3	4	3	1	2	1	2
Torrance Tests of Creative Thinking Figural Originality	(GC)	7	3	4	3	1	2	1	2
Torrance Tests of Creative Thinking Verbal Fluency	(GC)	7	3	4	3	1	2	1	2
Torrance Tests of Creative Thinking Verbal Originality	(GC)	7	3	4	3	1	2	1	2

Source: *CSE Elementary School Test Evaluations*, Los Angeles, Calif.: UCLA Graduate School of Education 1970, p. 6.

TO EDUCATIONAL OBJECTIVES

ADMINISTRATIVE USABILITY										NORMED TECHNICAL EXCELLENCE						TOTAL GRADES
Administration			Scoring	Interpretation						Stability	Internal Consistency	Alternate Form	Replicability	Range of Coverage	Gradation of Scores	
Test Administration	Training of Admstr.	Administration Time		Norm Range	Score Interpretation	Score Conversion	Norm Groups	Score Interpreter	Can Decisions Be Made?							
0-2	0-1	0-1	0-2	0-1	0-1	0-2	0-1	0-1	0-3	0-3	0-3	0-3	0-1	0-3	0-2	Good Fair Poor
1	1	0	0	1	1	1	0	0	2	1	0	1	1	2	1	F G P P
1	1	1	0	1	1	1	0	0	2	0	0	0	1	2	1	F G F P
1	1	1	0	1	1	1	0	0	2	0	0	2	1	2	1	F G F P
0	0	1	1	1	1	2	0	0	1	0	0	0	0	1	2	P G P P
0	1	1	1	0	1	2	0	1	2	0	0	0	1	3	2	P F F P
1	1	1	0	1	1	1	0	0	2	0	0	1	1	2	1	F G F P
1	1	1	0	1	1	1	0	0	2	0	0	0	1	2	1	F G F P
1	1	1	0	1	1	1	0	0	2	0	0	1	1	2	1	F G F P
1	1	1	0	1	1	1	0	0	2	0	0	2	1	3	1	F G F P
1	1	1	0	1	1	1	0	0	1	0	0	2	1	3	1	F G P P

FIGURE 21.   COMPARISON OF BUDGET SUMMARY BY PROGRAMS
WITH BUDGET SUMMARY BY TRADITIONAL FUNCTIONS

Budget Summary by Program

Program Title	Budget
INSTRUCTIONAL PROGRAMS	
English, Language Arts and Reading	$ 942,116
Science (including health)	447,945
Mathematics	455,593
Social Studies	391,437
Physical Education, Intramurals and Inter-scholastic Athletics	303,415
Business	69,749
Foreign Languages	154,797
Unified Arts	126,292
Art	102,243
Music	144,067
Special Education	73,371
Vocational Education	49,064
Adult Education	10,413
INSTRUCTIONAL SUPPORT PROGRAMS	
Library	145,295
Guidance and Psychological Services	194,753
Health Services	97,597
Bond Principal and Interest	516,608
Operation and Maintenance of Plant	613,087
School Management	361,374
Central Office Management	311,121
Transportation	176,295
School Lunch	—
Non-Program	35,190
COMMUNITY SERVICES PROGRAMS	7,041
GRAND TOTAL	$5,728,863

Budget Summary by Traditional Function

Function Title	Budget
Board of Education	$ 23,275
Central Administration	196,180
Instruction	3,355,585
Community Services	6,000
Transportation	182,015
Operation and Maintenance of Plant	511,995
Undistributed Expenses	937,205
Debt Service	516,608
TOTALS	$5,728,863

Source: Pearl River School District, N.Y., *Brochure of 1970-1971 School Operating Budget,* p. 3.

FIGURE 22.   ILLUSTRATIVE PROGRAM STRUCTURE WITH
SIX-DIGIT PROGRAM CODES

		Program Code				
	Program Structure	Level I	Level II	Level III	Level IV	Level V
Level	Description					
I	District	None	—	—	—	—
II	Instruction	—	1	—	—	—
III	Regular Instruction	—	—	1	—	—
IV	English, K-12	—	—	—	10	—
V	Grade	—	—	—	—	00-12
IV	Social Studies, K-12	—	—	—	11	—
V	Grade	—	—	—	—	00-12
IV	Science, K-12	—	—	—	12	—
V	Grade	—	—	—	—	00-12
IV	Mathematics, K-12	—	—	—	13	—
V	Grade	—	—	—	—	00-12
IV	Nonprogram	—	—	—	00	—
III	Occupational Education	—	—	2	—	—
III	Special Education	—	—	3	—	—
III	Continuing Education	—	—	4	—	—
II	Supporting Services	—	2	—	—	—
III	Pupil Personnel Services	—	—	5	—	—
IV	Attendance	—	—	—	30	—
IV	Guidance	—	—	—	31	—
IV	Health	—	—	—	32	—
IV	Social Work	—	—	—	33	—
II	Community Services	—	3	—	—	—

Note: Program Level I (District) has not been provided a program code. The total of all program codes would equal the total district—Level I.

This illustration is based on a subject area program structure.

FIGURE 23.   ILLUSTRATIVE PROGRAM STRUCTURE
WITH THREE-DIGIT PROGRAM CODES

Program Structure		Program Code	
Level	Description	Level IV	Level V
I	District	—	—
II	Instruction	—	—
III	Regular Instruction	—	—
IV	English, K-12	15	—
V	Grades K-5	—	E
V	Grades 6-8	—	M
V	Grades 9-12	—	H
	Districtwide	—	D
IV	Science, K-12	20	—
V	Grades K-5	—	E
V	Grades 6-8	—	M
V	Grades 9-12	—	H
	Districtwide	—	D
IV	Social Studies, K-12	25	—
V	Grades K-5	—	E
V	Grades 6-8	—	M
V	Grades 9-12	—	H
	Districtwide	—	D
	Nonprogram	00	—

Note: In this figure program codes for program levels I through III have not been provided. The total for program level III can be determined by adding together all of the applicable program level IV categories. The same process can be followed for levels I and II.

FIGURE 24.   PURCHASE ORDER ILLUSTRATING PROGRAM CODING

PURCHASE ORDER
BOARD OF EDUCATION
CENTRAL SCHOOL DISTRICT

MAIL
INVOICE
TO

ATTENTION
ACCOUNTS PAYABLE

DATE 4	PURCH CLASS 29	PURCHASE ORDER 30
Dec. 4, 197X	3	4083

SCHOOL OR DEPARTMENT
Middle School + High School

VENDOR'S
NAME
AND
ADDRESS

A. C. Mullen & Co.
48 West 43rd Street
New York, New York

VENDOR CODE 10
2080

ZIP CODE 5 *10007*

DESC 35	APPROPRIATION CODE					AMOUNT	
	FUND 37	PROG 39	LOC 41	FUNC 43	OBJ 46	64	71
03	A0	25	H	220	300	15	—
03	10	25	H	220	300	25	—

Note

SHIP TO   *Central School District*
37 Pierce Avenue
Central, New York   59601

FOLD

REMARKS

PURCHASER IS TAX EXEMPT.
EXEMPTION CERTIFICATE ON
REQUEST.

REQUESTED BY   *W. F.*   TOTAL   *40 —*

REQUISITION NO. *1042*	DELIVERY DATE	VIA		VENDOR'S REF. NO. *None*	QUOTATION NO.	QUOTATION DATE

QUANTITY	UNIT	DESCRIPTION	UNIT PRICE	AMOUNT
200	*ea.*	*Social Studies outline maps of Asia (Revised edition) 75 for Middle School 125 for High School*	*$0.20*	*$40.00*

IMPORTANT INSTRUCTIONS TO VENDOR

IF UNABLE TO FILL ORDER IN EXACT ACCORDANCE WITH ABOVE SPECIFICATIONS, PRICE AND CONDITIONS, REQUEST FURTHER INSTRUCTIONS BEFORE SHIPPING. ALL FREIGHT AND DELIVERY CHARGES MUST BE PREPAID. INVOICE AND PACKAGE MUST BEAR ABOVE ORDER NUMBER. YOUR INVOICE MUST APPLY TO THIS PURCHASE ORDER ONLY.

APPROVAL OF FUNDS
DATE
INITIALS

ESTIMATED TOTAL   *$40.00*

AUTHORIZED BY   *George G. Kinsey*
PURCHASING AGENT

FORM 183 (9-69) 3M B.O.

1. VENDOR'S COPY

FIGURE 25. ILLUSTRATIVE STANDARD LIST OF GENERAL SUPPLIES
(Partial list only)

Name of School   West High School

Item No.	Description	Quantity Required	Unit	Unit Cost	Total Cost
	Binders:				
1.	Flexible Cover—3 ring	150	each	3.60	540.00
2.	Hard Cover—2″—3 ring	200	each	4.80	960.00
3.	Punchless—Gussco—Blue	50	each	.40	20.00
4.	Punchless—Gussco—Green	50	each	.40	20.00
5.	Spring Back, Open Side—1″ Cap. #37 Elbe or equivalent	75	each	1.15	86.25
6.	Vernon Royal Line R-2971 or equivalent—3 ring	25	each	.45	11.25
7.	Blotter Pads, Desk—19 X 24 leather corners	250	each	.70	175.00
8.	Blotting Paper, Brown—100 lb. 19 X 24	500	each	.10	50.00
	Calendar Pad Refills—1970:				
9.	W 170—Work-A-Day	125	each	.80	100.00
10.	W 345—Work-A-Day	—	each	.42	--
11.	#46½—Everready	—	each	.84	—
12.	#58½—Everready	—	each	.93	—
13.	Calendar Stand—3⅝ X 6—Green Book-Opening, Loose-Leaf	25	each	1.27	31.75
14.	Calendar Stand & Pad—W 345C Book-Opening, Loose-Leaf	50	each	1.45	72.50
15.	Carbon Letter Sets—with One-Time Carbon—100/box	350	box	3.25	1137.50
16.	Carbon Paper, Colonial—Black 8½ X 11—100/box	200	box	1.15	230.00

Total $3434.25

FIGURE 26.   ALLOCATION OF WEST HIGH SCHOOL STANDARD
LIST OF GENERAL SUPPLIES BY PROGRAM

Program	Program* Code	Percent Estimated Usage	Budget** Allocation
English	15H	40	$1374
Science	20H	15	515
Social Studies	25H	25	859
Nonprogram	00	20	686
Total		100	$3434

*Program coding is based on Figure 23.

**For budget purposes figures are rounded to the nearest whole dollar.

FIGURE 27.   COUNTING STAFF MEMBERS—SCIENCE

	Actual Count of Staff Members	Count Based on Full-Time Equivalent Staff
Teacher A	1	1.0
Teacher B	1	1.0
Teacher C (works half-time)	1	0.5
Teacher D	1	1.0
Teacher E	1	1.0
Teacher F	1	1.0
Teacher G	1	1.0
Teacher H (works half-time)	1	0.5
Teacher I	1	1.0
Teacher J	1	1.0
Teacher K	1	1.0
Teacher L (works half-time)	1	0.5
Teacher M	1	1.0
Teacher N	1	1.0
Teacher O	1	1.0
Total	15	13.5

FIGURE 28.   PORTLAND PUBLIC SCHOOLS STAFF—
FULL-TIME-EQUIVALENCY STANDARDS

	Hrs/Day	Hrs/Wk	Days/Wk	Days/Yr	Wks/Yr	Hrs/Yr	FTE Standard
Classified Personnel							
a. Cafeteria	8	—	—	194	—	1552	1552 Hrs
b. Secretarial	—	37.5	—	—	52	1950	1950 Hrs
c. Custodial & maintenance	—	40	—	—	52	2080	2080 Hrs
d. Teacher aides & assistants	7.5	—	—	183	—	1372.5	1372.5 Hrs
Certificated Personnel							
a. Teachers	—	—	—	183	—	—	183 Days
b. Directors	—	—	—	193	—	—	193 Days
c. Administrators	—	40	—	—	52	2080	2080 Hrs

Source: *Procedure for the Preparation of the 1971 Educational Program*, Portland, Maine: Central Office Edition, Portland Public School System, July 9, 1970, p. 8.

FIGURE 29.   ALLOCATION OF FOURTH-GRADE
TEACHING STAFF BY PROGRAM

Program	(1) Hours Per Week	(2) Percent of Total	(3) Teaching Staff Allocation FTE
Language Arts	10	40	4.8
Science	3	12	1.5
Social Studies	4	16	1.9
Mathematics	5	20	2.4
Physical Education	3	12	1.4
Total	25	100	12.0*

*Total number of fourth-grade teachers—12.

Column 1, showing hours of instruction per week by program, is based on the analysis of time spent by one fourth-grade teacher.

Column 2 shows the percent of time spent on each program based on Column 1. For example, the percentage for Language Arts is computed as follows:

$$\frac{\text{Hours spent in Language Arts}}{\text{Total Hours}} = \frac{10}{25} = 40\%$$

Column 3 shows the FTE for each program. Language Arts is computed as follows:

$$\begin{array}{ccc} \text{Total no. of fourth-} & \times & \text{Percentage} & = & \text{FTE} \\ \text{grade teachers} & & \text{Language Arts} & & \text{Language Arts} \\ 12.0 & & 40\% & & 4.8 \end{array}$$

FIGURE 30.   ALLOCATION OF SALARIES BY PROGRAM
USING INDIVIDUAL SALARIES

Name	Position:	Grade:	Building:	Card No.:
Phillip Kinsey	Teacher	11th	High School	204

Program Code	Program Title	Current Year		Budget Year	
		FTE	Actual Salary	FTE	Budget Salary
	English				
	Science				
	Mathematics				
	Social Studies				
	Physical Education				
	Business				
	Total				

Note: This form could be placed on a 5" × 8" card for ease in preparation and use.

FIGURE 31.   ALLOCATION OF SALARIES BY PROGRAM
USING AVERAGE SALARIES

I. Computation of Average Teacher Salary

	Total Teacher Salaries	No. of Staff FTE	Average Salary
Current Year Actual	$1,203,500	150.2	$8013
Budget Year Estimate	$1,387,200	158.4	$8758

II. Allocation of Salaries by Program (Based on Illustration Shown in Figure 29)

Phillip Kinsey Program	Current Year		Budget Year	
	FTE	Actual Salary	FTE	Budget Salary
Science	0.5	$4006	0.3	$2627
Mathematics	0.5	4007	0.7	6131
Total	1.0	$8013	1.0	$8758

FIGURE 32.   COMPUTATION OF EMPLOYEE
BENEFIT PERCENTAGE

Description		Budget Amount
Teachers' Retirement		$305,000
Non-Teaching Retirement		75,000
Social Security		50,000
Health Insurance		38,000
Workmen's Compensation Insurance		4,250
	Total	$472,250

$$\frac{\text{Total Employee Benefit Budget}}{\text{Total Salary Budget}} \quad \frac{\$472,250}{\$2,977,000} = 15.86$$

15.86% = Employee Benefit Percentage

FIGURE 33.   ALLOCATION OF EMPLOYEE
BENEFITS TO PROGRAMS

Program Description	Program Code	Salary Budget	Employee Benefit Allocation
English, Grades K-5	15E	$ 290,000	$ 45,994
English, Grades 6-8	15M	73,000	11,578
English, Grades 9-12	15H	84,000	13,322
English, Districtwide	15D	22,000	3,489
Science, Grades K-5	20E	92,000	14,591
Science, Grades 6-8	20M	125,000	19,825
Science, Grades 9-12	20H	140,000	22,204
Science, Districtwide	20D	18,000	2,855
Totals		$2,977,000	$472,250

Note: Allocation is based on an Employee Benefit Percentage of 15.86%.

FIGURE 34.   SUMMARY WORKSHEET BY ACCOUNT CODE

Account Code Description Teaching—Textbooks	Fund A	Program (see below)	Building (see below)	Function 220	Object 398
Program \ Building	00 District- wide	01 North	02 West	03 East	Total
Nonprogram					
English					
Science					
Mathematics					
Social Studies					
Physical Education					
Business					
Foreign Language					
Unified Arts					
Art					
Music					
Totals					

FIGURE 35.   PERSONNEL AND BUDGET BY PROGRAM

Personnel Summary (in full-time-equivalent personnel)

Program Title: Social Studies, K-12 | | | Program Code: 63

Position Title	Actual	Recommended Budget	Change
Summary of Staff			
Certificated staff	26.9	26.4	−0.5
Noncertificated staff	—	—	—
Total	26.9	26.4	−0.5
Certificated Staff			
Elementary			
Curriculum coordinator	0.3	0.3	—
Classroom teachers, K	0.5	0.5	—
Classroom teachers, 1-5	9.9	9.3	−0.6
Total elementary	10.7	10.1	−0.6
Middle school			
Curriculum coordinator	0.3	0.3	—
Classroom teachers	6.2	5.4	−0.8
Total middle school	6.5	5.7	−0.8
High school			
Curriculum coordinator	0.4	0.4	—
Classroom teachers	9.3	10.2	+0.9
Total high school	9.7	10.6	+0.9

Program Budget

Program Title: Social Studies, K-12 | | | | | Program Code: 63

	Elementary	Middle School	High School	District-wide	Total
Certificated Staff					
Regular salaries	$109,131	$50,056	$123,084	$2,250	$284,521
Substitutes & overtime	3,025	1,815	3,630	—	8,470
Employee benefits	28,506	14,836	32,252	565	76,159
Total	$140.662	$66,707	$158,966	$2,815	$369,150
Noncertificated Staff					
Regular salaries	—	—	—	—	—
Substitutes & overtime	—	—	—	—	—
Employee benefits	—	—	—	—	—
Total	—	—	—	—	—
Other Expenses					
Equipment	$ 839	$ 200	$ 608	—	$ 1,647
Supplies	4,000	2,500	3,000	—	9,500
Textbooks	4,600	1,200	3,100	—	8,900
Purchased services	—	310	360	1,570	2,240
Total	$ 9,439	$ 4,210	$ 7,068	$1,570	$ 22,287
Grand Total	$150,101	$70,917	$166,034	$4,385	$391,437
Number of Students Served	1,531	910	1,247	3,688	3,688
Budget per Student Served	$98	$78	$133	$1	$106

FIGURE 36. PROGRAM BUDGET WORKSHEET

Function-Object Description	Function-Object Code	Total	Allocation by Program					
			English	Science	Mathematics	Social Studies	Physical Education	Non-program
Salaries, Certificated	220-110	240,000	120,000	40,000	30,000	20,000	30,000	—
Equipment	220-200	50,000	10,000	30,000	2,000	4,000	4,000	—
Supplies and Materials	220-300	70,000	5,000	20,000	10,000	25,000	10,000	—
Textbooks	220-398	30,000	15,000	5,000	3,000	7,000	—	—
Other Expenses	220-400	20,000	2,000	3,000	6,000	4,000	2,000	3,000
Tuition to Other Districts	220-501	10,000	—	—	—	—	—	10,000
Totals		3,125,000*	1,110,000	610,000	583,000	574,000	230,000	18,000

*This figure should agree with the total function-object budget total.

FIGURE 37.   ANNUAL SUMMARY OF ACTUAL
SALARY AND EMPLOYEE BENEFITS

Employee Name	Position Title	Salary Paid	Employee Benefits Paid	Distribution by Program		
				Program Code	Salary	Benefits
Totals		*	**		*	**

*These totals should agree with that in Figure 38.
**These totals should agree with that in Figure 38.

FIGURE 38.   SUMMARY BY PROGRAM

Program Description	Program Code	Salary	Employee Benefits	Total
Totals		*	**	

*This total should agree with those in Figure 37.

**This total should agree with those in Figure 37.

FIGURE 39.   ALLOCATION OF ACTUAL COST
OF A STANDARD SUPPLY LIST

Program	Program Code	(1) Percent Estimated Use	(2) Budget	(3) Actual
English	15 H	40	$1374	$1328.87
Science	20 H	15	515	498.33
Social Studies	25 H	25	859	830.55
Nonprogram	00	20	686	664.43
Total		100	$3434	$3322.18

Note: Based on illustration of West High School Standard Supply List shown in Figure 25.

Columns 1 and 2 show the budget allocation.

Column 3 shows the actual cost of these supplies as $3322.18. This actual cost was allocated to each program based on the percent of estimated use as shown in Column 1. For example, English is computed as follows:

$$\frac{\text{Total actual costs}}{\text{General supplies}} \times \frac{\text{Percent}}{\text{estimated}} = \frac{\text{English program}}{\text{allocation}}$$

$$\$3322.18 \quad \times \quad 40\% \quad = \quad \$1328.87$$

FIGURE 40.   SUMMARY JOURNAL OF
VOUCHER CHECKS BY PROGRAM

Fund	Month	Year	
Program Description	Program Code	Amount	Posted (✓)
Total		*	

*This total should agree with voucher check register total.

FIGURE 41.   PROGRAM COST WORKSHEET

Program Description			Program Code		Budget	
Month	Year	Posting Source	Current Month		Year-to-date	
July						
August						
September						
October						
November						
December						
January						
February						
March						
April						
May						
June						
Salary cost for year		/////	/////			
Employee benefit cost for year		/////	/////			
Total program cost for year		/////	/////			

FIGURE 42.   MONTHLY PROGRAM EXPENDITURES

Month:		Year:		
Program	Program Code	Budget	Year-to-date Actual	Unspent Balance

Note: A column to show current month actual expenditures could be added to this report if desired by a district.

| Totals | | | | |

FIGURE 43.   COMPUTER-PREPARED FINANCIAL REPORTS

Title and Use	Illustrative Report— See Figure	Information Shown
Revenue Reports		
Revenue ledger		
used by business office	44	Detail of each revenue account
Revenue report		
used by the school business administrator for reviewing revenues	45	Summary of revenues by program and source
Expenditure Reports		
Program		
used by the program director for program management	46	Costs for each program by function-object of expense and building. Note that this report does not show regular salaries and employee benefits which only show on the year-end report.
Building		
used by the building principal for building management	47	Cost for each building by function-object and program
Detail function-object		
used by the school business administrator for budget management	48	Cost for each function-object by program and building
Summary function-object		
used by the school business administrator for fiscal control of expenditures	49	Cost for each function-object
Expense ledger		
used by business office	50	Detail for each expense account.

FIGURE 44.   REVENUE LEDGER

GENERAL FUND

DEN ACCOUNT F P L	FN OBVEN	DESCRIPTION	REF.	I.D. DT	ESTIMATE ORIG	ESTIMATE REVS	RECEIPTS CURR	RECEIPTS TO DATE	UNRLD BAL
521A0	001464	SALES SUPPLS			20000	20000			
533A0	001464		031				35560	35560	15560−
530A0	001464			CR081120			35560	35560	15560−
				TOTAL	20000	20000	35560	35560	15560−
		SALES SUPPLS TOTAL			20000	20000	35560	35560	15560−
521A0	001469	SALES BK A E			30000	30000		4460	
533A0	001469		031				6644		
530A0	001469			CR070104			534		
530A0	001469			CR080119					
				TOTAL	30000	30000	7178	11638	18362
		SALES BK A E TOTAL			30000	30000	7178	11638	18362
521A0	001470	INSURANCE			100000	100000			
533A0	001470		031				53000	64851	
530A0	001470			CR070104			42439		
530A0	001470			CR074110			197032		
530A0	001470			CR081120					
				TOTAL	100000	100000	292471	357322	257322−
		INSURANCE TOTAL			100000	100000	292471	357322	257322−
521A0	001471	LOST BOOKS	031		80000	80000		8767	
533A0	001471	E2104R CORNISHO					350−		
577A0	001471	E4275T KENNY 0					350−		
577A0	001471			JE040130			3000		
510A0	001471			CR070104			800		
530A0	001471			CR070104			2500		
530A0	001471			CR072106			800	15832	
530A0	001471			CR078117			665	15832	64168
530A0	001471			TOTAL	80000	80000	7065		
		LOST BOOKS TOTAL			80000	80000	7065	15832	64168

ACCOUNTING REPORTS=BOCES FORM AF-0028-669=

FIGURE 45. REVENUE REPORT

GENERAL FUND

DEN	ACCOUNT	DESCRIPTION		ESTIMATE		RECEIPTS		UNRLD
				ORIG	REVS	CURR	TO DATE	BAL
		REVENUE FROM LOCAL						
592A0	001110	PROP TAXES		365704800	365704800		365726909	22109—
		PROP TAXES	TOTAL	365704800	365704800		365726909	22109—
592A0	001220	AD ED TUITN		980000	980000	14500	419065	560935
		AD ED TUITN	TOTAL	980000	980000	14500—	419065	560935
592A0	001230	SUMMER TUITN		70000	70000		77400	7400—
		SUMMER TUITN	TOTAL	70000	70000	—	77400	7400—
592A0	001340	HEALTH SERV		60000	60000			60000
		HEALTH SERV	TOTAL	60000	60000	—		60000
592A0	001420	PROP RENTAL		380000	380000	72085	177553	202447
		PROP RENTAL	TOTAL	380000	380000	72085—	177553	202447
592A0	001435	ADMISSIONS		465000	465000	103825	426330	38670
		ADMISSIONS	TOTAL	465000	465000	103825—	426330	38670
592A0	001450	INTEREST		3500000	3500000		193530	3306470
		INTEREST	TOTAL	3500000	3500000	—	193530	3306470
592A0	001452	INTEREST T+A		120000	120000			120000
		INTEREST T+A	TOTAL	120000	120000	—		120000

FIGURE 46. EXPENDITURE REPORT BY PROGRAM

GENERAL FUND

DEN	DESCRIPTION	APPROPRIATION ORIG	APPROPRIATION REVS	ENCUMBERANCES PLCD	ENCUMBERANCES LIQD	ENCUMBERANCES OPEN	EXPENSES CURR	EXPENSES TO DATE	TOTAL ENC+EXP	UNENC BAL
	SOCIAL STUD									
	220125TEACHING TCHR OVERTIM									
5	593A06308220125HIGH SCHOOL	42000	42000				5950	36226	36226	5774
8	TOTAL TEACHING TCHR OVERTIM	42000	42000				5950	36226	36226	5774
	220200TEACHING EQUIPMENT									
11	593A0630022202000DISTRICTWIDE	20000	20000							20000
	593A0630222202000EVANS PARK	25000	25000					11500	11500	13500
14	593A0630322202000FRANKLIN	10000	10000							10000
	593A0630422202000LINCOLN AVE	25000	25000					20000	20000	5000
	593A0630522202000NAURAUSHAUN	10000	10000					6555	6555	3445
17	593A0630722202000CENTRAL AVE	50000	50000		6450		6450	30345	30345	19655
	593A0630822202000HIGH SCHOOL	52500	63800	16300		16300		61512	77812	14012-
	593A0633022202000MIDDLE SCHL	30000	30000					6450	6450	23550
20	TOTAL TEACHING EQUIPMENT	222500	233800	16300	6450	16300	6450	136362	152662	81138
	220300TEACHING SUPPL + MTL									
23	593A0630022203000DISTRICTWIDE	62500	62500					1847	1847	60653
	593A0630222203000EVANS PARK	66800	66800		3280		3568	82343	82343	15543-
26	593A0630322203000FRANKLIN	74000	75300	2400	4560	2400	4317	88773	91173	15873-
	593A0630422203000LINCOLN AVE	56600	56600		2752		3363	102310	102310	45710-
	593A0630522203000NAURAUSHAUN	55400	55400		4018		4156	81600	81600	26200-
29	593A0630722203000CENTRAL AVE	35300	35300		2640		3276	101241	101241	65941-
	593A0630822203000HIGH SCHOOL	195100	198800	9000	10985	5450	11821	181883	187333	11467
	593A0633022203000MIDDLE SCHL	299500	299500	600		11980	1979	179241	191221	108279
32	TOTAL TEACHING SUPPL + MTL	845200	850200	12000	28235	19830	32480	819238	839068	11132
	220398TEACHING TEXTBKS K-6									
35	593A0630222203098EVANS PARK	31000	31000							31000
	593A0630322203098FRANKLIN	38500	38500					24658	24658	13842
38	593A0630422203098LINCOLN AVE	46000	46000					35600	35600	10400
	593A0630522203098NAURAUSHAUN	31500	31500					64455	64455	32955-
	593A0630722203098CENTRAL AVE	31000	31000					57686	57686	26686-
41	593A0633022203098MIDDLE SCHL	50000	50000					71358	71358	21358-
44	TOTAL TEACHING TEXTBKS K-6	228000	228000					253757	253757	25757-
	220399TEACHING TEXTBKS 7-12									
47	593A0630822203099HIGH SCHOOL	105000	105000	98898	98898		106257	240216	240216	135216-

ACCOUNTING REPORTS = BOCES FORM AF-0028-669 =

FIGURE 47.   EXPENDITURE REPORT BY BUILDING

GENERAL FUND

#	ACCOUNT	DESCRIPTION	APPROPRIATION ORIG	APPROPRIATION REVS	ENC PLCD	ENC LIQD	ENC OPEN	EXP CURR	EXP TO DATE	TOTAL ENC+EXP	UNENC BAL
2		MIDDLE SCHL									
5	593A08230211200 / 211200	SUPVN-PRINCP EQUIPMENT / DISTRICT MGT	20000	20000					4300	4300	15700
8	TOTAL	SUPVN-PRINCP EQUIPMENT	20000	20000					4300	4300	15700
11	593A00030211300	NO PROGRAM		6900							6900-
	593A08230211300 / 211300	DISTRICT MGT / SUPVN-PRINCP SUPPL + MTL	50000	50000				500	52468	52468	2468-
14	TOTAL	SUPVN-PRINCP SUPPL + MTL	50000	56900				500	52468	52468	4432
17	593A08230211400 / 211400	DISTRICT MGT / SUPVN-PRINCP OTHER EXPENS	140000	140000				1270	121328	121328	18672
20	TOTAL	SUPVN-PRINCP OTHER EXPENS	140000	140000				1270	121328	121328	18672
23	593A00030220125	NO PROGRAM — TEACHING TCHR OVERTIM	101000	101000				20575	116266	116266	15266-
26	593A06030220125	ENGLISH	14000	14000					3500	3500	10500
	593A06130220125	SCIENCE	36800	36800				5688	20038	20038	16762
	593A06430220125	PHYSICAL ED	274700	274700					301212	301212	26512-
29	593A06730220125	UNIFIED ARTS							13390	13390	13390-
	593A06930220125	MUSIC	38500	38500				45875	85838	85838	47338-
	593A07330220125	HEALTH SERV						6213	17938	17938	17938-
32	TOTAL	TEACHING TCHR OVERTIM	465000	465000				78351	558182	558182	93182-
35	593A00030220200	NO PROGRAM — TEACHING EQUIPMENT							7500	7500	7500-
38	593A06030220200	ENGLISH	30000	30000			19200		10050	29250	750
	593A06130220200	SCIENCE	80000	80000					68219	68219	11781
	593A06230220200	MATHEMATICS	101800	101800					73903	73903	27897
41	593A06330220200	SOCIAL STUD	30000	30000		6450		6450	6450	6450	23550
	593A06430220200	PHYSICAL ED	30000	30000		15000		15000	22730	22730	7270
	593A06630220200	FOREIGN LANG	20000	20000			9000			9000	11000
	593A06730220200	UNIFIED ARTS	20000	20000					22040	22040	2040-
44	593A06830220200	ART	67000	67000		32500		33333	33333	33333	33667
	593A06930220200	MUSIC	36500	36500					5520	5520	30980
47	TOTAL	TEACHING EQUIPMENT	415300	415300		53950	28200	54783	249745	277945	137355

FIGURE 48.   DETAIL EXPENDITURE REPORT BY FUNCTION-OBJECT

GENERAL FUND

DEN ACCOUNT	DESCRIPTION	ORIG	REVS	PLCD	LIQD	OPEN	CURR	TO DATE	ENC+EXP	UNENC BAL
593A06230220399	MATHEMATICS MIDDLE SCHL	45000	45000	98898	98898		106257	59642	59642	14642-
593A06308220399	SOCIAL STUD HIGH SCHOOL	105000	105000					240216	240216	135216-
593A06330220399	SOCIAL STUD MIDDLE SCHL	215000	215000				4302	151735	151735	63265
593A06508220399	BUSINESS HIGH SCHOOL	35000	35000		4080			35448	35448	448-
593A06608220399	FOREIGN LANG HIGH SCHOOL	95000	95000					131555	131555	36555-
593A06630220399	FOREIGN LANG MIDDLE SCHL	25000	25000		11940		12366	120703	120703	95703-
593A06708220399	UNIFIED ARTS HIGH SCHOOL	32500	32500					12366	12366	20134
593A06730220399	UNIFIED ARTS MIDDLE SCHL	20000	20000					16923	16923	3077
593A06908220399	MUSIC HIGH SCHOOL	30000	30000							30000
593A06930220399	MUSIC MIDDLE SCHL	45000	45000					45369	45369	369-
	TEXTBKS 7-12 TOTAL	1800000	1807600	98898	220981		221620	1789071	1789071	18529
593A00000220400	TEACHING OTHER EXPENS									
593A00002220400	NO PROGRAM DISTRICTWIDE	37200	37200					32075	32075	5125
593A00003220400	NO PROGRAM EVANS PARK	39000	39800					24436	24436	15364
593A00004220400	NO PROGRAM FRANKLIN	46400	46400	3000		3000		36200	39200	7200
593A00005220400	NO PROGRAM LINCOLN AVE	32200	32200					34263	34263	2063-
593A00007220400	NO PROGRAM NAURAUSHAUN	31200	31200		8000	995	8500	12568	13563	17637
593A00008220400	NO PROGRAM CENTRAL AVE	31000	31000				4744	24674	24674	6326
593A00030220400	NO PROGRAM HIGH SCHOOL	227500	379500		37500	65000	98332	442619	507619	128119-
593A00030220400	NO PROGRAM MIDDLE SCHL	68000	208000				11949	217864	217864	9864-
593A06000220400	ENGLISH DISTRICTWIDE							22290	22290	22290-
593A06002220400	ENGLISH EVANS PARK	8000	8000							8000
593A06003220400	ENGLISH FRANKLIN	10000	10000							10000
593A06004220400	ENGLISH LINCOLN AVE	6500	6500							6500
593A06005220400	ENGLISH NAURAUSHAUN	6500	6500							6500
593A06007220400	ENGLISH CENTRAL AVE	6500	6500							6500
593A06008220400	ENGLISH HIGH SCHOOL	64000	65300	1800	9995		3875	63680	63680	1620
593A06030220400	ENGLISH MIDDLE SCHL	45000	45000		4496		2906	7600	7600	37400
593A06010220400	ENGLISH DISTRICTWIDE	50000	50000				10130	51626	51626	1626-
593A06102220400	SCIENCE EVANS PARK	5000	5000							5000
593A06103220400	SCIENCE FRANKLIN	6000	6000				4795	5295	5295	705
593A06104220400	SCIENCE LINCOLN AVE	4000	4000							4000
593A06105220400	SCIENCE NAURAUSHAUN	4000	4000					4000	4000	
593A06107220400	SCIENCE CENTRAL AVE	120000	157500		36325		35990	112600	112600	44900
593A06108220400	SCIENCE HIGH SCHOOL	35000	55000		24560		26685	60839	60839	5839-
593A06130220400	SCIENCE MIDDLE SCHL						89800	111150	111150	111150-
593A06200220400	MATHEMATICS DISTRICTWIDE	8000	8000					2400	2400	5600
593A06202220400	MATHEMATICS EVANS PARK	10000	10000							10000
593A06203220400	MATHEMATICS FRANKLIN	6500	6500				510	510	510	5990
593A06204220400	MATHEMATICS LINCOLN AVE	6500	6500							6500
593A06205220400	MATHEMATICS NAURAUSHAUN	6500	6500							6500
593A06207220400	MATHEMATICS CENTRAL AVE	6500	6500					6500	6500	
593A06208220400	MATHEMATICS HIGH SCHOOL	35000	35000					3700	3700	31300

FIGURE 49. SUMMARY EXPENDITURES BY FUNCTION-OBJECT

GENERAL FUND

Ln	DEN ACCOUNT	DESCRIPTION	APPROPRIATION ORIG	APPROPRIATION REVS	ENCUMBERANCES PLCD	ENCUMBERANCES LIQD	ENCUMBERANCES OPEN	EXPENSES CURR	EXPENSES TO DATE	TOTAL ENC+EXP	UNENC BAL
2	593A0000021210I	CERT ISALARY	26460100	26460100				2114102	7320457	7320457	19139643
	593A0000021214 9	CERT ISALARY	270000	270000				36000	124000	124000	146000
	593A0000021215 0	NON CERT SAL	2874500	2874500				215704	1033753	1033753	1840747
5	593A0000021215 2	NCN CERT OT	300000	300000				550	25210	25210	274790
	593A086C0212300	SUPPL + MTL	200000	201927	87660	42830	104712	42830	79704	184416	17511
	593A0860021240 0	OTHER EXPENS	1100000	1190000		26900	334448	30300	206225	540673	649327
8		SUPPORT SVC									
		TOTAL	31204600	31296527	87660	69730	439160	2439486	8789349	9228509	22068018
11	593A0000021310I	CERT ISALARY	9069500	9069500				771088	2698808	2698808	6370692
	593A0000021314 9	CERT ISAL SUB	25000	25000				4000	4000	4000	21000
	593A0000021315 0	NON CERT SAL	1846000	1846000				180715	478138	478138	1367862
14	593A0710021320 0	EQUIPMENT	78000	78000	18100	71035	18100	71035	71035	89135	11135-
	593A0710021330 0	SUPPL + MTL	2320000	2420882	329416	105997	432565	146600	420921	853486	1567396
	593A0710021340 0	OTHER EXPENS	162000	162000					11460	11460	150540
17		LIBRARY									
		TOTAL	13500500	13601382	347516	177032	450665	1173438	3684362	4135027	9466355
20	593A0000022110	SAL-C-1/2KDG	6674300	6674300				542120	1897420	1897420	4776880
	593A0000022111	CERT ISAL K-6	75328100	75328100				5806513	20431807	20431807	54896293
	593A0000022112	CERT ISAL7-12	145818900	145818900				11352621	40463184	40463184	105355716
23	593A0000022114	CERT ISAL SUM	500000	500000				13500	455000	455000	45000
	593A0000022120	CERT ISAL HOM	500000	500000					52500	52500	447500
	593A0690022125	OVERTIME	1450000	1450000				117913	262952	262952	1187048
26	593A0000022149	CERT ISAL SUB	5800000	5800000				430000	920000	920000	4880000
	593A0000022150	NON CERT SAL	7481000	7481000				645983	1889820	1889820	5591180
	593A006C0822152							2313-			
29	593A0690022020 0	EQUIPMENT	2885000	3745019	68667	453514	607675	474909	1901483	2509158	1235861
	593A0720822030 0	SUPPL + MTL	9222500	10077664	536007	2919804	3082069	1136175	5302690	8384759	1692905
	593A0000022030 1	PERS IPTY DAM		25000				11380	11380	11380	13620
32	593A0000022039 7	TEXTBOOK LAW	500000	500000	32367	173232	67254	123674	196682	263936	236064
	593A0690522039 8	TEXTBKS K-6	1447500	1478520	9675	242093	346763	267003	663286	1010049	468471
	593A0690022039 9	TEXTBKS 7-12	2238000	2173000	39174	328139	230433	317327	1017743	1248176	924824
35	593A0850022040 0	OTHER EXPENS	2570000	2814847	13665	328275	420027	482009	887010	1307037	1507810
	593A0000022040 10	OTHER EXPENS	200000	200000							200000
	593A0760022050 1	SPEC IED	400000	400000							400000
38	593A0770822052 5	SERV IBOCES	13446500	13446500				1317039	2634078	2634078	10812422
		TEACHING									
		TOTAL	276461800	278412850	699555	4445057	4754221	23035853	78987035	83741256	194671594
41											
44											
47											

FIGURE 50. EXPENSE LEDGER

GENERAL FUND

DEM	ACCOUNT (F P L FN OBVEN)	DESCRIPTION	REF. I.D. DT	APPR. ORIG	APPR. REVS	ENC. PLCD	ENC. LIQD	ENC. OPEN	EXP. CURR	EXP. TO DATE	TOTAL ENC+EXP	UNENC BAL
2	523A0640422020 0	PHYSICAL ED LINCOLN AVE										
	563A0640422020 0	P										
5	567A0640422020 0		4487GOLDSTEIN 01082 0581603						6190	49080		
		PHYSICAL ED LINCOLN AVE TOTAL		33500	33500				6190	55270	55270	21770–
11	521A0640522020 0	TEACHING EQUIPMENT										
	523A0640522020 0	PHYSICAL ED NAURAUSHAUN		33000	33000					51910		
	563A0640522020 0	P										
14		PHYSICAL ED NAURAUSHAUN TOTAL		33000	33000					51910	51910	18910–
17	521A0640722020 0	TEACHING EQUIPMENT										
	523A0640722020 0	PHYSICAL ED CENTRAL AVE		33000	33000					28410		
20	563A0640722020 0	P								28410		
		PHYSICAL ED CENTRAL AVE TOTAL		33000	33000					28410	28410	4590
26	521A0640822020 0	TEACHING EQUIPMENT										
	523A0640822020 0	PHYSICAL ED HIGH SCHOOL		340000	340000					238600		
	563A0640822020 0	P							90720			
29	56 A0640822020 0		5940AMERICAN A0125 03114629				90720					
	568A0640822020 0		11052ATLAS ATHLETIC 03115520				14500		14500			
	567A0640822020 0		84327RE TECARR 01332053486 29						14500			
32	577A0640822020 0		84327R TECARR 02782005348 630						14500–			
	579A0640822020 0		84327R E TECARR01332 629									
		PHYSICAL ED HIGH SCHOOL TOTAL		340000	340000		105220		105220	343820	343820	3820–
38	521A0640430222020 0	TEACHING EQUIPMENT										
	523A0640430222020 0	PHYSICAL ED MIDDLE SCHL		30000	30000					7730		
	563A0640430222020 0	P							15000			
41	56 A0640430222020 0		5940AMERICAN A0115 03135617				15000		15000	22730		
		PHYSICAL ED MIDDLE SCHL TOTAL		30000	30000		15000		15000	22730	22730	7270
47	521A0650822020 0	TEACHING EQUIPMENT										
	523A0650822020 0	BUSINESS HIGH SCHOOL		280000	301500							

ACCOUNTING REPORTS = BOCES FORM #F-0028-669 =

FIGURE 51.   DESCRIPTION OF EXISTING PROGRAM

Description of Existing Program	Page 1 of 2

Program Title	Program Code	Program Level

Brief Summary of Program

Student Text Materials

Teacher's Resource Guides

No. of Certificated Staff (FTE)	No. of Noncertificated Staff (FTE)

Hours of Instructional Time Provided Each Student
    Hours per day   Days per week   Total hours per year

No. of Teaching Stations Required

Description of Test Data Available for This Program

FIGURE 51.   DESCRIPTION OF EXISTING PROGRAM (continued)

Description of Existing Program		Page 2 of 2	
Program Title	Program Code	Program Level	
Current Student Enrollment Grade/Course	No. of Students	No. of Sections	Average/ Section
Projected Student Enrollment (List each grade or course separately)	1st Year	2nd Year	3rd Year
Multi-Year Financial Plan	1st Year	2nd Year	3rd Year
Salaries			
Employee Benefits			
Equipment			
Supplies and Workbooks			
Textbooks			
Purchased Services			
Total			
Number of Certificated Staff (FTE)			
Number of Noncertificated Staff (FTE)			
Cost per Student Enrolled			
Prepared by	Date	Reviewed by	Date

FIGURE 52.   PROGRAM CHANGE PROPOSAL

Program Change Proposal	Page 1 of 2
Program Title	**Program Code**

Type of Program Change
- [ ] New program
- [ ] Change in existing program
- [ ] Expansion of existing program
- [ ] Deletion within existing program

Target Group

Description of Change

Rationale for Change

Predicted Achievement as a Result of Change

Number of Students Affected and Grade Level

Evaluation Procedures

Impact on Space and Facilities

Impact on Student's Time

Implementation Schedule

Responsibility for Change

Development   Approval   Accomplishment

FIGURE 52.   PROGRAM CHANGE PROPOSAL (continued)

Program Change Proposal		Page 2 of 2	
Program Title		Program Code	
Projected Budget	1st Year	2nd Year	3rd Year
No. of certificated staff			
Certificated staff budget			
No. of noncertificated staff			
Noncertificated staff budget			
Employee benefits			
Equipment			
Supplies and workbooks			
Textbooks			
Purchased services			
Total			
Allocation of Projected Budget Development			
Operations			
Total			
Prepared by		Date	
Reviewed by	Date	Comments (Attach additional pages if necessary)	

FIGURE 53.   PROGRAM ANALYSIS MEMORANDUM

Instructions— Prepare a Part I Form for Each Separate Study		Analysis No.

Part I—General Background Data

Program Title: Program Code _____

1. Statement of Problem:

2. Program Objectives:

3. Description of Pupils to Be Served:

4. List of Alternatives or Options to Be Analyzed:

   Alternative No.   Description

FIGURE 53.   PROGRAM ANALYSIS MEMORANDUM (continued)

Instructions—
Prepare a Separate
Part II for Each
Alternative Identified
in Part I

Analysis
No.

Part II—Analysis of Each Alternative

Description of Alternative: Alternative No. _____

1. Constraints: (legal, geographic, demographic, administrative, political, technological, financial, State Department of Education regulation, and local School District Board Policy)

2. Assumptions:

3. Related Research Findings:

4. Related School District Studies:

5. Test Data Available:

FIGURE 53.   PROGRAM ANALYSIS MEMORANDUM (continued)

Analysis No.

Part II—Analysis of Each Alternative

Description of Alternative: Alternative No. _____

6. Impact on Other Programs:

7. Space and Facilities Requirements:

8. Statistical Data:

	This year	1st year	2nd year	3rd year
• Number of students affected				
• Student time (in hours) for this program -in the classroom -at home -extracurricular				
• No. of certificated staff— teachers, administrators (in full-time-equivalent number of staff)				
• No. of noncertificated staff— clerical, teacher aides, custodial and maintenance (in full-time-equivalent number of staff)				
• Class size				
• Size of school				
• Teacher-pupil ratio				
• Ratio of administrators and clerical workers to pupils				

FIGURE 53.   PROGRAM ANALYSIS MEMORANDUM (continued)

	Analysis No.

Part II—Analysis of Each Alternative

Description of Alternative: Alternative No. _____

	This year	1st year	2nd year	3rd year
9. Estimated Cost (show details of computations):				
• Salaries				
• Employee benefits (retirement, social security, health, insurance, etc.)				
• Equipment				
• Supplies				
• Textbooks				
• Purchased services				
• Building and facilities				
Total				
Less: offsetting revenues				
Net estimated costs				
10. Distribution of Estimated Cost (shown in item 9 above) by one-time developmental and installation costs and operations costs:				
• Developmental and installation costs (net of offsetting revenues)				
• Operations costs (net of offsetting revenues)				
• Net estimated costs				

FIGURE 53.   PROGRAM ANALYSIS MEMORANDUM (continued)

	Analysis No.

Part II—Analysis of Each Alternative

Description of Alternative: Alternative No. _____

11. Anticipated Benefits. Show predicted specific growth of learner's
    knowledge, skill, and attitudes, including corallary benefits to
    other programs.

Predicted Benefit	Predicted Measure of Effectiveness	Time Required to Achieve Results

12. Anticipated Disadvantages—Legal, political, student impact

Prepared by _____   Date Prepared _____

Review by _____   Date Reviewed _____

Note: Reviewers may attach comments to this document

FIGURE 53.   PROGRAM ANALYSIS MEMORANDUM (continued)

Instructions— Prepare a Part III Form for Each Separate Study	Analysis No.

Part III—Recommended Alternative

1. Recommended Alternative:

2. Major Factors Influencing Recommendation:

3. Plan to Implement Alternative Selected:
   - Assignment of responsibility
     -Development of program
     -Preparation of event schedule
     -Installation
     Evaluation   { District
                    { Outside resources
     Progress reports
   - Event schedule for installation (key dates)
   - Evaluation schedule
   - Progress report schedule

Prepared by _____ Date _____

Reviewed by _____ Date _____

Note: Reviewers may attach comments to this document

FIGURE 54.   ILLUSTRATIVE CONTENTS OF A MULTI-YEAR PLAN

I Introduction

II Summary of Findings and Conclusions

III Supporting Data

    A. Projected School Operating Expenditures

    B. Revenue Prospects

    C. The Budget Process and Format

    D. Capital and Operating Costs

    E. Educational Technology

IV Exhibits

    A. Teachers' Salary Schedule 1968-1969

    B. Annual Rates of Increase—5 Years, 13 Years

    C. Actual School Expenditures 1962/63-1968/69

    D. Selected School Personnel Statistics

    E. Teachers' Salary History

    F. Projection of School Operation Expense

    G. School Operating Revenue by Source

    H. School Building Revenue by Source

    I. Breakdown of Mil Rate

    J. Comparison of Town Expenses, Local Taxes, Grand List, and Mil Rate 1962/63-1968/69

    K. Westport Grand List 1959/60-1968/69

    L. Percent Distribution of Households in Westport by Cash Income Groups 1962-1967

    M. Comparison of Increase in Effective Buying Income per Household and Tax Rate in Westport 1962/63-1968/69

    N. Comparison of Westport's School Tax Rate and Tax Resources with 12 Connecticut Towns—1966

    O. Selected Statistics of Local School Systems 1956-1966

    P. Selected Statistics of School Revenue Receipts by Source 1967-1968

    Q. State Sales Tax and State Aid to Westport Schools

    R. Five-Year Projection of School and Town Expense and Taxes

    S. Cost of TV Installation

    T. Time Table for Achieving Complete Program Budget

    U. Proposed Foreign Language Instruction Operating Budget 1970-1971

V Appendices

    A. Policy of the Westport Board of Education on Advisory Committees to the Board of Education

    B. Charge of the Westport Board of Education to the Advisory Committee on a Long-Range School Budget

Source: *Report of the Advisory Committee on a Long-Range School Budget to the Board of Education, Westport, Connecticut,* Table of Contents, 1969.

FIGURE 55.   COMPARISON OF FUNCTION-OBJECT BUDGET DOCUMENT,
PROGRAM BUDGET DOCUMENT, AND PPBS SUMMARY DOCUMENT

Components of PPBS	Function-Object Budget Document	Program Budget Document	PPBS Summary Document
Objectives	None	None	Objectives are displayed in relationship to the program budget
Priorities	None	None	Priorities are shown
Description of existing program	None	None	Existing program is described
Program changes	None	None	Program changes are included
Program analysis	None	None	Program analyses that were completed are part of this document
Evaluation	None	None	Evaluation results are shown
Multi-year fiscal plan	None	None	Multi-year fiscal plan is included in this document
Budget	Shows budget by traditional functions categories, i.e.: Board of education Central administration Instruction Community service Transportation Operation & maintenance of plant Undistributed expenses Debt service	Shows budget breakout as defined by the program structure, i.e.: Mathematics, grades K-12 Science, grades K-12 Reflects budget for *purposes* of programs and their intended *outcomes*	Same as program budget document

FIGURE 56.   1969-70 PHILADELPHIA PROGRAM BUDGET

PROPOSED EXPENDITURES BY PROGRAM

	(1) Actual Fiscal 1967-1968	(2) Adjusted Budget Fiscal 1968-1969	Proposed Budget Fiscal 1969-1970	Federal Education and Antipoverty Programs, etc. 1969-1970
Early childhood education	$ 4,597,966	$ 5,860,200	$ 7,421,800	$11,326,579
Elementary education	57,367,284	62,419,800	74,117,200	6,554,892
Junior high education	30,808,692	33,337,400	40,649,200	933,898
Senior and technical high education	37,125,809	44,055,200	50,099,000	2,961,479
Special education	11,146,700	14,574,000	17,129,800	419,360
Community education	3,430,018	3,102,400	3,894,000	4,536,432
Health and pupil services	6,925,582	7,467,600	8,168,800	1,273,180
Instructional services	5,249,797	6,161,200	7,246,100	1,067,692
Plant operations and maintenance	20,879,921	25,679,000	27,696,600	
General services	8,055,577	7,624,500	9,159,200	
Transportation	4,079,113	4,026,600	4,484,400	
Planning	1,088,769	1,587,000	1,894,900	2,415,488
School district management	3,568,851	3,401,100	4,450,000	
Debt service	14,292,395	20,700,000	27,900,000	
Contingency			1,500,000	
	$208,616,474	$240,000,000	$285,811,000	$31,489,000

(1) Redistributed according to program composition for Fiscal 1969-1970.
(2) Refer Table II. Page 8.
Source: *The Proposed Operating Budget of the School District of Philadelphia*, 1969-1970, p. 18.

PROPOSED EXPENDITURES BY PROGRAM

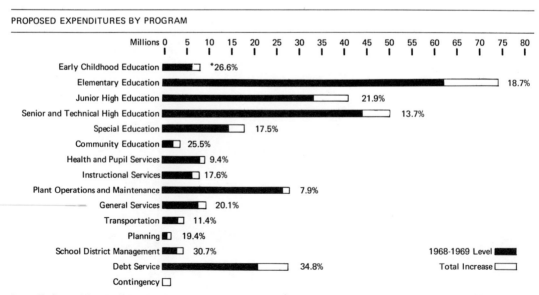

Source: *The Proposed Operating Budget of the School District of Philadelphia*, 1969-1970, p. 19.   *% Increase to 1968-1969 Level.

FIGURE 57.   PROGRAM BUDGET FOR FISCAL YEAR 1970-71
DADE COUNTY PUBLIC SCHOOLS, MIAMI, FLORIDA

SUMMARY OF REGULAR PROGRAMS

	Elementary Instruction	Middle/Junior High Instruction	Senior High Instruction	Total
Kindergarten	$ 3,185,406	—	—	$ 3,185,406
Primary	24,423,396	—	—	24,423,396
Intermediate	22,422,460	—	—	22,422,460
Supplementary services	4,335,726	—	—	4,335,726
Art	—	$ 897,944	$ 477,623	1,375,567
Business education	—	278,908	1,984,386	2,263,294
Driver training	—	—	698,021	698,021
Foreign language	—	904,832	1,600,120	2,504,952
Home economics	—	1,023,129	897,204	1,920,333
Industrial arts	—	1,708,396	1,137,776	2,846,172
Language arts	—	5,573,616	5,609,447	11,183,063
Mathematics	—	5,393,080	3,177,149	8,570,229
Music	—	1,331,226	556,126	1,887,352
Physical education	—	3,237,043	2,160,349	5,397,392
Science	—	3,573,008	2,636,722	6,209,730
Social studies	—	3,615,227	3,618,114	7,233,341
Vocational training	—	896,544	2,674,577	3,571,121
Co-curricular	128,402	272,010	745,924	1,146,336
	$54,495,390	$28,704,963	$27,973,538	$111,173,891
Adult instruc-tion/support				7,359,568*
				$118,533,459

*Does not include salary increases or employee benefits which are included in Un-allocated Resources (Other).
Source: *Program Budget for Fiscal Year 1970-1971,* Dade County Public Schools, Miami, Florida, pp. 4-7.

FIGURE 57.   PROGRAM BUDGET FOR FISCAL YEAR 1970-71
DADE COUNTY PUBLIC SCHOOLS, MIAMI, FLORIDA (continued)

SUMMARY OF SPECIAL PROGRAMS*

	Elementary School	Middle/ Junior High School	Senior High School	Inter-Level/ Systemwide	Total
Compensatory					
Projects	—	—	—	—	—
Instructional administration*	—	—	—	$ 200,563	$ 200,563
				$ 200,563	$ 200,563
Cuban Refugee					
English as a second language	$1,240,946	$ 495,563	$ 162,987	$ —	$ 1,899,496
Spanish for native speakers	599,605	237,595	226,298	—	1,063,498
Pupil personnel services*	—	—	—	126,706	126,706
Instructional administration*	—	—	—	76,694	76,694
	$1,840,551	$ 733,158	$ 389,285	$ 203,400	$ 3,166,394
Drug Abuse					
Instruction	$ 48,121	$ 21,905	$ 19,274	$ 58,400	$ 147,700
Program development*	—	—	—	37,300	37,300
Staff development*	—	—	—	65,000	65,000
	$ 48,121	$ 21,905	$ 19,274	$ 160,700	$ 250,000
Exceptional Child					
Emotionally disturbed	$ 441,036	$ —	$ —	$ —	$ 441,036
Hearing impaired	294,436	58,581	—	—	353,017
Homebound/hospital	96,199	47,762	108,109	—	252,070
Learning disabilities	407,459	—	—	—	407,459
Mentally handicapped	1,569,005	564,246	153,140	—	2,286,391
Physically handicapped	294,436	105,859	23,639	—	423,934
Speech therapy	312,875	288,394	83,971	—	685,240
Socially maladjusted	58,680	713,031	102,997	—	874,708
Visually handicapped	141,558	58,581	59,102	—	259,241
COPE center	—	—	—	72,754	72,754
Pupil personnel services*	—	—	—	255,965	255,965
Instructional administration*	—	—	—	119,879	119,879
Program development	—	—	—	68,664	68,664
	$3,615,684	$1,836,454	$ 530,958	$ 517,262	$ 6,500,358
Reading Remediation					
Corrective reading	$1,110,623	$ 214,820	$ 37,307	—	$ 1,362,750
Remedial reading	1,770,955	—	—	—	1,770,955
	$2,881,578	$ 214,820	$ 37,307	—	$ 3,133,705

*Support elements of special programs which have been earmarked to support such programs have been so allocated. These support costs do not in the main represent the full costs of these special programs and in particular omit necessary auxiliary services, other instructional, facilities and administrative support. In addition, many of the students served by these special programs are also either fully or partially served by regular instructional programs.

FIGURE 57.   PROGRAM BUDGET FOR FISCAL YEAR 1970-71
DADE COUNTY PUBLIC SCHOOLS, MIAMI, FLORIDA (continued)

SUMMARY OF SUPPORT PROGRAMS

	Elementary School	Middle/ Junior High School	Senior High School	Inter-Level/ Systemwide	Total
Summer					
Summer instruction	$ 954,600	$ 803,281	$ 900,709	—	$ 2,658,590
Instructional administration*	199,581	167,019	190,133	—	556,733
Operations services*	21,666	18,072	20,262	—	60,000
Program evaluation*	—	—	—	$ 14,954	14,954
	$1,175,847	$ 988,372	$1,111,104	$ 14,954	$ 3,290,277
	$9,561,781	$3,794,709	$2,087,928	$1,096,879	$16,541,297
Auxiliary Services					
School food**	$ 64,035	$ 8,005	$ 8,005	$ 161,357	$ 241,402
Transportation	462,855	893,257	1,231,202	114,626	2,701,940
	$ 526,890	$ 901,262	$ 1,239,207	$ 275,983	$ 2,943,342
Instructional Support					
Educational media	$ 4,869,111	$ 2,109,631	$ 2,076,923	$ 660,946	$ 9,716,611
Pupil personnel services	1,179,976	2,727,226	2,068,251	767,029	6,742,482
Instructional administration	7,531,501	3,832,763	3,085,831	—	14,450,095
Staff development	—	—	—	1,652,833	1,652,833
Program development	—	—	—	1,874,509	1,874,509
Program evaluation	—	—	—	374,710	374,710
	$13,580,588	$ 8,669,620	$ 7,231,005	$ 5,330,027	$34,811,240
Facilities Support					
Plant operations	$ 6,529,615	$ 2,794,512	$ 2,499,887	$ 454,686	$12,278,700
Plant maintenance	2,683,320	1,413,826	1,117,589	939,064	6,153,799
Plant construction	—	—	—	122,219	122,219
Plant security	—	—	—	1,328,940	1,328,940
Plant management	—	—	—	93,411	93,411
	$ 9,212,935	$ 4,208,338	$ 3,617,476	$ 2,938,320	$19,977,069
Administrative Support					
Business services	—	—	—	$ 1,236,596	$ 1,236,596
Financial services	—	—	—	750,728	750,728
Information services	—	—	—	1,503,954	1,503,954
Personnel services	—	—	—	1,568,763	1,568,763
Management	—	—	—	1,963,863	1,963,863
	—	—	—	$ 7,023,904	$ 7,023,904
	$23,320,413	$13,779,220	$12,087,688	$15,568,234	$64,755,555

**Does not include funds or federal lunch/milk subsidies.

FIGURE 58. PROGRAM BUDGET FOR PUBLIC

PROGRAM AREA	PERSONNEL				CONTRACTED		
	Professional		Civil Service & Other				
	No. Staff	Salaries	No. Staff	Salaries	Rentals	Consul- tants	Printing
INSTRUCTIONAL SERVICES							
Kindergarten	25.	208,733.					
Elementary	132.	1,384,227.	3.	42,137.			
Adult Education	1.	102,509.	1.	9,918.	100.		2,700.
Art	15.2	171,805.	.5	2,919.		300.	
Business	7.6	107,931.	2.5	18,102.	12,020.		
English-Language Arts	48.7	556,210.	2.	15,782.		1,350.	
Foreign Languages	33.	354,492.	1.	5,973.			
Homemaking	14.	146,393.				300.	
Industrial Arts	15.	193,599.	.33	2,391.			
Mathematics	30.2	353,110.	1.	8,198.	4,500.	3,000.	
Music	13.	157,787.	.4	2,270.	560.	100.	
Physical Education	27.	331,234.	1.	7,476.	13,780.		
Remedial Instruction	11.6	116,594.					
Science	27.8	346,662.	1.5	9,949.		750.	
Social Studies	31.2	342,544.	1.	8,239.			
Special Education	14.	156,407.	1.	7,270.	8,800.		
Summer School		37,300.		2,700.			1,300.
Tech.-Voc. Education		69,412.		52,984.		1,200.	
Supplementary Education		19,686.		6,180.			
Unallocated	5.8	68,667.		13,003.	100.		11,700.
Subtotal: Instructional Services	452.1	5,225,302.	16.23	215,491.	39,860.	7,000.	15,700.
SUPPORT SERVICES							
Administration	3.	72,223.	12.	104,770.			6,000.
Athletics (subsidy)							
Attendance			1.	10,862.		10,000.	
Audiovisual	2.	29,639.	3.5	23,166.	18,000.		
Guidance	21.6	274,786.	6.	28,043.	2,500.		
Health			8.	62,680.			
Library	25.	191,951.	5.13	36,433.	2,200.		
Psychological Services	12.	176,112.	3.	19,170.		7,200.	
Research & Development							
School Lunch (subsidy)						1,500.	
School Plant			61.5	535,696.	101,375.		
Heating & Lighting Plant			5.	25,039.			
Student Body Activities		9,400.					
Supervision	15.	256,723.	20.1	158,485.	14,265.	3,000.	
Transportation							
Subtotal: Support Services	78.6	1,010,834.	125.23	1,004,344.	138,340.	21,700.	6,000.
Grand Total	530.7	6,236,136.	141.46	1,219,835.	178,200.	28,700.	21,700.

Source: *Program Budget for Public Schools of Brookline, Mass., 1970.*

SCHOOLS OF BROOKLINE, MASS., 1970

SERVICES			SUPPLIES		OTHER EXPENSES			FURNITURE & EQUIPMENT	TOTAL BUDGET REQUEST
Building Repairs & Modernizations	Field Trips	Other	General	Text-books	Travel	Tuition and Other	Postage; Express; Dues		
1,090.	2,300.		2,500.		405.			3,500.	218,528.
1,635.	11,350.		21,860.		1,000.			18,000.	1,480,209.
			2,525.	4,000.	250.		750.	500.	123,252.
1,600.	700.	950.	30,575.	1,130.	490.		25.	3,700.	214,194.
	50.	4,840.	5,000.	1,950.	330.			16,773.	166,996.
1,400.	2,700.		9,814.	45,700.	1,370.		100.	4,000.	638,426.
10,450.	650.		3,760.	10,320.	1,260.		11.	3,000.	389,916.
2,700.	1,000.	300.	5,440.	1,883.	540.		11.	5,900.	164,467.
	550.	2,550.	16,655.	900.	500.		11.	13,000.	230,156.
330.	450.		9,600.	15,330.	800.		30.	8,500.	403,848.
1,072.	1,850.	7,150.	3,375.	1,025.	480.		36.	7,000.	182,705.
6,350.	3,050.	15,410.	12,755.	600.	810.		500.	7,000.	398,965.
			880.	2,730.	400.				120,604.
2,350.	3,000.	1,000.	30,225.	12,525.	630.		11.	22,000.	429,102.
845.	4,200.	500.	6,340.	20,405.	800.		25.	2,000.	385,898.
	2,500.	37,859.	6,650.	1,159.	390.	2,500.		4,600.	228,135.
	1,500.		1,300.	500.					44,600.
	2,500.		5,678.		1,100.			2,525.	135,399.
		5,280.	3,700.			2,200.			37,046.
		2,000.	16,424.	15,340.		4,656.	345.		132,235.
29,822.	38,350.	77,839.	195,056.	135,497.	11,555.	9,356.	1,855.	121,998.	6,124,681.
			7,125.		4,170.		2,450.	1,800.	198,538.
						84,016.			84,016.
					100.				20,962.
		26,180.	61,200.		1,300.		800.	39,500.	199,785.
2,200.	200.		900.	1,125.	2,600.		85.	8,200.	320,639.
200.		24,875.	3,700.		1,725.			400.	93,580.
1,275.		2,920.	63,200.		850.		350.	10,000.	309,179.
		550.	6,544.		1,400.	2,600.	75.	4,000.	217,651.
		21,000.							21,000.
						45,797.			47,297.
202,035.		21,000.	148,900.		1,700.			4,248.	1,014,954.
		3,337.	30,750.					150.	59,276.
	600.	307.	2,700.					4,000.	17,007.
14,360.			9,590.		3,950.		4,255.	4,710.	469,338.
						30,610.			30,610.
220,070.	800.	100,169.	334,609.	1,125.	17,795.	163,023.	8,015.	77,008.	3,103,832.
249,892.	39,150.	178,008.	529,665.	136,622.	29,350.	172,379.	9,870.	199,006.	9,228,513.

FIGURE 59.   PROGRAM BUDGET, PEARL RIVER SCHOOL DISTRICT

PEARL RIVER SCHOOL DISTRICT

PEARL RIVER, NEW YORK

VOTE WEDNESDAY MAY 6, 1970

10 A.M. — 10 P.M.

SCHOOL OPERATING BUDGET 1970-71 BY PROGRAM

Requiring a tax levy of $3,145,183
on an estimated assessed evaluation of $36,833,020
to provide a 1970-71 operating budget of $5,728,863

COSTS ARE DISPLAYED FOR THE FIRST TIME BY PROGRAM

This budget has been

EXTENSIVELY REVIEWED

By the Board of Education
By the Citizens' Budget Advisory Committee

THIS BASIC BUDGET   REFLECTS CURRENT SALARY RATES AND DOES NOT INCLUDE MONIES FOR NEGOTIATED SALARY INCREASES subject to negotiations now in progress.

— **Establishes** reading as a top priority area
— **Establishes** health with emphasis on drug abuse as a priority area
— **Reduces** one elementary principal
— **Satisfies** some staffing needs through reassignment of personnel
— **Excludes** non-essentials

TAX RATES

This year's budget with current salary rates*	1970-71 Estimated	$85.39	per $1000 assessed value
Last year's approved budget	1969-70 Actual	$79.33	per $1000 assessed value

*Should a settlement on teachers and clerical salaries be reached before budget vote date, that settlement will be communicated to you immediately.

A BUDGET SENSITIVE TO PEARL RIVER'S NEEDS

MAY 6 SCHOOL BUDGET AND BOARD ELECTION

FIGURE 59.   PROGRAM BUDGET, PEARL RIVER SCHOOL DISTRICT (continued)

April 10, 1970

TO THE VOTERS:

The proposed 1970-71 School Operating Budget, which has been developed after careful consideration of its tax implications, reflects the need for improving our instructional programs in accordance with a system of priorities. Reading has been established as our top priority, while health education—with emphasis on drug abuse—has been established as a priority area. A significant increase in expenditures has been made in these two areas.

Newly adopted procedures have increased our ability to analyze the budget on a subject area basis and to make program and fiscal decisions in relation to our priorities.

In order to keep the tax rate increase to a minimum, we have deferred a number of program changes which, while desirable, are not absolutely necessary.

The total dollar increase over the revised 1969-70 budget* is $284,836 or 5% more. Approximately 96% or $274,000 of this increase is mandated as follows:

Rockland County Board of Cooperative Educational Services (BOCES)	$97,000	Middle School health program (mandated by New York State)	$15,000
Retirement, social security and other employee benefits costs	85,000	Debt Service (for the bonds issued passed by the voters on November 12, 1969 and High School litigation settlement)	77,000

Monies have been allocated to maintain the Central Avenue school next year on a limited basis for community and recreation purposes. It may be necessary to temporarily use this building in the event the elementary classroom additions have not been completed by the beginning of the coming school year. A citizens' committee is presently studying the disposition of this building and will make a recommendation to us regarding this matter. The final decision will be made, however, by you at a future referendum.

The 1970-71 budget requires an estimated tax increase of 8%, as compared to last year's 1% increase in tax rate. This 8% includes $97,930 for 1969-70 negotiated staff settlements reached after the budget adoption in May 1969. This budget does not include monies beyond existing salary levels for the staff because contract negotiations have not been completed for groups other than the custodians. Should a settlement be reached before the May 6th budget vote that settlement and its budget implications will be communicated to you immediately.

The Operating Budget as outlined in this brochure is a direct result of contributions made by the entire staff as well as by members of the Citizens' Budget Advisory Committee.

Program goals, descriptions of existing programs and their proposed changes, staff allocations, and supporting fiscal data have been prepared in complete detail. Should you wish to study and review this detailed information it is available on request by visiting our administrative offices or by calling 735-4091.

Three meetings will be held at various schools within the district to discuss this proposed budget. We urge you to attend.

Henry C. Leidel, Jr., President

Roberts W. Smithem, Vice President
Andrew D. McCahill

Francis J. Nilan, Jr.
Lee N. Starker

---

*The original 1969-70 budget was adjusted as follows:

1.	Original 1969-70 budget	$5,214,133
2.	Negotiated staff settlements reached after the budget adoption in May 1969	97,930
3.	Settlement of the High School litigation	100,000
4.	Incomplete purchase orders carried forward from June 30, 1969 as required by New York State Department of Audit and Control	31,964
5.	Adjusted 1969-70 budget	$5,444,027

2

FIGURE 59.   PROGRAM BUDGET, PEARL RIVER SCHOOL DISTRICT (continued)

PEARL RIVER SCHOOL DISTRICT

Summary of 1970-71 Budget by Program

Program Title	1969-70 Budget	1970-71 Budget
INSTRUCTIONAL PROGRAMS		
English, Language Arts and Reading	$ 811,547	$ 942,116
Science, (including health)	393,246	447,945
Mathematics	445,507	455,593
Social Studies	384,932	391,437
Physical Education, Intramurals and Interscholastic Athletics	317,203	303,415
Business	56,229	69,749
Foreign Languages	141,182	154,797
Unified Arts	135,074	126,292
Art	100,658	102,243
Music	135,715	144,067
Special Education	52,628	73,371
Vocational Education	43,130	49,064
Adult Education	14,113	10,413
INSTRUCTIONAL SUPPORT PROGRAMS		
Library	135,032	145,295
Guidance and Psychological Services	158,540	194,753
Health Services	97,369	97,597
Bond Principal and Interest	439,333	516,608
Operation and Maintenance of Plant	553,145	613,087
School Management	351,756	361,374
Central Office Management	343,246	311,121
Transportation	161,394	176,295
School Lunch	—	—
Non-Program	168,899*	35,190
COMMUNITY SERVICES PROGRAMS	4,149	7,041
GRAND TOTAL	$5,444,027	$5,728,863

Total Budget Increase — $284,836

---

*Includes $100,000 High School litigation settlement and $27,300 for refund of prior year's taxes.

3

FIGURE 59.   PROGRAM BUDGET, PEARL RIVER SCHOOL DISTRICT (continued)

INSTRUCTIONAL PROGRAMS

ENGLISH, LANGUAGE ARTS AND READING PROGRAM

The English, Language Arts and Reading Program is our No. 1 priority area for 1970-71. We plan to improve reading by:

* Increasing the time devoted to reading instruction in grades 7 and 8 by reducing the amount of required instructional time in special areas such as industrial arts, homemaking, music and art.
* Reorganizing the middle school 8th grade program to allow a full time reading specialist to concentrate on students having basic reading deficiencies.
* Expanding the middle school developmental reading program at grades 6 and 7 through the addition of a full time reading specialist and the reallocation of existing staff members.
* Adding teacher aides who will assist elementary school classroom teachers.
* Adding elementary school reading specialists to work with teachers in improving their teaching skills as well as working with students having remedial reading problems.

We plan to improve our English program by:

* Increasing the number of English teachers on the high school staff to provide for increasing enrollments.
* Modifying the English elective program at the 12th grade.

		Number of Staff	1970-71 Budget
CERTIFICATED STAFF (Includes substitutes, overtime, and employee benefits)		58.9	$882,520
Classroom Teachers	42.6		
Reading Specialists	14.3		
Speech Therapist	1.0		
English Coordinator	1.0		
NON-CERTIFICATED STAFF (Includes substitutes, overtime and employee benefits)		5.9	33,929
Teacher Aides	5.9		
EQUIPMENT			828
SUPPLIES			13,308
TEXTBOOKS			7,274
CONTRACT SERVICES			4,257
Total			$942,116

SCIENCE, (Including HEALTH) PROGRAM

The Health portion of the Science Program is our No. 2 priority area for the coming year. This focus will enable us to provide modern health instruction in the critical areas of drug abuse, smoking and alcoholism, and family life education by:

* Adding one teacher for a state-mandated health program at the 6th grade and changing the 12th grade health program to the 10th grade level.
* Providing an in-service training course for classroom teachers in the area of health education.

We plan to improve the Science Program by:

* Expanding the introductory physical science course in the 8th grade.
* Modifying existing high school schedule to provide for a regents and non-regents program.
* Adding teaching time to accommodate increasing high school enrollments.

		Number of Staff	1970-71 Budget
CERTIFICATED STAFF (Includes substitutes, overtime, and employee benefits)		26.3	$412,524
Classroom Teachers	25.3		
Science Coordinator	1.0		
NON-CERTIFICATED STAFF (includes substitutes, overtime and employee benefits)		0.4	2,012
Teacher Aides	0.4		
EQUIPMENT			5,849
SUPPLIES			16,700
TEXTBOOKS			6,050
CONTRACT SERVICES			4,810
Total			$447,945

NOTE: For each program the number of staff is shown on a full-time-equivalent basis. Elementary teachers have been prorated to programs based on the amount of teaching time spent in each subject area.

4

FIGURE 59.   PROGRAM BUDGET, PEARL RIVER SCHOOL DISTRICT (continued)

MATHEMATICS PROGRAM

Substantial improvements have been made in the Mathematics Program over the past two years. To maintain present program levels, changes include:

*Adding teaching time at the high school to accommodate increasing student enrollments.

*Adding teaching time at the middle school to maximize the effectiveness of cooperative teaching arrangements.

		Number of Staff	1970-71 Budget
CERTIFICATED STAFF (Includes substitutes, overtime, and employee benefits)		27.2	$420,174
Classroom Teachers	26.2		
Mathematics Coordinator	1.0		
NON-CERTIFICATED STAFF (Includes substitutes, overtime, and employee benefits)		0.6	3,736
Teacher Aides	0.6		
EQUIPMENT			4,583
SUPPLIES			16,550
TEXTBOOKS			7,710
CONTRACT SERVICES			2,840
Total			$455,593

SOCIAL STUDIES PROGRAM

The Social Studies Program will be continued at the present level at the elementary schools and modified at the middle and high schools. These modifications include:

*Eliminating teaching time at the middle school and reallocating it to the reading area in order to expand the developmental reading program.

*Reorganizing the high school social studies program and providing a variety of 12th grade elective courses.

*Adding teaching time to accommodate increasing student enrollments at the high school.

		Number of Staff	1970-71 Budget
CERTIFICATED STAFF (Includes substitutes, overtime, and employee benefits)		26.4	$369,150
Classroom Teachers	25.4		
Social Studies Coordinator	1.0		
EQUIPMENT			1,647
SUPPLIES			9,500
TEXTBOOKS			8,900
CONTRACT SERVICES			2,240
Total			$391,437

5

FIGURE 59. PROGRAM BUDGET, PEARL RIVER SCHOOL DISTRICT (continued)

PHYSICAL EDUCATION, INTRAMURALS, AND INTERSCHOLASTIC ATHLETICS PROGRAM

Since the Physical Education Program has been significantly improved over the past few years, we plan to make relatively few changes in this area during the coming year. These changes include:

*Eliminating teaching time at the middle school and reallocating it to the new 6th grade health program that has been mandated by the state.

*Eliminating a physical education teacher at the high school.

*Adding interscholastic gymnastics at the high school to replace the existing intramural program in gymnastics.

		Number of Staff	1970-71 Budget
CERTIFICATED STAFF (Includes substitutes, overtime, and employee benefits)		15.4	$257,699
Classroom teachers	0.6		
Physical Education teachers	13.8		
Physical Education Coordinator	1.0		
NON-CERTIFICATED STAFF (includes substitutes, overtime, and employee benefits) — for custodial overtime			3,666
EQUIPMENT			2,750
SUPPLIES			17,100
TEXTBOOKS			—
CONTRACT SERVICES (Includes fee for athletic officials, fees for police and fire officials, reconditioning of athletic equipment, athletic dues and fees, and bus transportation for teams)			22,200
Total			$303,415

BUSINESS EDUCATION PROGRAM

We plan to continue the Business Education Program at its present level with three modifications. These include:

*Adding an office practice course that provides training in basic office and clerical procedures for vocationally oriented students.

*Transferring consumer math courses from the Business Department to the Math Department.

*Adding teaching time to accommodate increasing student enrollments.

		Number of Staff	1970-71 Budget
CERTIFICATED STAFF (Includes substitutes, overtime, and employee benefits)		4.0	$62,609
Classroom teachers	4.0		
EQUIPMENT			3,555
SUPPLIES			1,550
TEXTBOOKS			935
CONTRACT SERVICES			1,100
Total			$69,749

6

FIGURE 59.   PROGRAM BUDGET, PEARL RIVER SCHOOL DISTRICT (continued)

FOREIGN LANGUAGE PROGRAM

In order to improve the Foreign Language Program we plan to modify it by:

*Revising selection procedures for students beginning the study of foreign language in the 7th grade.

*Eliminating teaching time at the middle school and reallocating it to the developmental reading program.

*Revising student placement procedures in foreign language courses at the high school level.

*Providing revised textbooks where needed.

*Adding teaching time for accommodating increasing student enrollments at the high school.

	Number of Staff	1970-71 Budget
CERTIFICATED STAFF (Includes substitutes, overtime and employee benefits)	9.6	$142,823
Classroom teachers 8.6		
Foreign Language Coordinator 1.0		
EQUIPMENT		400
SUPPLIES		5,400
TEXTBOOKS		3,775
CONTRACT SERVICES		2,399
Total		$154,797

UNIFIED ARTS (INDUSTRIAL ARTS, HOMEMAKING, DRIVER EDUCATION AND MECHANICAL DRAWING) PROGRAM

We plan to maintain Unified Arts (Industrial Arts, Homemaking, Driver Education and Mechanical Drawing) Program and staff at current levels with the exception of:

*Adding a 12th grade elective for boys in the field of home economics.

*Modifying the middle school unified arts program to implement an elective system in grades 7 and 8.

*Reducing unified arts teaching time at the middle school and reallocating it to improve the developmental reading program.

	Number of Staff	1970-71 Budget
CERTIFICATED STAFF (Includes substitutes, overtime and employee benefits)	7.0	$112,719
Classroom teachers 7.0		
EQUIPMENT		3,842
SUPPLIES		8,000
TEXTBOOKS		971
CONTRACT SERVICES		760
Total		$126,292

7

FIGURE 59.   PROGRAM BUDGET, PEARL RIVER SCHOOL DISTRICT (continued)

ART PROGRAM

We plan to maintain the existing Art Program with some modifications. These include:

   *Changing the 7th and 8th grade program to an elective one.

   *Reducing teaching time at the middle school and reallocating it to improve the developmental reading program.

   *Providing special art classes for high school students on an audit basis.

		Number of Staff	1970-71 Budget
CERTIFICATED STAFF (Includes substitutes, overtime and employee benefits)		6.6	$ 90,421
Classroom teachers	0.6		
Art teachers	5.0		
Art Coordinator	1.0		
EQUIPMENT			2,346
SUPPLIES			8,794
TEXTBOOKS			—
CONTRACT SERVICES			682
Total			$102,243

MUSIC PROGRAM

We plan to improve the Music Program by:

   *Implementing an elective vocal Music Program for 7th and 8th grade students at the middle school. Reduction of teaching time associated with this change will be reallocated into the developmental reading program.

   *Adding an advanced music theory course to the high school to provide an in-depth instructional sequence for students in this area.

   *Providing for the scheduling of band, orchestra, and chorus as part of the regular school day at both the middle and high schools.

   *Adding a teacher at the high school to implement the expanded program in this area.

		Number of Staff	1970-71 Budget
CERTIFICATED STAFF (Includes substitutes, overtime and employee benefits)		8.6	$137,002
Classroom teachers	0.6		
Music teachers	7.0		
Music Coordinator	1.0		
EQUIPMENT			1,900
SUPPLIES			2,775
TEXTBOOKS			1,340
CONTRACT SERVICES			1,050
Total			$144,067

8

FIGURE 59.   PROGRAM BUDGET, PEARL RIVER SCHOOL DISTRICT (continued)

SPECIAL EDUCATION PROGRAM

We plan to maintain the Special Education Program by:

*Providing for increasing enrollments in BOCES programs.

	1970-71 Budget
CONTRACT SERVICES (Contract with BOCES provides educational services to 49 students)	$73,371

VOCATIONAL EDUCATION PROGRAM

We plan to maintain the Vocational Education Program by:

*Providing for increasing enrollments in BOCES programs.

	1970-71 Budget
CONTRACT SERVICES (Contract with BOCES provides educational services to 90 students. These students attend our High School one-half day and attend BOCES classes the other one-half day.)	$49,064

ADULT EDUCATION PROGRAM

The Adult Education Program will remain essentially the same for the 1970-71 school year.

	1970-71 Budget
CERTIFICATED STAFF (Includes substitutes, overtime, and employee benefits)	$ 8,134
NON-CERTIFICATED STAFF (Includes substitutes, overtime and employee benefits)	704
EQUIPMENT	—
SUPPLIES	665
TEXTBOOKS	300
CONTRACT SERVICES	610
Total	$10,413

NOTE: The cost of this program is fully paid for by registration fees.

FIGURE 59.   PROGRAM BUDGET, PEARL RIVER SCHOOL DISTRICT (continued)

INSTRUCTIONAL SUPPORT PROGRAMS
LIBRARY PROGRAM

We plan to improve the existing Library Program by:

*Increasing the library book budget.

		Number of Staff	1970-71 Budget
CERTIFICATED STAFF (Includes substitutes, overtime and employee benefits)		6.0	$ 99,879
Librarians	5.0		
Library Coordinator	1.0		
NON-CERTIFICATED STAFF (Includes substitutes, overtime and employee benefits)		2.9	19,816
Senior Library Clerk	0.8		
Teacher Aides	0.8		
Typists	1.3		
EQUIPMENT			780
SUPPLIES (Includes purchase of library books)			23,200
TEXTBOOKS			—
CONTRACT SERVICES			1,620
Total			$145,295

GUIDANCE AND PSYCHOLOGICAL PROGRAM

We plan to improve the Guidance and Psychological Services Program by:

*Adding one psychologist who will work primarily with students, parents, and teachers at the middle and high school levels.

*Reallocating the time of the existing psychologist to the elementary level in order to allow him to devote the majority of his time to working with students, parents, and teachers at this level.

		Number of Staff	1970-71 Budget
CERTIFICATED STAFF (Includes substitutes, overtime and employee benefits)		8.0	$153,368
Psychologists	2.0		
Guidance Counselors	6.0		
NON-CERTIFICATED STAFF (Includes substitutes, overtime and employee benefits)		3.0	19,000
Senior Typists	2.0		
Typist	1.0		
EQUIPMENT			—
SUPPLIES			3,525
TEXTBOOKS			—
CONTRACT SERVICES (Includes contract services with BOCES).			18,860
Total			$194,753

HEALTH SERVICES PROGRAM

We plan to maintain Health Services at the existing levels but will modify the program by:

*Employing a part time physician to replace nine school physicians presently providing school medical services. This approach will provide greater continuity of service and improved preventative procedures in student health.

		Number of Staff	1970-71 Budget
CERTIFICATED STAFF (Includes substitutes, overtime, and employee benefits)		4.6	$63,896
Nurse-Teachers	4.6		
NON-CERTIFICATED STAFF (Includes substitutes, overtime, and employee benefits)		1.6	27,286
School Physician (Part-time)	0.5		
Typists	1.1		
EQUIPMENT			965
SUPPLIES			950
TEXTBOOKS			—
CONTRACT SERVICES (Includes contract health services with other districts as required by law)			4,500
Total			$97,597

FIGURE 59.   PROGRAM BUDGET, PEARL RIVER SCHOOL DISTRICT (continued)

BOND PRINCIPAL AND INTEREST

This program has been modified by:

*Providing for the first installment of the high school litigation settlement.

*Providing for the first installment on the bonds for the recently approved building program.

	1970-71 Budget
CONTRACT SERVICES (Debt service for existing building program, $441,408; new building program, $45,000; High School litigation settlement, $26,700 and interest on tax anticipation notes, $3,500)	$516,608

OPERATION AND MAINTENANCE OF PLANT PROGRAM

We plan to maintain Operation and Maintenance of Plant Program at existing levels except to modify it by:

*Implementing a comprehensive preventative maintenance program.

*Providing an alarm system at the high school.

	Number of Staff	1970-71 Budget
NON-CERTIFICATED STAFF (Includes substitutes, overtime, and employee benefits)	27.1	$243,242
Superintendent of Buildings & Grounds 1.0		
Senior Head Custodians (1 at High School		
and 1 at Middle School) 2.0		
Head Custodians 6.0		
Custodians 5.8		
Cleaners 2.3		
School Matron 1.0		
Senior Clerk 1.0		
Building Mechanics 3.0		
Courier 1.0		
Groundsmen 4.0		
EQUIPMENT		3,760
SUPPLIES (Includes custodial cleaning supplies and grounds maintenance supplies)		29,000
TEXTBOOKS		—
CONTRACT SERVICES (Includes contract maintenance, contract cleaning, insurance and utilities)		337,085
Total		$613,087

SCHOOL MANAGEMENT PROGRAM

We plan to modify and improve the School Management Program by:

*Reallocating existing central office administrative time to provide administrative support for the middle school.

*Eliminating one elementary principal due to the closing of Central Avenue Elementary School.

	Number of Staff	1970-71 Budget
CERTIFICATED STAFF (Includes substitutes, overtime, and employee benefits)	10.2	$220,832
Principals 6.0		
Assistant Principals 2.0		
Assistant to the Principal 0.6		
High School Deans 1.6		
NON-CERTIFICATED STAFF (Includes substitutes, overtime, and employee benefits)	17.8	114,954
Secretarial Assistant 1.0		
Senior Stenographer 1.0		
Senior Typists 7.0		
Typists 1.3		
Teacher Aides 6.5		
Clerk 1.0		
EQUIPMENT		1,000
SUPPLIES		3,000
TEXTBOOKS		—
CONTRACT SERVICES (Includes contracted services for data processing at BOCES, $14,873)		21,588
Total		$361,374

11

FIGURE 59.   PROGRAM BUDGET, PEARL RIVER SCHOOL DISTRICT (continued)

CENTRAL OFFICE MANAGEMENT PROGRAM

We plan to modify the Central Office Management Program by:

*Reducing central office staff and reallocating it to provide needed administrative support at the middle school.

	Number of Staff	1970-71 Budget
CERTIFICATED STAFF (Includes substitutes, overtime, and employee benefits)	4.4	$116,375
Superintendent of Schools — 1.0		
Assistant Superintendent—Instruction — 1.0		
Assistant Superintendent—Business — 1.0		
Assistant to Superintendent—Personnel — 1.0		
Administrative Assistant — 0.4		
NON-CERTIFICATED STAFF (Includes substitutes, overtime, and employee benefits)	11.8	108,869
District Clerk — 0.2		
District Treasurer — 0.2		
Secretarial Assistants — 5.0		
Senior Typists — 1.8		
Typists — 1.8		
Senior Account Clerk — 1.0		
Account Clerk — 0.8		
Telephone Operator — 1.0		
EQUIPMENT		2,400
SUPPLIES		10,885
TEXTBOOKS		—

CONTRACT SERVICES—Includes the following items:

Legal Services	$ 7,500
Independent Audit	1,800
District Meetings	3,500
Recruitment and Negotiations	17,000
Office Equipment Leases	11,000
Data Processing	9,000
BOCES Administration	7,050
Consultants	3,000
Other	12,742 72,592
Total	$311,121

TRANSPORTATION PROGRAM

We plan to maintain the Transportation Programs at existing levels, except to modify this program by:

*Increasing the late activity bus from three days a week to four days a week for students involved in extra-curricular activities or after school studies.

	Number of Staff	1970-71 Budget
NON-CERTIFICATED STAFF (Includes substitutes, overtime and employee benefits)	1.0	$ 9,935
Bus Driver — 1.0		
EQUIPMENT		5,000
SUPPLIES		600
TEXTBOOKS		—
CONTRACT SERVICES (Includes contract bus services)		160,760
Total		$176,295

SCHOOL LUNCH PROGRAM

We plan to modify the School Lunch Program by:

*Moving the preparation of elementary lunches to the new kitchen at Franklin Avenue School.

*Increasing the prices of all Type "A" lunches in order to continue the program on a self-supporting basis.

NON-PROGRAM

This program has been modified by:

	1970-71 Budget
EQUIPMENT	$ 2,050
SUPPLIES	3,448
TEXTBOOKS (Textbooks for non-public school students. This cost is fully reimbursed by New York State.)	5,000
CONTRACT SERVICES (Includes $20,000 for refund on prior year's taxes a s result of changes in assessments.)	24,692
Total	$35,190

These items are shown here because they could not be allocated to programs.

COMMUNITY SERVICES PROGRAMS

	1970-71 Budget
NON-CERTIFICATED STAFF (Custodial overtime for use of buildings by community groups)	$7,041

FIGURE 59.   PROGRAM BUDGET, PEARL RIVER SCHOOL DISTRICT (continued)

PEARL RIVER SCHOOL DISTRICT

CERTIFICATED STAFF*

	Actual 1969-70	Proposed 1970-71	Change
Central Office Administration	5.0	4.4	−0.6
Building Administration	9.0	8.6	−0.4
Teachers	203.1	210.2	+7.1
TOTAL	217.1	223.2	+6.1

Summary of Certificated Staff Changes
(In full-time-equivalent personnel)

Elementary	Changes	Net Change	High School	Changes	Net Change
Classroom Teachers, Grade 1-5	−2.0		Physical Education Teacher	−1.0	
Principal, Central Avenue	−1.0		Classroom Teachers	+4.8	
Music Coordinator—reallocation of time to High School	−0.2		Psychologist	+0.3	
Reading Specialists	+1.5		Dean	+0.3	
Psychologist	+0.4				
Total Elementary		−1.3	Total High School		+4.4

Middle School			District Wide		
Classroom Teachers (Reading Specialist, Net after reallocations)	+1.7		Administrative Assistant, reallocation to the Middle School		−0.6
Health Teacher (Mandated by State of New York)	+1.0				
Psychologist	+0.3		TOTAL		+6.1
Assistant to Principal (Reallocation from Central Office)	+0.6				
Total Middle School		+3.6			

NON-CERTIFICATED STAFF*

(Does not include food service personnel. These salaries are budgeted in a separate School Lunch Fund)

	Actual 1969-70	Proposed 1970-71	Change
Clerical	31.8	30.8	−1.0
Custodial, Maintenance and Transportation	28.6	27.1	−1.5
Teacher Aides and Monitors	9.5	14.2	+4.7
TOTAL	69.9	72.1	+2.2

*Note: Part time personnel are included on the basis of full-time-equivalent personnel.

HOW MANY PUPILS WILL BE SERVED?

Actual 1969-70 Enrollment	3667
Budgeted 1969-70 Enrollment	3591
Total Increase	+76

	Actual 1969-70 Enrollments	Estimated 1970-71 Enrollments	Change
Elementary Schools (grades K-5)	1581	1531	−50
Middle School (grades 6-8)	897	910	+13
High School (grades 9-12)	1189	1247	+58
TOTAL	3667*	3688	+21

*Budgeted enrollment was 3591.

13

FIGURE 59.   PROGRAM BUDGET, PEARL RIVER SCHOOL DISTRICT (continued)

SUMMARY 1970-71
PEARL RIVER SCHOOL DISTRICT BUDGET

RECEIPTS

DESCRIPTION	Revised BUDGET 1969-70	BUDGET 1970-71	Change
State Aid	$2,180,370	$2,522,000	+341,630
Other Receipts (Admissions, Building Use for Rentals, Earnings on Investments)	77,670	61,680	−15,990
Fund Balance From Previous Year	317,394	0	−317,394
Property Taxes	2,868,593	3,145,183	+276,590
TOTALS	$5,444,027	$5,728,863	+284,836

EXPENDITURES

DESCRIPTION			
Board of Education	$ 36,880	$ 23,275	−13,605
Central Administration	202,906	196,180	−6,726
Instruction (Salaries, Equipment, Supplies, Textbooks)	3,176,060	3,355,585	+179,525
Community Services (Building Use)	3,500	6,000	+2,500
Transportation	171,134	182,015	+10,881
Operation and Maintenance of Plant	474,366	511,995	+37,629
Undistributed Expenses (Data-Processing, Retirement, Social Security, Health Insurance, Other Insurance and BOCES Rentals)	939,548	937,205	−2,343
Debt Service	439,633	516,608	+76,975
TOTALS	$5,444,027	$5,728,863	+284,836

A detail comparison of the 1969-70 budget with the proposed 1970-71 budget is available upon request from the Administration Office or by calling 735-4091.

HOW IS THE TAX ESTABLISHED?

Year	Total Tax Levy ÷	Total District Assessed = Valuation	Tax Rate Per $1,000 Assessed Valuation
Estimated 1970-71	$3,145,183	$36,833,020 (Based on Estimate Made by the Town of Orangetown)	$85.39
Actual 1969-70	$2,866,433	$36,133,020	$79.33

14

FIGURE 59.   PROGRAM BUDGET, PEARL RIVER SCHOOL DISTRICT (continued)

Propositions For Wednesday May 6, 1970 Vote

SCHOOL BUDGET PROPOSITION

RESOLVED: That the Board of Education of Union Free School District No. 8, Town of Orangetown, County of Rockland, be authorized to expend the sums set forth herein during the school year 1970-71 and to levy the necessary tax therefor, and that the said Board be authorized to transfer unexpended balances in any item to meet necessary expenditures in any items of any function.

BOARD OF EDUCATION MEMBER—Election of one member of the Board of Education for a full term of five (5) years to fill a vacancy to occur through the expiration of the term of Dr. Lee N. Starker and election of one member of the Board to fill the un-expired term of four (4) years of John J. Bernardi.

RENTAL TO BOCES PROPOSITION

SHALL the Board of Education, pursuant to Section 1958 of the Education Law, enter into a rental agreement with the Board of Cooperative Educational Services of Rockland County to rent one classroom in the High School for a term of one year at the annual rental of $2,310, payable monthly in advance.

PUBLIC LIBRARY BUDGET PROPOSITION

RESOLVED: That the Library Board be authorized to expend annually the sums herein set forth; and that the Board of Education be empowered to levy the necessary tax therefor; and that the Library Board be authorized to transfer unexpended balances in any item to meet any necessary expenditures in any item of any group.

These propositions presented by Pearl River Union Free School District No. 8 will appear on the ballot for machine vote. Additional propositions may be presented by voters. Such propositions must be presented by petition supported by signatures of 150 qualified voters to the Clerk of the Board no later than six (6) days before the election (by 5:00 P.M., April 29, 1970).

LIBRARY BOARD MEMBER—Election of one member of the Board of the Pearl River Public Library for a full term of five (5) years, to fill a vacancy to occur through the expiration of the term of Leighton J. Cree.

PETITIONS FOR BOARD CANDIDATES

Petitions for candidates for Board of Education and Public Library Board of Trustees vacancies must be filed in the Office of the Clerk of the District not later than 14 days prior to the date of the election (April 22, 1970 at 5:00 P.M.) Such petitions require signatures of at least 25 qualified voters.

Candidates will be voted on at the District Election, May 6, 1970.

REGISTRATION REQUIRED

Only voters registered for School District Elections May Vote

TWO VOTER REGISTRATION DAYS WILL BE HELD

Saturday, April 25, 10 A.M. — 3 P.M.
Tuesday, April 28, 4 P.M. — 10 P.M.

at regular voting places

You are registered if you registered or voted at the annual meeting on May 8, 1968 or thereafter. Permanent personal registration is in effect for all who vote in School Elections once every two years.

IMPORTANT: Town election registration does not qualify voter for School District Elections.

VOTER QUALIFICATIONS

You may register to vote in school district elections if you meet the following qualifications:

*United States Citizen

*Aged 21 years, or over

*School District Resident For 30 Days Prior To May 6, 1970

WHERE TO VOTE —

Wednesday, May 6, 10 A.M. — 10 P.M.

DISTRICT NO. 1 — LINCOLN AVENUE SCHOOL
All addresses West of N.J. and N.Y. Railroad tracks.

DISTRICT NO. 2 — CENTRAL AVENUE SCHOOL
All addresses between N.J. and N.Y. Railroad tracks and the center of Middletown Road (North-South).

DISTRICT NO. 3 — HIGH SCHOOL
All addresses East of the centerline of Middletown Road (North-South) and the Eastern boundary of School District.

15

FIGURE 59.   PROGRAM BUDGET, PEARL RIVER SCHOOL DISTRICT (continued)

PEARL RIVER SCHOOL DISTRICT

Operating Budget Vote Wednesday – May 6, 1970

IMPORTANT FACTS FOR VOTER

PUBLIC NEIGHBORHOOD DISCUSSION MEETINGS
SCHOOL BUDGET   LIBRARY BUDGET

—FRANKLIN AVENUE, THURSDAY, APRIL 23, 8 P.M.

—LINCOLN AVENUE, THURSDAY, APRIL 30, 8 P.M.

—MIDDLE SCHOOL, MONDAY, MAY 4, 8 P.M.

LISTEN: EACH THURSDAY, 12:15, WKQW, 1300 on Dial
For School News and Announcements on "PEARL RIVER SCHOOLS NEWS REPORT"

VOTE: MAY 6, 1970

10 A.M. — 10 P.M.

REGISTRATION FOR THOSE NOT REGISTERED, SATURDAY, APRIL 25, 10 A.M. — 3 P.M.

TUESDAY, APRIL 28, 4 P.M. — 10 P.M.

SCHOOL
DISTRICT
37 Franklin Avenue
Pearl River, N.Y. 10965

NON-PROFIT
U.S. POSTAGE
P A I D
Permit No. 203
Pearl River, N.Y.

Address Correction Requested

FIGURE 60.   PPBS INSTALLATION PLANNING FORM, PERSONNEL INVOLVED

District	Date Prepared		Prepared by			Page 1 of 1	
Personnel Involved	Planning	Develop-ment	Installa-tion	Opera-tions	Evalua-tion	Task Force Team	Other Team(s)
Community involvement Agencies and organizations							
Parents							
Program management Superintendent and board of ed.							
Ass't. Supt.—instruction							
Ass't. Supt.—business							
Ass't. to Supt.—personnel							
Curricular/instructional—personnel Instructional supervisors							
Principals							
Teachers							
Support service personnel Buildings and grounds							
Transportation							
School lunch							
Accounting							
Purchasing							
Students							
Technical/outside assistance Independent educ. auditor							
University							
Fiscal auditor							
Consultants							
County office							
State department							

FIGURE 61.   PPBS INSTALLATION PLANNING FORM, TASKS OR ACTIVITIES

District	Date Prepared	Prepared by	Page of

No.	Task or Activity	Personnel Involved			Start	Finish	Est. Days Req.
		Preparation	Review	Approved			

FIGURE 62.   PPBS INSTALLATION FORM, MANPOWER USAGE—MAN DAYS

Personnel Involved	May	Jun	Jul	Aug	Sept	Oct	Nov	Dec	Jan	Feb	Mar	Apr	May	Jun	Jul	Aug	Sept	Oct

District _____   Date Prepared _____   Prepared By _____   Page ___ of ___

FIGURE 63.   PPBS INSTALLATION PLANNING FORM, BUDGET

No.	Task or Activity	2nd qtr	3rd qtr	4th qtr	1st qtr	2nd qtr	3rd qtr	4th qtr	1st qtr	2nd qtr	3rd qtr	4th qtr	TOTAL

District   Date Prepared   Prepared by   Page 1 of 1

FIGURE 64.   TENTATIVE PLAN FOR IMPLEMENTATION OF PPBS,
FOLSOM-CORDOVA UNIFIED SCHOOL DISTRICT,
CALIFORNIA

1.0 Appoint PPBS Task Force
    1.1 Set forth the various points of view to be included.
    1.2 Set up the number of participants from each area.
    1.3 Set the maximum number.
    1.4 Assign people to position.
    1.5 Written directive from the Board designating the PPBS task force by name and including their major charge, distributed throughout the district.

2.0 Orient Task Force Personnel
    2.1 Prepare a basic orientation program for general interest: teachers organizations, communications, teachers, task force, department chairmen.
        2.1.1 Prepare objectives for this orientation.
        2.1.2 Prepare strategies for this orientation.
        2.1.3 Prepare visual and written materials to accomplish objectives.
        2.1.4 Prepare assessment to determine if objectives are met.
    2.2 Prepare an intermediate-level introduction (for task force and department chairmen).
        2.2.1 Prepare objectives for this orientation.
        2.2.2 Prepare strategies for this orientation.
        2.2.3 Prepare visual and written materials to accomplish objectives.
        2.2.4 Prepare assessment to determine if objectives are met.
    2.3 Prepare a plan for orientation.
        2.3.1 Set up a calendar for implementation.
            2.3.1.1 Schedule meetings with teachers, faculty in schools.
            2.3.1.2 Schedule meetings with department chairmen in schools.
            2.3.1.3 Schedule meetings with subcommittees of CAC.
            2.3.1.4 Schedule meetings with community.

3.0 Identify Constraints (Budgetary, Statutory, Political) by Task Force
    3.1 Budgeting resources
        3.1.1 Allocation of personnel and time.
        3.1.2 Preparation of, or review of, the budget.
    3.2 Statutory constraints
        3.2.1 Write contract requirements by the State and for the State.
        3.2.2 Write contract requirements by the district and for the district.
    3.3 Political constraints
        3.3.1 Board of Education directives
            3.3.1.1 Board of Education action items from minutes.
        3.3.2 Administrative directives and concerns
            3.3.2.1 Administrative regulations
            3.3.2.2 Personnel organizations concerns
                3.3.2.2.1 Teachers organizations
                3.3.2.2.2 Classified organization

FIGURE 64.   TENTATIVE PLAN FOR IMPLEMENTATION OF PPBS,
FOLSOM-CORDOVA UNIFIED SCHOOL DISTRICT,
CALIFORNIA (continued)

3.3.2.2.3 Administrative organization

3.3.2.3 Community concerns (areas and groups)

3.3.2.3.1 Mather Air Force Base

3.3.2.3.2 Folsom

3.3.2.3.3 Cordova

4.0 Evaluate Current Status by the Task Force

4.1 Philosophy and goals (at levels I, II, III, IV, V, VI)

4.1.1 Evaluate the system for community involvement and district philosophy and goals.

4.1.2 Evaluate CAC philosophy and goals and any other goals used in the district.

4.1.3 Evaluate administrative regulations on curriculum development for goals.

4.1.4 Evaluate Sacramento County Course of Study philosophy and goals.

4.1.5 Other materials impinging upon decisions that are to be made in this area.

4.2 Objectives

4.2.1 Evaluate the district objectives (at levels I, II, III, IV, V, VI).

4.2.2 Evaluate the CAC objectives and any objectives developed and used or planned to be used in the district.

4.2.3 Evaluate the administrative regulations on curriculum development for objectives.

4.2.4 Evaluate the Sacramento County Course of Study objectives.

4.2.5 Other materials impinging upon the decisions that are to be made in this area.

4.3 Assessment systems

4.3.1 Evaluate the district assessment program.

4.3.2 Evaluate the administrative regulations in the areas of assessment.

4.3.3 Evaluate the use and benefit to the district of the State Regulation Tests.

4.3.4 Evaluate the use and benefit to the district of any county school evaluation.

4.3.5 Evaluate the assessment programs and procedures in use or planned for use in the district by departments, grade levels, or larger groups.

4.3.6 Evaluate other assessment materials or procedures which will impinge upon the decisions that are to be made in this area, i.e., W.A.S.C. program.

4.4 Program documentation (explanation of what this is)

4.5 Fiscal system

4.5.1 Evaluate the policy and administrative regulations in this area.

4.5.2 Evaluate the present fiscal planning.

4.5.3 Evaluate the present fiscal programming.

4.5.4 Evaluate the present fiscal budgeting.

4.6 Systems and procedures (what this is)

FIGURE 64 (continued)

4.7 Available resources
    4.7.1 Available people with required skills in our districts
        4.7.1.1 To develop goals.
        4.7.1.2 To develop objectives.
        4.7.1.3 To develop assessment procedures.
        4.7.1.4 To develop a fiscal system.
        4.7.1.5 To develop systems and procedures.
        4.7.1.6 To carry out program documentation.
    4.7.2 Available consultant possessing required skills outside the district
        4.7.2.1 List skills, titles, and name for P.M.M.
        4.7.2.2 List skills, titles, and name for Sacramento County School.
        4.7.2.3 List skills, titles, and name for Education Res. Org.
        4.7.2.4 List skills, titles, and name for Department of Corrections.
        4.7.2.5 List skills, titles, and name for Sacramento State College.
        4.7.2.6 List skills, titles, and name for U. C. Davis.
        4.7.2.7 List skills, titles, and name for U. of P.
        4.7.2.8 List skills, titles, and name for other agencies or individuals in the community.
        4.7.2.9 List skills, titles, and name for other agencies or individuals outside of the community.
5.0 Identify and Document Inadequacies between Current Practices and Those Required for PPBS
    5.1 List the specific inadequacies identified.
    5.2 Establish the priority of items identified above.
    5.3 List each suggestion to improve each inadequacy in the priority list.
6.0 Develop Communications Plan
    6.1 Write the objectives for this function.
    6.2 Identify the groups or individuals that must be informed.
        6.2.1 List the groups and individuals to be informed.
        6.2.2 List the three to seven types of communication media to be used.
        6.2.3 Outline each of the types of communication media and list under each of the media the groups and individuals to be informed.
    6.3 Establish a list of the items and information to be communicated to the groups and individuals.
        6.3.1 Establish a communication calendar.
            6.3.1.1 Indicate the person responsible for each of the items identified on the calendar.
7.0 Make Presentations on a Continuing Basis to Staff and Non-Staff Groups (See Develop Communications Plan 6.0)
8.0 Prepare Implementation Plan (Identify Tasks and Schedules)
    8.1 List the tasks to be performed in implementing PPBS.
    8.2 List the tasks to be performed in order of their performance and assign responsibilities to people and write their name opposite the task.

FIGURE 64 (continued)

8.3 Prepare calendar for the implementation of PPBS. Indicate the function and the name of the person performing the function and during what time span.

9.0 Develop Training Plan

9.1 Write behavioral objectives and assessment for the training plan.

9.2 Prepare the strategies to achieve the 9.1 objectives.

9.3 Write the resources necessary to carry on strategies in 9.2.

9.4 Write the resources we have available.

9.5 Write the match, mis-match 9.3-9.4.

9.6 List alternatives to 9.3 and 9.4.

9.7 Select a plan of implementation

9.7.1 Prepare a calendar.

9.7.2 Assign responsibilities.

9.7.3 Assign resources.

10.0 Conduct Seminars and Workshops (Implementation Plan 9.0)

11.0 Assign Tasks (Sec. 8.0 and 9.0)

12.0 Document Existing Program Structure (what does this mean, get help)

12.1 Propose existing program element.

12.2 Group elements in behavioral order.

13.0 Develop Goals

13.1 (See attached 4.0 Goals)

13.2 (See attached Community Involvement System) Id. #C-1.

13.3 Curriculum Development Plan, see Ad. Reg. #.

13.4 Establish levels of goals to be developed and for what.

13.4.1 List levels of goals to be written.

13.4.2 List the areas for which goals are to be prepared.

13.4.3 Assign responsibility (person's name) for each area and each level.

13.4.4 Set a time period in which 13.4.1 and 13.4.2 are to be completed.

14.0 Develop Objectives and Evaluative Criteria

14.1 (See 4.0 attached)

14.2 (See Community Involvement Plan, Id. #C-1 and #C-2)

14.3 (See 5-year program #C-2)

14.4 (See Curriculum Development Plan, See Administrative Regulation #)

14.5 Establish (Same as for goals except objectives, see 14.4).

14.6 Assessment of objectives

14.6.1 Every objective will have at least one means of assessment to determine the extent to which it was achieved.

14.6.1.1 Spell out this area in detail—get help.

14.6.2 Each objective shall have at least one quantitative means of measuring the degree to which it is met.

14.6.3 Each objective's measurement shall be assessed by three or more teachers in the field and certified by them as being a true assessment. (Their three signatures will attest.)

FIGURE 64 (continued)

14.6.4 Each objective assessment shall be scored the same by three teachers in the field taking the assessment, and shall be certified as such by their signatures. (Develop a notice.)

14.6.5 "The standards for developing assessment instruments," measures, scales, and judgments are set forth in a brief one-sheet document.

14.6.6 Develop a booklet to assist those attempting assessment of objectives.

    14.6.6.1 The booklet should contain the following specific information:

        14.6.6.1.1

        14.6.6.1.2

        14.6.6.1.3

14.6.7 Establish a workshop to assess objectives.

    14.6.7.1 Write objectives for the workshop.

    14.6.7.2 Write strategies for the workshop.

    14.6.7.3 Identify resources necessary for strategies.

    14.6.7.4 Identify resources available.

    14.6.7.5 Assessment plan for the program

    14.6.7.6 Revise program as indicated.

    14.6.7.7 Plan a follow-up in-service plan to meet objectives not met as indicated in 14.6.7.4

        14.6.7.1 Same function as outlined in 14.6.7.1—14.6.7.7.

15.0 Develop Program Description Packages (see all material up to this point). (Review and evaluate and revise procedures.)

16.0 Develop procedures (see all material up to this point). (Review, evaluate, and revise procedures.)

17.0 Develop Program Structure, (We have one), (Revise), (Get help).

18.0 Develop Program Coding (Revise as per accumulated notes and comments).

19.0 Develop Budgets and Multi-Year Financial Plan (Review-revise-evaluate-check multi-year), (Need help).

20.0 Manage resources (What does this mean in this context?), (Look for help)

21.0 Assess Results (How? Against what? Look for help.)

FIGURE 65.   INSTRUCTIONAL OBJECTIVES EXCHANGE (IOX)
CATALOG, LOS ANGELES, CALIFORNIA

1. READING, K-3 — This collection emphasizes word recognition, comprehension, and study skills. Each of these areas is respectively subdivided into the major categories of phonetic and structural analysis, literal, interpretive, critical and vocabulary comprehension, and the work skills of alphabetizing, reading rate, organization, and use of references, pictorial and graphic material. (313 objectives, 1 item per objective)

2. READING, 4-6 — This collection treats the areas of word recognition, comprehension and study skills. Each of these areas provides objectives for the sub-categories to develop and extend the skills acquired in grades kindergarten through three. (148 objectives, 1 item per objective)

3. READING, 7-12 — This collection stresses structural analysis, critical comprehension, and study skills. Objectives for selected phonetic analysis skills are also included, as well as extensive coverage of the major sub-categories. (93 objectives, 1 item per objective)

4. LANGUAGE ARTS, K-3 — Contents of this collection include writing skills, simple paragraph and letter forms, grammar skills, listening and speaking skills. (84 objectives, 1 item per objective)

5. LANGUAGE ARTS, 4-6 — Contents of this collection include structure and types of sentences, parts of speech, capitalization, punctuation, linguistics (word analysis), composition, literature. (194 objectives, 1 item per objective)

6. LANGUAGE ARTS, 7-9 — Contents of this collection include reference skills, listening and speaking skills, composition, literature. (159 objectives, 1 item per objective)

7. ENGLISH GRAMMAR, 7-12 — This collection contains objectives and evaluation items for English grammar in secondary schools. Although there are some objectives which deal with the traditional approach, the main concentration is on the Roberts transformational approach. The sections are: traditional, syntax, morphology, and phonology. (84 objectives, 6 items per objective)

8. ENGLISH SKILLS, 7-9 — This collection contains objectives and evaluation items for the teaching of English skills in junior high school. Content areas include: speech, composition, mass media, reference skills, and mechanics and conventions. Grammar is not included in this collection. (76 objectives, 1 item per objective)

9. ENGLISH SKILLS, 10-12 — This collection contains objectives and evaluation items for the teaching of English skills in high school. Content areas include: speech, composition, mass media, reference skills, and mechanics and conventions. Grammar is not included in this collection. (37 objectives, 6 items per objective)

10. ENGLISH LITERATURE, 7-9 — This collection is designed to develop the students' ability to analyze literature and to evaluate its effects. Content areas include poetry and the novel. (16 objectives, 6 items per objective)

11. ENGLISH LITERATURE, 10-12 — This collection is designed to develop the students' ability to analyze literature and to evaluate its effects. Content areas include: poetry, the novel, drama, short story, and non-fiction. (34 objectives, 6 items per objective)

12. MATHEMATICS, K-3 — This collection emphasizes the introduction of concepts and skills. The content area includes sets; numbers, numerals and numeration systems; operations and their properties;

FIGURE 65 (continued)

measurement; geometry, relations, functions, and graphs; probability and statistics; applications and problem solving; and mathematical sentences, order, and logic. (174 objectives, 4 items per objective)

13. MATHEMATICS, 4-6 — This collection covers intermediate concepts and skills. The content area includes sets; numbers, numerals, and numeration systems; operations and their properties; measurement; geometry, relations, functions, and graphs; probability and statistics; applications and problem solving; and mathematical sentences, order, and logic. (233 objectives, 4 items per objective)

14. MATHEMATICS, 7-9 — This collection covers those concepts and skills structural to the discipline of mathematics. The content areas include sets; numbers, numerals, and numeration systems; operations and their properties; measurement; geometry, relations, functions, and graphs; probability and statistics; applications and problem solving; and mathematical sentences, order and logic. (265 objectives, 2 items per objective)

15. GENERAL MATHEMATICS, 10-12 — This collection emphasizes general concepts and skills. Objectives are included for the following categories: sets; numbers, numerals and numeration systems; operations and their properties; measurement; geometry; probability, graphs, and statistics; applications and problem solving; order and logic. (123 objectives, 6 items per objective)

16. BUSINESS EDUCATION (Bookkeeping), 7-12 — This collection treats the basic procedures and concepts fundamental to the bookkeeping cycle: journalizing; posting; preparing a trial balance; financial statement; balancing and ruling accounts. Objectives for the handling of banking transactions; receiving, disbursing and recording cash transactions; handling payroll records; recording accrual deferred expenses and depreciation; and bookkeeping vocabulary are also included. (17 objectives, 6 items per objective)

17. BUSINESS EDUCATION (Business Law), 7-12 — This collection is an introduction to the basic concepts and skills of Business Law. The objectives are organized in the following categories: legal foundations, the laws of contracts, property, negotiable instruments, insurance and agency. (37 objectives, 6 items per objective)

18. BUSINESS EDUCATION (General Business), 7-12 — This collection is designed to familiarize the student with some of the concepts which he will find most useful in the business world. Content areas include such topics as money and banking, consumer buying, credit, economic risks (insurance), money management, communication services, and transportation and shipping services. (35 objectives, 6 items per objective)

19. BUSINESS EDUCATION (Secretarial Skills), 7-12 — This collection emphasizes basic stenographic skills: typing, shorthand, office machines, filing, telephone answering and processing and basic forms of business English. Also included are objectives covering the fundamentals of office behavior and appearance. (46 objectives, 6 items per objective)

20. HOME ECONOMICS, 7-9 — This collection is divided into the following categories: child development, clothing and textiles, consumer practices, foods and nutrition, home management and family economics. (74 objectives, 6 items per objective)

21. HOME ECONOMICS, 10-12 — This collection is divided into the following categories: child development, clothing and textiles, consumer practices, foods and nutrition, home management and family economics. (48 objectives, 6 items per objective)

isoningING

FIGURE 65 (continued)

22. AUTO MECHANICS, 10-12 — This collection reflects major behavioral objectives required in a comprehensive course in automotive tune-up and repair. (185 objectives, 1 item per objective)

23. ELECTRONICS, 7-12 — This collection is an introduction to basic concepts and skills of electronics. It is organzied into the following categories: fundamentals; direct current circuits; primary and secondary batteries; magnetism; electro-magnetic induction; direct current generators; alternating current single phase circuits; transformers; and regulators. (50 objectives, 1 item per objective)

24. GENERAL METALS, 7-12 — This collection is an introduction to concepts and skills in general metals. It is divided into the following categories: properties of metal, operations and functions, cutting and shearing, filing, cutting holes, grinding, bending metal, forming metal, metal spinning, threaded fasteners, soldering, riveting, sheet metal seams, polishing and buffing metal surfaces, and decorating metal. (90 objectives, 6 items per objective)

25. MECHANICAL DRAWING, 7-12 — This collection is an introduction to concepts and skills in mechanical drawing. It is divided into the following categories: basic drafting skills, beginning lettering, making the drawing, orthographic projections, dimensioning, scale drawing, pictorial drawing, dimensioning pictorial drawings, section drawing, auxiliary views, the draftsman and the shopman, thread conventions and thread symbols, assembly and detail drawing, reference and constructions. (85 objectives, 1 item per objective)

26. WOODWORKING, 7-12 — This collection introduces basic skills and emphasizes the processes involved in woodworking. It is divided into the following categories: tool care and use, rough stock, squaring up stock, making and fastening joints, and miscellaneous finishing processes. (56 objectives, 6 items per objective)

27. AMERICAN HISTORY, 7-12 — This collection emphasizes political, social, and economic concepts, problems and fundamental issues in American history from the pre-Revolutionary period to modern times. (19 objectives, 6 items per objective)

28. GEOGRAPHY, K-9 — This collection reflects major social science concepts in the discipline of geography. (97 objectives, 1 item per objective)

29. BIOLOGY, 10-12 — This collection emphasizes processes of inquiry and laboratory work, either directly or indirectly. Although this sequence is based on the Biological Sciences Curriculum Study (BSCS), the objectives are designed to make them serviceable to any program. (15 objectives, 6 items per objective)

30. SPANISH, 7-12 — This collection is an introduction to the basic concepts and skills structural to the discipline of Spanish. It includes objectives covering key functions of understanding, speaking, reading, and writing. (74 objectives, 6 items per objective)

31. MUSIC, K-6 — This collection reflects major concepts, fundamentals and applications in music appreciation. (97 objectives, 1 item per objective)

32. HEALTH (Nutrition), K-6 — This collection reflects the major concepts related to Nutrition—Man and His Food. Content area includes daily food choices using the four food groups, nutrients from food, how the body uses food, food processing, consumer education in advertising and merchandising, and cultural and social uses of food in man's environment. (24 objectives, 6 items per objective)

FIGURE 65 (continued)

33. PHYSICAL EDUCATION, K-3 — The content area includes perceptual motor, sensory motor, locomotor skills, non-locomotor skills, balance, eye-foot skills, eye-hand skills, and dance. (44 objectives, 3 items per objective)

34. SELF CONCEPT, K-12 — This is a collection of affective objectives which deal with the learner's self concept. Objectives are grouped according to three grade ranges (K-3, 4-6, 7-12), and a self-report inventory or observational indicator is provided to measure each objective. Subdimensions frequently employed in the measures are peer, scholastic, family, and general. (Approximately 20 objectives)

35. ATTITUDE TOWARD SCHOOL, K-12 — This is a collection of affective objectives which deal with the learner's attitude toward school. Objectives are grouped according to three grade ranges (K-3, 4-6, 7-12), and a self-report inventory or observational indicator is provided to measure each objective. Subdimensions frequently employed in the measures are attitudes toward teacher, school subject, learning, peers, social structure and climate, and general. (Approximately 40 objectives)

36. POTENTIAL USES OF IOX OBJECTIVES — This booklet explains alternate schemes for employing operationally stated objectives in a school setting (no charge for single copies accompanying orders).

bibliography

Ackoff, Russell L. "Towards a Quantitative Evaluation of Urban Services." *Public Expenditure Decisions in the Urban Community*. Washington, D.C.: Resources for the Future, Inc., 1962.

Advisory Commission on School District Budgeting and Accounting. *Conceptual Design for a Planning, Programming, Budgeting System for California School Districts*. August 1969.

Alioto, Robert F., and J. A. Jungherr. "Using PPBS to Overcome Taxpayers' Resistance." *Phi Delta Kappan, 51* (November 1969).

Allen, James E., Jr. "Preparing the Way for a New Era of Advancement in Education." In *1969-1970 AASA Official Report*. Washington, D.C.: AASA, 1970.

American Association of School Administrators 1969-1970 Official Report. Washington, D.C.: AASA, 1970.

Armstrong, D. Robert. *A Systematic Approach to Developing and Writing Behavioral Objectives*. Tucson, Ariz.: Educational Innovation Press, 1968.

Barnard, Chester I. *The Functions of the Executive*. Cambridge, Mass.: Harvard University Press, 1966.

Baumol, William J. "Neumann Morgenstern Cardinal Utility." *Economic Theory and Operations Analysis*. Englewood Cliffs, N.J.: Prentice-Hall, 1961.

Bennis, Warren G., Kenneth D. Benne, and Robert Chin, eds. *The Planning of Change: Readings in the Applied Behavioral Sciences*. New York: Holt, Rinehart and Winston, 1962.

Bhaerman, Robert. "In Quest: The Danger of Program Budgeting." *American Teacher, 55,* no. 2 (October 1970).

Blau, Peter. *The Dynamics of Bureaucracy: A Study of Interpersonal Relations in Two Government Agencies,* rev. ed. Chicago: University of Chicago Press, 1955.

Bruner, Jerome S. "Learning and Thinking." In Alice and Lester D. Crow, eds., *Vital Issues in American Education*. New York: Bantam Books, 1964.

Burkhead, Jesse. "The Theory and Application of Program Budgeting to Education." *National Education Association School Finance Conference*. Washington, D.C., April 6, 1965.

Business Week. "How Colleges Cope with the Red Ink." November 21, 1970.

Campbell, Roald F., Luvern L. Cunningham, and Roderick F. McPhee. *The Organization and Control of American Schools*. Columbus: Charles E. Merrill, 1965.

Carlson, Richard O., et al. *Change Process in the Public Schools.* Eugene, Ore.: University of Oregon Press, 1965.

Churchman, C. West, et al. "Weighting Objectives." *Introduction to Operations Research.* New York: Wiley, 1957.

Clark, Kenneth B. "Alternative Public School Systems." *Equal Educational Opportunity.* Cambridge, Mass.: Harvard University Press, 1969.

Coleman, James S. "Toward Open Schools." *The Public Interest.* Fall 1967.

Coleman, James S., et al. *Quality of Educational Opportunity.* Washington, D.C.: U.S. Office of Education, 1966.

Cook, Desmond L. *Program Evaluation and Review Technique: Applications in Education.* OE-12024, Coop. Research Monograph, no. 17. Washington, D.C.: U.S. Department of Health, Education, and Welfare, 1966.

Cyphert, Frederick R., and Walter L. Gant. "The Delphi Technique: A Case Study." *Phi Delta Kappan, 52*, no. 5 (January 1971).

Davis, Joseph L., and Martin W. Essex. *Educational Evaluation.* Columbus, Ohio: State Superintendent of Public Instruction, 1969.

Drucker, Peter J. *The Age of Discontinuity.* New York: Harper & Row, 1969.

Durstine, Richard M. "An Accountability Information System." *Phi Delta Kappan, 52,* no. 4 (December 1970).

Durstine, Richard M., and Robert A. Howell. *Toward PPBS: Program Budgeting in a Small School District.* Boston: New England School Development Council, 1970.

Education Turnkey Systems. *Performance Contracting in Education: The Guaranteed Student Performance Approach to Public School System Reform.* Champaign, Ill.: Research Press, 1970.

Education, USA. "PPBES (Planning, Programming, Budgeting, Evaluation System), Vandalism, and the Voucher Plan." Washington, D.C.: National School Public Relations Association, November 2, 1970.

Education Vouchers: A Preliminary Report on Financing Education by Payments to Parents. Cambridge, Mass.: Center for the Study of Public Policy, 1970.

"Excerpts from the President's Special Message to Congress on Education Reform." *The New York Times*, March 4, 1970. © The New York Times Company.

Financial Accounting: Definition, Classifications, and Codes for Local and State School Systems (Handbook II, Revised). Washington, D.C.: National Center for Educational Statistics, U.S. Office of Education, 1970.

Financial Accounting for Local and State School Systems (Handbook II). Bulletin No. 4. Washington, D.C.: State Educational Records and Report Series, U.S. Office of Education, 1957.

Fisher, Gene H. *The World of Program Budgeting.* Speech presented at conference on program budgeting and cost analysis, UCLA, June 2, 1966. Santa Monica, Calif.: The Rand Corporation, 1966.

Ford, Walter J. "Revised North Rockland School Budget Discussed." *The Journal News* (Rockland County, N.Y.), May 13, 1970.

Friedman, Milton. "The Role of Government in Education." *Capitalism and Freedom.* Chicago: University of Chicago Press, 1962.

Gallup, George. "How the Nation Views the Public Schools: A Study of the Public Schools of the United States." Princeton, N.J.: *Gallup International,* as sponsored by CFK Ltd., Fall 1969.

Gardner, John W. *Excellence: Can We Be Equal and Excellent Too?* New York: Harper & Row, 1961.

Gardner, John W. *The Recovery of Confidence.* New York: Norton, 1970.

Gorham, William. "Notes of a Practitioner." *The Public Interest,* no. 8 (Summer 1967). © National Affairs 1967.

Governmental Accounting, Auditing, and Financial Reporting. Chicago: Municipal Finance Office Association, 1968.

Greenwood, Frank. *Managing the Systems Analysis Function.* New York: American Management Association, 1968.

"Group Approach Harnesses Youth's Creativity." *Management in Practice.* New York: American Management Association, 1970. © American Management Association, Inc., 1970.

Haga, Enoch, ed. *Automated Educational Systems.* Elmhurst, III.: The Business Press, 1967.

Haggart, S. A., et al. *Program Budgeting for School Planning: Concepts and Applications.* Englewood Cliffs, N.J.: Educational Technology Publications, 1971.

Hartley, Harry J. *Educational Planning-Programming-Budgeting: A Systems Approach.* Englewood Cliffs, N.J.: Prentice-Hall, 1968.

Hartley, Harry J. *PPBS History, Rationale, and Theory.* Speech presented at New England School Development Council Information Conference on PPBES, Nashua, N.H., February 1970.

Hartman, W., et al. *Management Information Systems Handbook: Analysis-Requirements-Determination-Design and Development-Implementation and Evaluation.* New York: McGraw-Hill, 1968.

Harvard Business Review, eds. *New Decision Making Tools for Managers.* Cambridge, Mass.: Harvard University Press, 1963.

Hatry, Harry P., and John F. Cotton. *Program Planning for State County City.* State-Local Finances Project. Washington, D.C.: The George Washington University, January 1967.

Herbers, John. "Survey Finds Voters Across the Nation Opposed Bonds or Taxes for Education." *The New York Times,* November 8, 1970.

Hite, Herbert. "A Model for Performance Certification." In Robert C. Burkhart, ed., *The Assessment Revolution: New Viewpoints for Teacher Evaluation.* Sponsored by N.Y.S. Education Dept., Division of Teacher Education and Certification, and Buffalo State University College, Teacher Learning Center.

Hoepfner, Ralph, et al. *CSE Elementary School Test Evaluations.* Los Angeles: Center for the Study of Evaluation, UCLA Graduate School of Education, 1970.

Howe, Harold, II. "The Frustrations of Progress." *1967-1968 AASA Official Report.* Washington, D.C.: American Association of School Administrators, 1968.

Instructional Objectives Exchange. *Biology, 10-12.* Los Angeles: Center for the Study of Evaluation, U.C.L.A. Graduate School of Education, 1970.

Instructional Objectives Exchange, *Social Science, K-9.* Los Angeles: Center for the Study of Evaluation, U.C.L.A. Graduate School of Education, 1970.

Jaeger, Richard M., as quoted in "Testing Policies, School Span Under Fire." *Education, USA.* Washington, D.C.: National School Public Relations Association, November 9, 1970.

James, H. Thomas. *The New Cult of Efficiency and Education.* Horace Mann Lecture, University of Pittsburgh, 1968. Pittsburgh: University of Pittsburgh Press, 1969.

Jencks, Christopher. "Is the Public School Obsolete?" *The Public Interest,* Winter 1966.

Jones, David M. "PPBS—a Tool for Improving Instruction." *Educational Leadership. Journal of the Association for Supervision and Curriculum Development*, National Education Association, Washington, D.C. *28,* no. 4 (January 1971).

Kent, Arthur E., and Wesley F. Gibbs, "Why Skokie Switched to PPBS Grade Level Array." *Nation's Schools*, January 1970.

Knezevich, Stephen J. *Symposium on Organization and Resource Allocations Required by School Systems Desiring to Implement PPBS.* Speech at AASA National Academy for School Executives, Lake Tahoe, Nevada, August 1969.

Knezevich, Stephen J., ed. *Administrative Technology and the School Executive.* Washington, D.C.: American Association of School Administrators, 1969.

Knezevich, Stephen J., and Glen G. Eye, eds. *Instructional Technology and the School Administrator.* Washington, D.C.: American Association of School Administrators, 1970.

Krathwohl, David R., et al. *Taxonomy of Educational Objectives: The Classification of Education Goals, Handbook II: Affective Domain.* New York: David McKay, 1964.

Lessinger, Leon. "Engineering Accountability for Results in Public Education." *Phi Delta Kappan, 52,* no. 4 (December 1970).

Levin, Henry M. "The Failure of the Public Schools and the Free Market." *The Urban Review,* June 1968.

Levine, Donald M. "The Emergence of the Planning, Programming, Budgeting, Evaluation System (PPBES) as a Decision and Control Technique for Education." *Research Corporation of the Association of School Business Officials,* October 1969.

Levine, Donald M. *Some Problems in Planning-Programming-Budgeting for Education.* Cambridge, Mass.: Harvard University Press, May 1969.

Levinson, Harry. "Management by Whose Objectives?" *Harvard Business Review,* July-August 1970.

Lippett, Ronald, Jeanne Watson, and Bruce Westley. *The Dynamics of Planned Change.* New York: Harcourt Brace Jovanovich, 1958.

Lyden, Fremont J. and Ernest G. Miller, eds. *Planning-Programming Budgeting: A Systems Approach to Management.* Chicago: Markham, 1967.

McCleery, William. "One University's Response to Today's Financial Crisis." Interview with William G. Bowen, *University: A Princeton Quarterly,* Winter 1970-1971, © Princeton University.

McGhan, Barry R. "Accountability as a Negative Reinforcer." *American Teacher, 55,* no. 3 (November 1970).

Mager, Robert F. *Preparing Instructional Objectives.* Palo Alto, Calif.: Fearon, 1962.

Mattox, Frank. "Setting New Education Communications Priorities." Quoted in *Trends,* National School Public Relations Association, December 15, 1970.

Merriman, Howard O. "Profile of a School District's Department of Evaluation— Present and Future." *Educational Evaluation: Official Proceedings of a Conference.* Columbus, Ohio: Department of Education, 1969.

Miles, Matthew B., ed. *Innovation in Education.* New York: Teachers College, Columbia University, 1964.

Miller, Donald R. *An Introduction to Planning-Programming-Budgeting Systems,* Operation PEP, San Mateo County Superintendent of Schools. San Mateo, Calif.: California Board of Education, March 1969.

Myers, Miles. "The Unholy Marriage—Accountants and Curriculum Makers." *American Teacher, 55,* no. 3 (November 1970).

New York State School Boards Association Newsletter, 12, no. 2 (November 1970).

Novick, David, ed. *Program Budgeting: Program Analysis and the Federal Budget.* Cambridge, Mass.: Harvard University Press, 1965.

An Operational Model for the Application of Planning-Programming-Budgeting Systems in Local School Districts, Pre-Pilot Test Version. Williamsville, N.Y.: The Western New York School Development Council, 1970.

"PPBS—A Communication Jack-in-the-Box." *Trends,* National School Public Relations Association, December 15, 1970.

PPBS Pilot Project Reports from the Participating 5 States, 5 Counties, and 5 Cities. State-Local Finances Project. Washington, D.C.: The George Washington University, February 1969.

Planning for Educational Development in a Planning, Programming, Budgeting System. Washington, D.C.: Committee on Educational Finance, National Education Association, 1968.

Planning, Programming, Budgeting System Implementation in Two New York State School Districts: Spring Valley Public Schools, Pearl River Public Schools. New York: Peat, Marwick, Mitchell & Co., June 1970.

Ponti, Irene Y. *A Guide for Financing School Food and Nutrition Services.* Chicago, Ill. American School Food Service Association and The Research Corporation of the Association of School Business Officials, 1970.

Preliminary Compilation of Behavioral Objectives. New York: The Read System, Litton Educational Publishing, Inc., 1970.

Procedure for the Preparation of the 1971 Education Program. Portland, Maine: Portland Public School District, July 1970.

Pyhrr, Peter A. "Zero-Base Budgeting." *Harvard Business Review*, Cambridge, Mass., *48*, no. 6 (November-December 1970).

Report of the Advisory Committee on a Long-Range School Budget to the Board of Education. Westport, Conn.: 1969.

Report of the Advisory Committee on School Goals to the Board of Education. Westport, Conn.: June 1969.

Report of the First National Conference on PPBES in Education. Chicago: Research Corporation of the Association of School Business Officials, June 10, 1969.

Rescher, Nicholas. *Delphi and Values.* Santa Monica, Calif.: The Rand Corporation, September 1969.

Saylor, Galen. "National Assessment: Pro and Con." *The Record,* Teachers College, Columbia University, *71,* no. 4 (May 1970).

"School Board OKs $116 Million Budget, 73¢ Tax Hike." *The San Francisco Examiner,* August 6, 1969.

Schwartz, Ron. "Accountability." *Nation's Schools, 85,* no. 6 (June 1970).

Silberman, Charles E. *Crisis in the Classroom: The Remaking of American Education.* New York: Random House, 1970. © Charles E. Silberman.

Stahl, Robert. "PPBS and the Teacher." *The Challenge of Planning-Programming-Budgeting Systems,* Supplementary Research Report No. 104, Burlingame, California Teachers Association, 1969.

Sweigert, Roy, Jr., and Donald Kase. *Assessing Educational Needs of California: A Progress Report.* A paper prepared for the Region III Conference on Title III of ESEA, Denver, Colorado, March 1969.

Temkin, Stanford. "An Evaluation of Comprehensive Planning Literature with an Annotated Bibliography." *Research for Better Schools, Inc.,* Philadelphia, Pa., 1970.

Thelen, Herbert. *Dynamics of Groups at Work*. Chicago: University of Chicago Press, 1954.

Three Human Forces in Teaching and Learning. Washington, D.C.: NTL Institute for Applied Behavioral Science, 1961.

Toffler, Alvin. *Future Shock*. New York: Random House, 1970. ©Alvin Toffler.

Townsend, Robert. *Up the Organization*. New York: Knopf, 1970. © Robert Townsend.

Trump, J. Lloyd. "Focus on Change: Guide to Better Schools." In Alice and Lester Crow, eds., *Vital Issues in American Education*. New York: Bantam Books, 1964.

Underwood, Kenneth E. "Just What Will You Be Accountable For?" *The American School Board Journal, 58,* no. 3 (September 1970).

Walberg, Herbert J. "Curriculum Evaluation: Problems and Guidelines." *The Record, 71,* Teachers College, Columbia University (May 1970).

Wald, H. Richard. "Reconciling Organizations and Personal Goals." *Personnel Journal,* January 1970.

Watson, Goodwin, ed. *Change in School Systems*. Washington, D.C.: National Training Laboratories, National Education Association, 1967.

Watson, Goodwin, ed. *Concepts for Social Change*. Washington, D.C.: National Training Laboratories, National Education Association, 1967.

Watson, Goodwin, ed. "Resistance to Change." *Concepts for Social Change*. Washington, D.C.: NTL Institute for Applied Behavioral Science, 1967.

Winter, Ralph E. "Desperate Educators." *The Wall Street Journal,* June 15, 1970.

index

71 72 73 74   7 6 5 4 3 2 1